In Praise of Gina

'Being a first-time mum was so difficult; I just felt completely all over the place and didn't have a clue to start with. It is so much easier this time. I am just totally sooo loving Gina's routines with two children. I have no idea how it would be possible without structure and the benefits are amazing.'   *Fee*

'I have found that having a routine helps organise my day immensely, leaving me more time for my children. They thrive, not only on the structured meals and sleeps as per Gina's routines, but they also know what's coming next. We are all happy thanks to Gina Ford!'   *Amy*

'The CLB book was a saviour for me being a breast-feeder, and the section on how to increase your milk supply was just what I needed. Before following the routines I felt I could never satisfy Evie. Then a friend lent me Gina's book; I followed it and it worked.'   *Jo*

'Just wanted to share how much I actually love CLB and Gina Ford! It's now 7.20pm and all three of my little ones are tucked up in bed peacefully sleeping! Thank you Gina, once again, for a third contented little baby!'   *Anna*

*To all the thousands of parents who have shared
their babies with me – without you and your
babies this book would not have been possible.*

The
Contented
Baby with
Toddler Book

Gina Ford

Vermilion
LONDON

1 3 5 7 9 10 8 6 4 2

Published in 2009 by Vermilion, an imprint of Ebury Publishing
A Random House Group company

The Random House Group Limited Reg. No. 954009

Addresses for companies within the Random House Group can be found at
www.rbooks.co.uk

A CIP catalogue record for this book is available from the British Library

The Random House Group Limited supports The Forest Stewardship
Council (FSC), the leading international forest certification organisation. All our
titles that are printed on Greenpeace approved FSC certified paper carry the FSC logo.
Our paper procurement policy can be found at www.rbooks.co.uk/environment

Mixed Sources
Product group from well-managed
forests and other controlled sources
www.fsc.org Cert no. TT-COC-2139
© 1996 Forest Stewardship Council

Designed and set by seagulls.net
Printed in the UK by CPI Mackays, Chatham, ME5 8TD

ISBN 9780091929589

Copies are available at special rates for bulk orders.
Contact the sales development team on 020 7840 8487 for more information.

To buy books by your favourite authors and register for offers, visit www.rbooks.co.uk

Please note that conversions to imperial weights and measures
exact.

of general guidance in relation to
not to be relied on for medical,
specific circumstances and in
ing, stopping or starting any
nation given is correct and up to
hange, and the reader should
s. The author and publishers
directly or indirectly from
ined in this book.

Contents

Acknowledgements

I would like to say a very special thank you to my editor Clare Hulton, who was the inspiration behind this book and has been a constant source of great ideas and helpful suggestions. I would also like to express my thanks to my publisher Fiona MacIntyre, who has always encouraged my career as an author and has had such faith in my work, and to Cindy Chan and all the team at Random House whose hard work has contributed to the book. My agent Emma Kirby is owed a huge thank you for all the support she has given me, and for her continued dedication and guidance. I would also like to say a big thank you to my website editor Kate Brian and technical editor Yamini Franzini for the wonderful support they have given me personally and for doing such a great job of taking care of the website while I was writing this book. Laura Simmons, one of the founder members of Contentedbaby.com, deserves a very special thank you for all her hard work in ensuring that the routines within this book are clear and concise.

Finally, I would like to thank all of you for your continuing support, particularly those of you who have taken time to get in touch to tell me of your experiences using my routines, and to send me your opinions and suggestions. I'd like to take the opportunity to send my special thanks to every one of you and my love to all your contented babies and toddlers.

Introduction

It's 10 years since my first book, *The Contented Little Baby Book*, was published. Since then many mothers have been in touch to tell me how helpful they have found it, and I have continued to be touched by the number of you who have taken the time to express your appreciation. Those first 'Contented Babies' are now approaching their 11th year, and it gives me great pleasure that my first book still seems as relevant today as it was in 1999. Many of you have requested advice about following routines when a second baby comes along, and I have written *The Contented Baby with Toddler Book* in response to your questions.

When your second baby arrives, trying to meet the demands of two small children can be as challenging as it was adapting to life with your first baby, and establishing routines for both children will help to ease the transition. During my career I looked after more than 300 babies and soon learned how vital routines are for both mothers and babies. Your babies, toddlers and older children will thrive on consistent and healthy routines – nutritious meals at regular intervals, plenty of sleep, fresh air and exercise, social playtime, one-to-one attention and cuddles.

I very much hope that the advice in this book will help you to provide both the stability for an older child adapting to life with a new sibling, and the routines that promise a contented little baby.

If you have used the Contented Little Baby (CLB) routines with your first baby, you will know that during the first year they change many times. When starting the routines this time around, it is important not to assume that your second baby will follow the routines the same way as your first baby did. Remember that the whole aim of the CLB routines is to allow for the individual needs of each baby to be met.

If you didn't follow a routine with your first baby, but have decided to try a routine-based approach with your second, you might be a little apprehensive. There are many myths surrounding routines these days, the main ones being that babies are forced to eat and sleep to a strict timetable. While this may be true of some routines, it is not the case with the CLB routines.

The CLB routines are unique because they are created to meet the natural sleep and feeding needs of all healthy, normal babies. They also allow for the fact that some babies need more sleep than others, and that some may be able to go for longer between feeds than others. The aim of the routines is not to push your baby through the night without a feed, but to structure the feeding and sleeping during the day in order to keep your baby's night-time waking to a minimum. By doing this, he will wake and feed quickly before settling back to sleep. The routines also ensure that once your baby is capable of going one longer spell between feeds, this will happen in the middle of the night, not during the day.

'Is it really possible to establish the CLB routines with a second baby?' is a question that I am frequently asked. I know from personal experience of helping to care for many second and third babies that sometimes the joy of having a second baby can be over-shadowed when the mother becomes overly anxious about how she is going to cope. Caring for a newborn baby and a boisterous toddler can seem pretty daunting when you think of all that it entails. Trying to establish breast-feeding and regular sleep times for a newborn while juggling mealtimes, school runs and play dates, and not disrupting a toddler's bath and bedtime routine, are just some of the main concerns that many of the mothers I worked with shared with me. If you are worried, and simply can't imagine how it will be possible to establish a routine that will result in a happy and contented baby and toddler, please trust and believe me when I say that it *is* possible. The important thing to remember is that the CLB routines change nine times during the first year. That is the beauty of my routines, and why they are so successful. Unlike traditional routines, the CLB routines take into account the different needs of all babies, and allow you to structure the feeding and sleeping advice to suit the individual needs of your baby.

Here I have created a set of routines and guidelines that will help you cope in the months ahead, and help you meet the needs of both your baby and your toddler. Yes, there will be times when establishing the routines may be very challenging, and even some days when it all goes totally wrong, but by being consistent and persistent you will, in the long-term, reap the rewards of having two happy and contented children.

Gina

1

Preparing for the Second Baby

Parents often ask me for advice about having a second child and want to know how they can use my routines to satisfy the wants and needs of a baby and a toddler at the same time. In my experience, establishing a good routine for both children is vital when you are trying to spread yourself between the two, without either your baby or toddler feeling overlooked or missing out. Looking after two children will obviously be much harder work than looking after just one, but I am confident that the routines and advice in this book, which have been tried and tested by the thousands of members on my website, will help you to avoid many of the pitfalls that lots of parents experience when the second baby comes along.

If you have spent some time thinking about how you will deal with a second child, and about the implications for your family life and finances, you will have a clearer idea of what to expect and this will make the transition far easier for you, your partner and your children.

Are we ready for another child?

I've come across some parents who have been so delighted by the experience of having their first child that they can hardly wait to have a second. However, many others do have concerns about how they will find the reserves of time and energy to devote to another baby. You may know that you want your child to have a sibling, but be concerned about how you will cope physically, emotionally or financially. These are all important issues that you should take time to discuss openly with each other.

Emotional concerns

Dealing with one child is demanding, but when you have two it can seem as if you lose those last small gaps of precious time for yourself. It can be a lonely business looking after small children at home, whether you have opted to be a stay-at-home mother or whether you are on maternity leave. Having a second child is not the complete shock to the system that a first baby can be, as you will know what to expect and will have already made many lifestyle changes. However, you may find that it isn't as easy to get things done once you have two children, and your life starts to revolve around your children more.

Even if you got by happily with your first child, having a second baby may leave you feeling as though you can no longer manage. Think about the support you have available, and whether you may need to get some extra help for a while. Women who have a strong support network of family or friends tend to find it easier to cope with life at home with young children as there is always someone to lend a sympathetic ear or to come to the rescue in times of crisis. Talk to your friends who have more than one child about how they manage, and consider offering to do some babysitting or childcare swaps so that you begin to build a support network ready for your new arrival.

It is perfectly natural to worry about how you will spread yourself between your toddler and new baby, how you will establish their routines, and how they will get on with one another. Discussing these concerns with your partner is important, as it will ensure that you are both aware of the problems that may arise. Couples sometimes tell me that they seem to argue more after the birth of a second child, as they both feel exhausted and run down. I know how hard it can be to fit caring for a newborn around dealing with a toddler, and that is why I have written this book with adapted routines for a baby and toddler. Encourage your partner to read the book as well so that you are both dealing with any problem situations in the same way.

Financial concerns

You won't need to spend quite as much money when you are expecting your second child because you will have bought the basic baby equipment first time around. If you still have your first child's baby clothes, you will be able to reuse those, too. However, depending on the age gap between your children, your first child may still be sleeping in a cot and using a buggy, in which case there may well be some additional expenses. If your children are close in age, you will have them both in nappies for some time, and, if these are disposable, you may not realise quite how quickly these costs can mount up. If you have thought through the additional out-goings involved, though, there should not be too many surprises.

Couples sometimes feel they need to move house when they are expecting a second child in order to have more space. Your monthly overheads are likely to increase if you are moving to a larger home, and there are costs involved in moving whether you are renting or buying. If you haven't budgeted carefully, the extra expenditure can come as a shock. I have seen how this can make the arrival of a second baby more difficult than it needs to be for some parents. Money problems are one of the main things that couples argue about, and the joy of having a new addition to the family can be completely overshadowed by financial concerns if you haven't thought this through.

Work matters

Women who have found it relatively easy to return to work after their first child may find that things don't slot into place so neatly after the second. Some may make the decision to reduce their hours or stop work altogether for a while. If you are going to become a stay-at-home mother, there will be financial implications and you need to think about this. Some women say they find they spend less money when they are not at work, but you are still likely to have to make some sacrifices if you cut out one income. If you are used to holidays or meals out on a regular basis, to beauty treatments or nights away, you may find that you have to change your lifestyle and cut out some of these luxuries because you can no longer afford them on one salary.

If you do go back to work, either full- or part-time, the costs of childcare will rise when you are paying for two children, and again this is something you need to take into consideration.

Getting pregnant again

Once you've decided you want a second child, you need to consider the age gap. People think that, having looked after so many babies, I must know the perfect age gap between children. In fact, I've worked with some parents who have had their children as close together as possible, and others who have left it many years before having a second child. I believe the age gap itself is less important than the level of agreement between the couple that the time is right, how well they have prepared for a second child and the personalities of the children themselves.

There are advantages and disadvantages to each age gap, and your decision about this may end up being as much to do with circumstances as choice. If you are an older mother, and aware of your biological clock, you may not feel you can sit around waiting for the ideal opportunity and may want to try to get pregnant again as soon as possible. Others who have wanted their children close together may find that they end up having to wait far longer than they had anticipated to get pregnant for a second time.

A close age gap: 11–15 months

For parents who have two children very close in age, it can be more like dealing with twins. You will have two very young children in nappies, and your toddler will still need a lot of your attention. She will need lifting and carrying, and help with feeding. It can seem as if your entire day is spent servicing the needs of your children and life is a whirl of nappy changing and feeding. It can be exhausting trying to get out and about with them both, and at first it will take a lot longer to get anything done.

Despite this, there are some clear advantages to having your children this close together. Although it may be tough at the time, at least it means the years of nappy changing and feeding are over much more quickly rather than being spread out over a number of years. Another advantage of this close age gap is that there tends to be less jealousy when the new baby arrives because the toddler is too young to feel that her role in the family is being taken over. As they get older, children this close in age are more likely to enjoy doing the same things and this can make life easier.

An average age gap: 18 months to three years

Most couples tend to aim for a gap of 18 months to three years between their children, but the way a first child deals with a new baby varies considerably from either end of this age range.

Although it is probably the most popular age gap, in my experience it is often more difficult if your toddler is between the ages of 18 months and two years when her baby brother or sister is born. Many changes occur in a toddler's life at this stage: she is learning new skills, such as how to talk and dress herself, and may be learning how to use the potty at around this time, too. These are milestones in your toddler's life, and helping her through them can be time-consuming. She may find these developmental changes more difficult if you can't give her the attention and encouragement she needs; equally, attempting to cope with a demanding toddler when you are looking after a little baby can be frustrating for you. You and your toddler may end up losing patience with one another and it is hardly surprising that this is a time when many toddlers start having tantrums.

If this is the age gap between your children, try to minimise the changes you introduce into your toddler's life when your baby is very small. If she is ready, potty-train her before the baby comes along (see page 16 and *Potty Training in One Week*), and help her learn to dress herself – this will make all the difference. You also need to reassure your toddler that having a new baby doesn't mean you love her any less. It is important to get your baby into a good routine as quickly as possible as this will leave you free to devote time to your toddler and address her needs.

If your child is at the upper end of this age bracket (closer to age three) when the baby is born, things are likely to be easier because she will be more independent and will need less concentrated attention. It is also easier to explain to a child of this age that the new baby is not taking her place in the family, and she will be able to understand when you tell her that you still love her.

A wide age gap: three or more years

If you have a big age gap between your children, initially the main problem you are likely to experience is having to adapt your life back to living with a baby. By the time your child is three, you will have moved on from focusing your family life around a baby's feeding and sleeping routines, and returning to a world of nappies, hours of feeding and night-time wakings can come as quite a shock.

The main bonus of having a bigger age gap is that your child will usually have some degree of independence. She may have her own circle of friends at nursery or school, and is likely to have started to enjoy spending time with other children. There is usually less jealousy with a bigger age gap, because the older child will not feel that her role in the family is being taken over by the new baby. It can be more of a problem if the older child is not used to spending time with other children of her own age and has been very focused on her life at home with her parents – if you feel this may be the case, try to address it during pregnancy. If your older child is going to start nursery or a playgroup, try to make sure this doesn't coincide exactly with the arrival of the new baby so that she has some time to get used to it first.

Having a larger age gap does help solve some of the concerns parents often express about how they will divide themselves between their two children. It is easier for parents to split their time between a baby and an older child; the older child has her parents' attention when the baby is sleeping, or in the evenings once the baby is in bed, and the baby is able to have all the attention during the day when the child is at nursery or at school.

Coping with your pregnancy and your toddler

Women often admit that they had at least a moment of panic after the initial joy on discovering they were pregnant for the second time. The reality of the positive pregnancy test can suddenly make all your concerns about how you are going to cope seem a lot more real. For the first time, you may wonder how you will deal with being pregnant when you have a toddler, let alone how you will cope once you have two small children. It is not unusual to feel this way, and being prepared can help you ease your way through this.

When to tell your toddler

Don't be tempted to tell your toddler you are expecting a baby until you are at least four months pregnant. Although it is not something anyone likes to dwell on, as many as one in four pregnancies will end in miscarriage and this is most common in the first 12 weeks of pregnancy. It is probably worth waiting until you have got through the first few months before telling your toddler the news.

It is important to remember that, although your toddler may know she is about to have a new baby brother or sister, her understanding of what this means will depend on her age. Younger children don't always realise that the new baby will be a permanent addition to the family, and even older children are unlikely to have much idea of the way a new baby will change your family life.

Of course, the other thing to bear in mind is that, once they have started talking, toddlers have little in the way of discretion when it comes to who they talk to and what they talk about. If you don't want the milkman, the supermarket cashier or the nursery assistant to know you are pregnant, it may be advisable not to tell your toddler for a while!

What to tell your toddler

Once you have decided the time is right, you will want to explain that your child is going to have a new baby brother or sister, and that the baby is growing in Mummy's tummy. You should aim to introduce the idea of the new baby gently and gradually, and to follow your toddler's lead on this. Try to keep the message positive, and to emphasise what fun it will be to be a big brother or sister, but don't be surprised if your child seems less than impressed by the news. Some toddlers will be genuinely interested, will want to talk about the baby and will ask lots of questions. They may enjoy being involved in your pregnancy, perhaps talking to the baby or giving it 'kisses' through your tummy, and they may want to help to choose baby clothes and get the baby's room ready. However, not all toddlers will react this way. If your child doesn't seem interested, don't feel you have to keep trying to explain things as this may make her feel pressured. A toddler who is under the age of two and a half will still have a fairly limited understanding of what is about to happen, so don't bombard her with information. You should be aiming to create a scenario of gentle change rather than turmoil. There is a wide variety of children's story books available that can help toddlers understand about 'Mummy having a baby' and give them some idea of what to expect.

Coping with morning sickness

If you are suffering from morning sickness or nausea, having to feed your toddler can be a real challenge. When you're pregnant with your first child, it is relatively easy to avoid having to spend too much time in the kitchen, but once you've got a hungry toddler in tow, this is much more difficult. Although it's called 'morning' sickness, the reality is that many pregnant women experience sickness and nausea throughout the day and, if you're feeling this way, the last thing you'll want to do is cook.

This is when batch cooking and freezing can make all the difference. If there are times of the day when you usually feel better, try to get some of your cooking done then. Sometimes particular foods and smells trigger nausea and if you can avoid cooking food that makes you feel really ill without upsetting your toddler's balanced diet, that may help.

The good news is that nausea and sickness are generally associated with the first three months of pregnancy, and after that the symptoms are likely to improve. Unfortunately this isn't always the case for everyone. If you are in the minority who feel sick throughout your pregnancy, you may need to get your husband or friends to batch cook for your freezer so that all you have to worry about is heating up food for your toddler at mealtimes.

Coping with tiredness

Many women feel completely exhausted in early pregnancy, and it is hard to entertain a bouncy toddler when all you want to do is lie down and sleep. As with morning sickness, extreme tiredness is usually a symptom of early pregnancy, although you will also have less energy at the end of your pregnancy when you are quite large. You may want to find some quiet games to play with your toddler that don't involve too much jumping about. If your toddler feels she is getting all your attention playing with her dolls or building blocks, she is less likely to notice that you are not running around the garden. I know mothers worry about children watching too much TV but, if you are completely exhausted, it may be helpful to let your toddler watch a DVD or some children's television now and again.

If your toddler still has a nap in the day, I know it can be tempting to use the time when she is asleep to catch up with some housework, but do try to use these opportunities to get some rest yourself. It is vital to make sure you look after yourself properly. If your toddler is no longer napping in the day, you can relax by enjoying some quiet time together perhaps looking at a book or doing a jigsaw.

If you are feeling very tired, you should also make the most of whatever childcare you have available. If your toddler spends some time at a playgroup or nursery, or even with friends or relatives, use the time to relax and recuperate rather than rushing about trying to get things done.

Antenatal appointments

I know many women have no choice but to take their toddlers with them to antenatal appointments, and this may help them to feel more involved. However, it is not much fun for a toddler to sit in a surgery or hospital waiting room so, if it's an option, let friends or family take care of her instead. It is not a good idea to take a toddler to an ultrasound scan because you will be unable to look after your toddler while you are being scanned. And some toddlers might find the dark room and strange-looking equipment frightening.

Preparing your toddler for the new arrival

I always advise trying to prepare your toddler before the new baby arrives, but what you tell her will depend on her age. At just over a year, your toddler will have little understanding of pregnancy, babies or siblings. At three or four, she may have friends with baby brothers and sisters and may be looking forward to having one of her own.

If you have friends or family who have young babies, it is a good idea to invite them round so that your toddler gets used to babies. One problem parents often face is over-exuberant toddlers who want to play with their younger siblings or cuddle them, but have no idea how carefully babies have to be handled. If your toddler has spent some time with other babies before her own brother or sister comes along, she will have seen how gently people handle them. Take some time to explain that newborn babies are small and fragile, and that they need a lot of gentle handling. It is also useful to prepare your toddler for the newborn baby's crying; she may not get distressed by it if she knows it is the only way the baby has of getting attention and that it doesn't mean that her little brother or sister is in pain or unwell.

If you are planning to breast-feed, you may want to talk about this to your toddler. If you have friends with young babies, she may be used to the idea of breast-feeding, but if she has never seen it before, you need to explain that the new baby will feed from your breasts, just like she did as a baby.

Get her involved

Now that she is going to be a big sister, your toddler may enjoy making some decisions for the new baby. If you are going shopping to buy new equipment for the baby, or if you are decorating a nursery, you can get her involved in the choices and talk about them together.

However, a word of caution here: it may be a good idea to involve your toddler, but you don't want her to feel too aware of how the central focus in the family is shifting. If you are out shopping for the baby together, you may want to make sure she chooses something small as well (even if it is something you need to buy her anyway, such as socks or toothpaste), and maybe let her choose it for herself.

Establish some ground rules

Your toddler will see your tummy growing and learn that its size prevents you from doing some activities. For example, you may not be able to run very fast any more or get involved in rough and tumble games. Now is also the time to replace any activities you are going to want to put a stop to later in pregnancy or when you are trying to breast-feed your newborn baby – for example, playing ball in the sitting room or bedroom. If you find other ways of spending time with your toddler, or some less vigorous activities that you can enjoy together, she may not feel that your pregnancy or the new baby are threatening her fun.

Try not to disrupt her life

Your toddler is used to being the focus of the family, with everything seeming to revolve around her. Things are about to change very rapidly, and the more secure and confident she feels, the easier it will be for her to handle this. Try to keep things in her life as normal as possible during your pregnancy and to maintain her routine of playgroups or visits to the library, toddler gym or music classes. If you need to make changes that could feel important to her, do this either well before or well after the new baby arrives.

Moving into a new bedroom

I know parents often want to move their toddler into a new room when they have a second child. Think carefully about how you present this, as you want your toddler to see it as her moving into a new bedroom rather than the baby taking over her old one. Let her have some say in the decoration, which doesn't have to be expensive; just a fresh coat of paint or a few pictures on the wall can go a long way to making her feel that this is an exciting new place to be. As with any changes, if you are planning to move your toddler into a new room you should do this at least two months before the baby is due, so that she has time to adjust. If your toddler and baby are going to be sharing a room, see pages 238–9 for advice.

Moving your toddler into a bed

Mothers often tell me that they have to move their toddler into a bed once they have a second child because they need her cot for the new baby. Moving into a bed is a big deal for a young child, and certainly, if your toddler is under 30 months old, it may be worth investing in a cot bed, or buying or borrowing a second cot instead. You don't want your toddler to feel she is being pushed aside by a new baby who is now sleeping in her cot. There are also some practical considerations here, such as having to deal with a toddler getting out of bed if she hears the new baby waking for a feed in the night.

Teaching your toddler to dress and undress

If your toddler is old enough, encourage her to try to dress herself. Establishing this before the baby is born will help you and give your toddler something to do during the morning and evening routines, when you are feeding the baby and trying to keep her occupied. By the age of about 14 months, most toddlers will have learned how to pull off their socks, but the majority will not be able to remove the rest of their clothes until they are aged between 18 and 24 months. By the time they reach 30 months, toddlers are usually capable of getting themselves dressed and undressed, although they will still need some help with buttons and poppers.

It is easiest to help a toddler learn how to dress and undress herself if you take it one stage at a time, starting with one or two items of clothing that she finds easiest and moving on gradually.

Potty-training

Mothers who have problems with potty-training their toddlers often tell me that they are in a hurry to get it over and done with before their second baby comes along. It is true that it can be more convenient not to have to deal with two lots of nappies, but it may be far worse to have to deal with one lot of nappies and endless accidents. If you are going to potty-train your toddler before you give birth, do it well in advance. If you end up leaving it until you are in the late stages of pregnancy, your toddler will pick up on any stress you feel about getting it all done in time, and you may find that it suddenly takes far longer than you would have expected.

I always tell parents that the key to successful potty-training is not just that their child should be ready, but that they should be ready, too. If you are in the last stages of pregnancy and your toddler is showing signs of being ready to come out of nappies but is still under the age of two, I would suggest delaying potty-training. It is worth waiting until the new baby is three or four months old and you are all more settled. It is very common for potty-trained toddlers to regress when a new baby is born, and this is far less likely to happen if you wait a while.

Get your partner to spend some time alone with your toddler

Your toddler should not feel that her life has been turned upside down by the new baby. For children who spend their days at nursery or with a nanny, you may assume that this will be less acute, but if you're the one who usually feeds your toddler her supper or reads her a story and puts her to bed, she may feel she is being pushed aside if these tasks are suddenly handed over to her daddy. Make their time together into something special that your toddler looks forward to, and that way she will feel it is a good thing if she gets to spend more time with Daddy once the baby is born.

New childcare arrangements

If you are going to employ a new nanny or mother's help, or send your child to nursery after the baby arrives, you should start this at least a few months before you are due to give birth. Toddlers do not always adapt easily to change and they will be far happier if this is something that has been instigated before the new baby arrives. If you can make it seem like a privilege only available to your toddler because she is older, she is far less likely to feel that she is being shunted out of the way. Arranging this while you're pregnant will also give you some precious time to yourself in the final months.

Find some activities your toddler can do alone

Try to encourage some activities that your toddler can do on their own, such as play dough, drawing or doing jigsaws, so that you know she will be able to occupy herself for short spells while you are looking after the baby. She should see these as fun activities, so that she looks forward to them. Boys and girls can both enjoy having a baby doll of their own, too. If the doll has a bottle, nappies, a bath and a Moses basket then your toddler can look after 'her baby' in just the same way that you are caring for her younger sibling.

Imagine what it is like for your toddler

Your toddler has been the centre of your attention throughout her entire life; older children are often said to be different in character to their younger siblings and although this may be a generalisation, it is true that their start in life is very different. The new baby will grow up having to share your time, love and affection, but this is not something your toddler has been accustomed to.

All the discussion about the new arrival can make your toddler feel as if her central role in the family is about to be taken over by this new baby. It will become gradually more and more apparent throughout your pregnancy that things are changing. When you meet friends and family, they will inevitably want to talk about the new arrival, and how you feel about it. They may want to look at your scan pictures or discuss your antenatal appointments, to ask whether you know the sex of your new baby or have decided on a name. It can feel as if everyone is less interested in your toddler than they used to be. If your child is younger, she may not be quite as aware of this, but older children may need extra reassurance as to how special and loved they are.

2

Preparing for the Birth

As the last few months of your pregnancy approach, it is time to make plans for the birth itself. This time around, it is not just about making sure that you are ready, but also that you have prepared your toddler for the changes ahead. You will have to think about who is going to look after her while you are in hospital, and whether you will need any extra help during your first few weeks at home with your newborn baby. You should also take the opportunity to sort out all your baby equipment, and you will probably find that you have most of what you need already. You may still be using some of it, depending on the age of your toddler, or you may have stored things away at the back of cupboards or in the loft. The last trimester of pregnancy is a good time to check that you have everything you need and that it is all in working order.

You will have discussed your plans for the birth with your midwife by this stage, and the way you feel about the approaching second birth may be partly dictated by your experience the first time around. If the birth of your first child was complicated or traumatic, you may feel nervous and determined that you want things to be different with your second. If the first birth went well, you are probably hoping for a similar experience. Of course, birth is often unpredictable and any plans that you make in advance may change. Once you know whether you are planning a hospital delivery, a home birth or an elective Caesarean, you will have a clearer idea of the arrangements you need to make for your toddler.

Your childcare plans

Arranging childcare for your toddler during labour and birth is an important part of your planning, and you will feel more secure once you have this sorted out. Many people turn to their families at this time, and it can be fairly straightforward if you have relatives nearby who will either come to your home or have your toddler to stay with them. It is not so easy if your family lives some distance away, although a relative still may be able to come and help out for a while. Even if you are not particularly close to your family, you may find that your parents or in-laws are happy to lend a hand, as the birth of a new baby is often a time when families pull together.

Alternatively, you may have friends who would be willing to look after your toddler and have her to stay for a night or two if necessary. Your toddler may really look forward to this, especially if your friends have children of a similar age. If she is already used to spending some time with a nanny or a childminder, this carer may be able to provide cover during the birth. This won't be so disruptive for your toddler as she will be used to this person looking after her when you aren't there.

Even if you are planning a home birth, you will need to think about childcare for your toddler. You will not want to be worrying about her when you are in labour, and there should be someone there to look after her. Sometimes women who have planned home births end up transferring to hospital, and you need to think through who will look after your toddler if this happens. Remember that seeing or hearing you in labour and giving birth could be disturbing for your toddler, so you may want to arrange for her to go to someone else's house during the birth and return home once her baby brother or sister is born.

Just in case of emergencies – a backup plan

Labour is never predictable and, however carefully you think you have prepared, things can happen unexpectedly. If your relatives are coming a week before your due date to look after your toddler, have an emergency backup plan just in case you go into labour earlier than expected. Do you have a friend or neighbour who could step in at short notice, if necessary, just until you can make other arrangements? It is worth having a few different options for emergency backup. Make sure you have all your friends' or neighbours' contact telephone numbers to hand together with a copy of your toddler's routine, and that your partner knows where to get hold of them, too.

Preparing your toddler for the birth

We all tend to associate hospitals with illness, and young children are no exception to this. If you are planning a hospital birth, make sure you have told your toddler that it is perfectly normal for babies to be born in hospital and that it doesn't mean that you or the baby are ill. Explain that babies are often born in the night and so she may get to stay with her granny or aunt or the family friend who is going to look after her. If you are expecting to have an elective Caesarean, so know that you will be spending a few days in hospital, tell her about this so that she knows what will happen. You may also want to explain that you will be quite tired when you come home.

Many mothers have never spent a night away from their toddlers, but the reality is that the first night spent away from your child often feels far more of a milestone to you than it does to them! If you suspect that your toddler is not going to be happy at the idea of staying with a relative or a friend, try to make it sound as if it will be fun and something in the way of a special treat. If it is possible, do a trial run beforehand so that she knows there is nothing to worry about. Try not to dwell on it all too much once you have explained who will look after your toddler while you have the baby. You don't want to worry her, and you risk doing this if she senses it is a big deal for you.

Preparing your toddler for the new baby

Once you have made your childcare arrangements, decide how you want your toddler to be told that the baby has arrived. Would you like the person caring for her to break the news or do you or your partner want to tell her yourselves? Perhaps you want to wait for your toddler to come to the hospital to see her new brother or sister. If you don't want your child told, make sure you have made your wishes clear to the person looking after her.

As well as understanding that she needs to be gentle with the new baby, make sure your toddler knows that it will be a while before the baby will be ready to play with her – toddlers are often disappointed to discover that their new brothers or sisters are actually rather boring and far from being a new playmate.

I often find that parents relax their routines as their children get older. But if you are about to have a new baby, it would make sense to establish a suitable routine prior to the arrival of the new baby that will fit in with the new baby's routine.

Getting things ready for the baby

You probably have most of the equipment you will need for your new baby already, but now is the time to make sure you can find it and that it is in good working order. Sometimes it is only when you go to look for a particular item that you remember lending it to someone, and you may have got rid of some equipment, too. If you have a small gap between children, you may still be using some things for your toddler.

Equipment checklist

I've put together this quick checklist to help you get the baby equipment ready, and ensure you haven't forgotten anything vital.

- **Cot and bedding:** If your toddler is still sleeping in her cot, you need to think about whether you are going to move her before the new baby arrives (see page 15). If you have a crib or Moses basket, you may choose to put the new baby in that for a while. However, this isn't a permanent solution as the baby will outgrow either in a matter of weeks. I would advise making a decision now about what you are going to do in the long-term, whether that involves getting a second cot for your new baby or a cot bed for your toddler. If you decide you'd rather put the new baby in the cot and move your toddler into a proper bed, make sure you allow plenty of time to do this before the baby arrives. You will also want to get out all the cot bedding now, and make sure that you have everything you need. You should have fitted bottom sheets, flat sheets, draw sheets and blankets.

- **Moses basket or crib:** A Moses basket or crib is very useful when your baby is tiny because it enables you to carry him around the house. Don't forget that you will need to get the bedding for your Moses basket or crib, too.

- **Changing station and changing mat:** You need to sort out a changing station for the new baby and you may find it useful to have more than one changing mat, especially if your toddler is still in nappies.

- **Pram/pushchair:** Your toddler will be out of her pram by now but, if she will still need to be pushed around, you will probably need to invest in a double buggy. There are many different types of double buggy on the market, and you need to think carefully about when you will be using it in order to work out which type will be best for you. If you spend a lot of time walking with your toddler in her buggy, you will need something sturdy. If you do most of your getting around in the car, and only use the buggy for short journeys, you will want something that is easy to fold and get into the car boot. Talk to any friends who have double buggies about the advantages and disadvantages of the type they have chosen. Try walking about with the buggy before you buy it. Double buggies can be awkward, so see how easy it is to get it through doorways or up and down steps. Try folding it up and opening it a few times to check how simple this is. Remember that you will have a baby and a toddler with you when you are doing this, so the easier it is the better.

Some parents prefer using buggy boards if they have an older child. A buggy board allows your toddler to stand on the back of the pram or buggy as you push it. Buggy boards can be useful and some people swear by them, but they may not be ideal if you are going to be doing a lot of walking as it can get uncomfortable having to lean over your toddler all the time. Not all buggy boards fit all makes of pram and pushchair, so make sure you get the right model.

- **Car seat:** Your toddler will probably be out of her baby car seat by now, but check that you still have it and that you remember how to fit it in the car. Don't forget to make sure it is in the car when you go to hospital to give birth. It may be helpful to leave it there a few weeks in advance.

- **Baby monitor:** You probably don't use this any more but once you've found it, make sure it is still working properly and that you have batteries, if it needs them.

- **Baby bath:** I don't feel this is an essential piece of equipment but, if you bought a baby bath for your first child, do get it out and use it again. You may have used a bath seat for your baby last time around, and again this will be useful if you still have it.

- **Sling:** I know many mothers find them helpful. If you had one for your first child, you may want to use it again. There is often a bit of a knack to getting a sling on properly, so it is a good idea to practise to make sure you remember how to do it.

- **Baby chair:** Baby seats can be very useful for babies once they are a couple of months old. If you have a bouncy chair, make sure that it is still firm and sturdy and that the safety strap is in place. If your chair has a removable cover, you will probably want to take this off and wash it.

- **Playpen:** If you have a playpen, it may come into its own when you have two children. A toddler should not be left in the playpen with his baby brother or sister, but it can be a useful way of keeping an over-exuberant toddler away from the baby. It goes without saying that babies and toddlers should never be left alone in a playpen for any length of time.

- **Baby clothes:** Young babies grow out of their clothes very quickly, and the garments you had for your toddler when she was born are probably still in good condition. Parents often like to buy one or two new items of clothing for the new baby, but it is not worth spending too much on baby clothes as your newborn will grow out of his first clothes in a matter of weeks. You're also likely to receive clothes as presents for the new baby, too. You may want to buy new items if you know your new baby is the opposite sex to your toddler, but bear in mind that the baby will probably live in Babygros at first anyway.

- **Preparing the nursery:** Finally, don't forget that your nursery should have full-length curtains with black-out linings to ensure the room is dark with no chinks of light that may wake the baby. You should have a chair or sofa in the room so that you can feed the baby in his room. I also advise having a fully fitted carpet in a baby's room rather than rugs that you might trip over in the dark. You may want to install a dimmer switch, or buy a plug-in night light, so that you can lower the lights when you are settling the baby in his cot.

Feeding equipment checklist

You will need to get together all the essentials for feeding your baby whether you intend to breast-feed or bottle-feed.

- **Nursing bra:** You may find the bras you had last time around don't fit quite as well now as you may not be exactly the same size. If you are going to invest in some new nursing bras, it is worth getting them fitted properly and you may want to wait until your milk has come in to ensure you get the right size. I always advise buying cotton nursing bras if possible, with wide, adjustable straps for support.

- **Supply of breast pads:** These are really useful in the early days and you may get through quite a lot of them, so stock up in advance.

- **Nipple cream or spray:** Try feeding without using a cream or spray at first to see how you go, even if you did use one first time around. I would always advise consulting your health visitor or breast-feeding counsellor if breast-feeding is painful, as this is most often caused by poor positioning of the baby on the breast.

- **Nursing pillow:** These shaped pillows can be useful as they bring the baby up to a good height for breast-feeding. I advise buying one with a removable cover. If you used it for your first baby, check it is still in good condition.

- **Electric breast pump:** I always encourage mothers to use an electric expressing machine rather than a hand pump because they are so much more efficient and can really help when you are trying to establish feeding. You can hire electric pumps, but don't forget

27

to talk to your midwife about this well in advance as there is a lot of demand for them. You will also need a stock of freezer bags to store frozen milk. Once you have some bags of breast milk in the freezer, they can be used to top up if the baby becomes restless when you are tired and your milk supply is low.

I always recommend having a stock of bottles and teats (see below) even if you are intending to breast-feed. If your baby is able to take a bottle of expressed milk, it means that you don't always need to be the one awake to feed the baby and it allows your partner to be more involved. It also gets your baby used to feeding from a bottle so you won't have problems when you need to introduce them at a later stage.

If you are going to be bottle-feeding, you will need:

- **Bottles and teats:** I recommend using wide-necked bottles and slow-flow teats for newborns. You may also want to stock up on some medium-flow teats as you will probably want to change your baby to these after about eight weeks.

- **Brushes:** For cleaning bottles and teats.

- **Formula milk:** Get a good supply to last you in the first few weeks.

- **Steriliser:** I usually suggest using a steam steriliser as they are quick and effective. If you had one last time around and are no longer using it, check that you have all the bits, including the instructions, and do a test run.

- If you have an electric bottle-warmer or a bottle-insulator, these may be useful but are not essential as a jug of hot water is just as effective.

Getting your home ready for the new baby

Once you've got out all the equipment you will need for your new baby and have made sure everything is in working order, you can start organising things at home. The first few months after the birth are often the most challenging as you will be getting used to balancing the needs of your new baby with caring for your toddler. You will find that you have very little spare time. The more organised you can be before the birth, the easier things will be once you get home with your new baby.

- Once you've sorted out the baby's equipment, get it all into place in the nursery or wherever you will use it. Make sure bed linen, muslins, towels and baby clothes are laundered and ready to use.

- Get in good supplies of all the essentials you will need for the baby. This includes nappies and baby wipes, cotton wool, sponges, baby wash and any baby oils, nappy or moisturising creams you will be using.

- It is a good idea to stock up on store-cupboard essentials to last you through the first month at least. This would include non-perishable groceries, such as tea, coffee and tinned goods, as well as cleaning materials, washing powder and kitchen and toilet rolls.

- You are not going to have much time to cook, so filling your freezer with as many home-cooked meals as you can will be a godsend once the baby comes along. It means you can still eat healthy meals and not have to resort to convenience foods that are often full of additives and preservatives. Spend some time at the end of your pregnancy batch cooking with your partner so that you have plenty of food in the freezer (see *Feeding Made Easy*). Try to have a selection of your toddler's favourite lunches and dinners in the freezer so that you always have something she will eat to hand.

● Now is the time for you or your partner to do any odd DIY jobs around the home, or get someone in if necessary. You don't want to be worrying about niggling problems around the house when you are looking after a new baby and a toddler, and you aren't going to want workmen coming in and out of the house at that time either.

● If you are expecting to give birth in the months before Christmas, get your cards written and presents bought and wrapped in advance. Trailing around the shops with a toddler and a small baby in tow will not be much fun, and the more preparation you have done in advance, the easier it will be. The same goes for any birth-days, anniversaries or other celebrations that are around the time of your due date or in the months directly after this. If you are organised, it really will make life much simpler.

Getting ready for the big day

When you gave birth the first time around, you probably had your hospital bag packed and ready weeks before the birth, but second-time mothers can find themselves throwing things into a plastic bag in the early stages of labour if they're not careful. It will make things much easier if you have your bag ready in advance.

Although you want your toddler to share the excitement of the new baby's arrival, it is not a good idea to let her help when you pack your hospital bag. In fact, I would suggest that you do this when your toddler is not around as it may make her worried about you going away.

Your hospital bag

You may want to make sure you have:

- Night clothes, slippers and dressing gown

- Underwear, including nursing bras and disposable knickers

- A change of clothing (don't forget that you will still need to wear maternity clothes for a while after the birth)

- Washbag containing soap, hairbrush and comb, shampoo, tooth-brush and toothpaste, face cloth, mirror, face and hand cream, tissues and any other toiletries you like

- Super-absorbent sanitary towels

- Towel

You will also want to pack some items for the birth itself. Your midwife or hospital will probably give you a list, but this may include:

- A copy of your birth plan

- Glucose tablets or energy drinks

- Warm socks

- Sponge

- Lip salve

- Massage oil

- Pillows

- Water spray

- Book or magazine

- Camera

- TENS machine, if you are using one

- Any food or snacks you may want if you are allowed to eat during labour

- A list of phone numbers of people to call with the news, or make sure their numbers are stored in your mobile phone, or your partner's

Finally, you will also want to pack for the baby. You will need:

- Three vests

- Three Babygros/nightdresses

- Two cardigans

- Swaddling blanket

- Two pairs of socks (only if using nightdresses)

- One packet of newborn nappies or, if you're planning to use reusables, 12 terry nappies plus liners

- Cotton wool

- Baby wash

- Hat

- Mittens

- Outdoor suit

Your toddler's bag

You may want to get your toddler involved in packing her overnight bag. She will enjoy this if she is looking forward to a sleepover at a friend's or relative's house, but it may not be advisable if she seems worried at the prospect of spending a night apart from you. She will need nightclothes, a couple of changes of clothing and a washbag with all her toiletries. Don't forget nappies and wipes if she isn't potty-trained, and pull-ups if she needs them at night. Packing some of her favourite things, such as books, crayons and paper, and favourite toys or games can be helpful. Remember you may need to make some last-minute additions if she has a special teddy she can't sleep without, or any other comforter she needs. Make sure whoever is going to be looking after your toddler is aware of her usual bedtime routine as this will help her settle.

If your toddler is going to stay the night with a friend or relative when you are in hospital, try to do one or two trial runs beforehand so that she is familiar with her new surroundings. This will also give your friend or relative a chance to see how the routine works. The same applies if the helper will be coming to look after your toddler at your home while you have the baby. Suggest that he or she spends one or two nights at your house to get familiarised with things, not least your toddler's routine.

I would recommend that you type up your child's routine with details of her feeding and sleeping patterns, as this will be helpful to whoever is going to look after her. You can leave this stuck somewhere prominent, such as the fridge door, so it is always at hand. It is also a good idea to have some of your toddler's favourite home-cooked meals in the freezer, so that you know she will be given something she really likes to eat while you are away. Very early on in my career I made the mistake of believing a toddler who assured me that she was allowed ice cream after lunch and tea, and a packet of Smarties every afternoon. I ended up having great difficulty trying to settle a very hyper toddler at bedtime. To avoid such a situation, list what treats your toddler is allowed and how often. If you are reassured that everything is organised, you will feel more relaxed about leaving her.

Organising paid help

I really do believe that having some kind of help in the first few weeks after the birth is a necessity rather than a luxury. If you don't have friends or family who can offer support and your partner has to work long hours, consider paying for some help, even if it is just for a few hours a week.

If you have the funds to pay for some extra childcare, there are a number of different options you may want to consider.

● **A mother's help** cannot be put in sole charge of the children, but can help with childcare and carry out some domestic duties around the house. This is a good option if you feel you could do with an extra pair of hands for a few hours a day.

- **An au pair** usually lives in and is paid 'pocket money' to help with household chores and childcare. An au pair should not have sole charge of young children.

- **A nanny** is a more expensive option, but usually has some child-care qualifications and can be given sole care of the children. A nanny may live in or out. Although nannies may be responsible for the children's clothes and bedrooms, they do not do domestic work unless it relates directly to the children, for example tidying the children's room and washing their clothes.

- **A childminder** usually looks after children in her own home. You should only use a registered childminder, who will have followed a basic course in first aid and childcare.

- **A maternity nurse:** You may want to employ a maternity nurse to help with your new baby. Maternity nurses usually live in for a few weeks after a new baby is born, and they will help you to establish a routine. They are not cheap, but they are usually on call 24 hours a day, five to six days a week. They do not look after older children.

- **A nursery:** It is not always easy to get a nursery place at the last minute, although if you are flexible and just looking for one or two sessions for your toddler, this may be easier to arrange.

It is important to employ the right person to look after your children. Personal recommendation is always a good thing, but you should make sure you have done your homework. Do always check references and ask for proof of qualifications. Talk to the carer first and let them meet your toddler so you can see how they interact with each other.

If your toddler has been at a playgroup or nursery, or with a childminder in the past, it is a good idea to carry this on if you can. It will give your toddler a sense of continuity, and will also give you some breathing space.

Alternative ways to get help

If you are on a tight budget and can't afford any paid help, there are some other options you may want to consider.

- If a local college runs childcare courses, families may be needed for work placements as part of the training. The students would need supervision and should not be left alone with babies, but they may be a real bonus when it comes to helping with your toddler or any older children, and they should be able to help with the baby as long as you are there, too.

- Ask your friends with young children whether any of them are in a babysitting circle, or would be interested in setting one up. You only need three mothers to make this work, as two of you can look after the children and give the third some time off. It will allow you to have some valuable space for yourself, and allow your toddler to spend time with other children.

- There is a government organisation in the UK called Sure Start (see page 325 for details) that provides help to parents. It runs children's centres, and can also offer support and outreach help to families who are identified as being in need.

The final days – waiting for labour

Most women don't give birth on their due date. If you are in paid work, you will probably have started your maternity leave, and you will want to try to make the most of these last days alone with your toddler. There should not be too much for you to do at this stage if you have been getting things ready during the last few months. You'll be quite large and tired by now anyway, and you may not have a great deal of energy. This is not necessarily the time for boisterous games or energetic sporting activity together, unless of course you are trying to bring on your labour, but you can still enjoy having fun with your toddler. Take some time to sit and read books, to do jigsaws together or play board games. She will find this reassuring, and it may be quite relaxing for you, too.

The one last thing you might want to do in the final days is buy a gift from the baby to your toddler. This may help to ease the new arrival for your toddler and can be given to her as soon as they first meet. It doesn't have to be anything large or expensive; you will know what she'd really like, whether it's a sticker book or building bricks. You can get something ready and maybe wrap it up so it feels like a special present. That way, when the baby arrives, your toddler will immediately start off with a positive feeling towards her younger brother or sister.

3

Birth and Beyond

When you gave birth to your first child, you could focus all your time and energy on caring for your tiny baby. This time around, you'll be balancing this with the needs of your older child. You know how much of your time your toddler takes up and you're also aware of how demanding it can be to care for a newborn baby. Trying to juggle both at the same time is not easy, but setting up a good structure as early as possible will make all the difference. This is why I stress the importance of establishing the routine you want your toddler to be in before the new baby comes along, and of making as many preparations as you can in advance, to help you through the first few months.

Recovery after birth

Having a baby is a physically exhausting experience, even for those mothers who have had a straightforward, natural labour. It will take time for your body to recover, and it is important to appreciate this. In my experience, some mothers try to do too much too quickly, feeling that they have to get their lives back to normal as soon as they possibly can. Shopping in John Lewis for missing baby equipment days after having a baby, or taking a newborn out for lunch in those early weeks, can be hugely counterproductive for both you and your baby. This is a time to rest and recuperate and, in the long-term, you will cope better if you have taken things gently at the start.

After a natural birth, the length of time you remain in hospital will depend on the well-being of you and your baby. Most women stay for a day or two after having their babies, but some are ready to leave on the same day. Being allowed home early should not be seen as a sign that life should get back to normal immediately.

Forty years ago, a woman would usually stay in bed for up to two weeks after giving birth and during this time she would be looked after and not expected to do anything other than feed her baby. We may not feel that this is necessary any more, but allowing yourself time to recover after the birth is vital, especially when you have an older child to care for as well.

From my personal experience, mothers who are realistic regarding their need for rest, and calm, not only recuperate more quickly but they fulfil the needs of their newborn baby and toddler more easily. A calm, peaceful home gives all the family time to adjust to the new arrival. I encourage mothers to minimise visitors in those early days, restricting guests to only close friends and family. Some mothers organise a visiting hour two or three times a week, and this is so much more manageable than a continual stream of well-meaning guests. There will be plenty of time to introduce your new baby to a wider circle of friends when he is a little bigger, and I feel strongly that it is far more preferable for a baby to have this attention when he is three or four weeks old than in the early days and weeks. After all, your baby has been cocooned in your tummy for nine months. Those first days are a period of enormous change for him, and the calmer and less stressful his new world, the better it is for you all. I believe that babies do not like to be passed around like parcels, and stimulated by unnecessary handling or by seeing different faces. Your baby needs to be getting to know you, and your immediate family, in those first few days.

For your toddler, too, it can be beneficial to minimise visitors to those who really know and love you. Your older child will already have to cope with the excitement and disruption of a new baby. If this is your second child, it will be the first time your older child has shared her parents' attention with a sibling. She will benefit from being given the time and space to do this gradually, without the additional disruption of a constant stream of visitors whose focus will be, inevitably, the new baby.

I've found that some women often try to do far too much immediately after the birth. Everyone wants to be the perfect mother, but you need to ensure your own needs are met if you're going to be at your best, and this means getting some rest. You should try to get a friend or relative to take your toddler to playgroup or nursery, and perhaps to take the baby and toddler out for a walk now and again, allowing you some time to recuperate. Thinking about yourself at this time is not selfish, it is sensible, and your family will all reap the benefits if you are not permanently exhausted.

Recovery after a Caesarean

If you've had a Caesarean section, you will have to stay in hospital for three or four days. It has become so common for women to have Caesareans now that we sometimes forget it is a major operation, and that it will take longer for your body to recover.

Although you will be able to get out of bed fairly soon after the operation, it is important to rest as much as you can. You will be given detailed information about what you can do and when, and you must stick to this. You should avoid any strenuous activity or heavy lifting, and it is generally advised that you should not drive for six weeks.

You will need help around the house when you arrive home. I know some mothers find the area around the scar can feel itchy and numb at first, and it will take some weeks for the incision to heal fully. Do discuss this with your midwife or health visitor.

In the longer term, being active will help your recovery but any physical activity should be low-key so that you do not overdo things.

Introducing your toddler to the new baby

The first meeting between your toddler and her new sibling is an exciting time, and I know mothers tend to want everything to go perfectly. It is true that first impressions are important, so try to strike the right note, but don't worry too much if things don't go quite to plan; it is the way your children get on in the longer term that really matters.

If the first meeting is going to take place in hospital, try to feed your baby before your toddler arrives, so that you are not feeding and cuddling the new baby when she walks in. This will enable you to make a big fuss of your toddler, and will help the children's first meeting to be a happy one. Ideally, introduce the toddler to the new baby in his cot, and look at him together. Then you can give your toddler the gift from the baby (see page 37). You could consider having a small treat for your toddler each time she comes to the hospital, since her interest in her new sibling is likely to be quite brief at this stage.

If you had a Caesarean, you may remain in hospital for a few days and therefore want your toddler to come to the hospital. It is not easy to be separated from your child for this length of time, although you may find it more difficult than she does.

A hospital ward can be an alien and rather daunting experience for your toddler, so if you're only spending a short time in hospital, you may prefer to wait until you get home to introduce your toddler to the new baby, rather than her coming to see you.

Arriving home

Bringing your new baby home for the first time is a big moment, but try to make sure that the focus is on your toddler during those first hours, particularly if you have been apart for a few days. It is preferable for your partner to carry the baby into the house as this will enable you to concentrate on your older child. Focus your attention on her. Ask her what she has been doing, and who she has seen, while you have been away. Most children are very excited to meet their new brother or sister, but occasionally a toddler can be either disinterested or obstreperous. Don't worry about this – she may become confused if she senses she is supposed to react in a certain way.

The first few weeks

You will feel tired following the birth, and looking after two children can feel overwhelming during the first few weeks. Mothers sometimes have unrealistic expectations about what they will be able to do when they are first at home with a new baby and a toddler. It will be easier to cope if you have prepared as much as you can in advance, and I firmly believe that how well you manage will be closely related to how much help you get (see page 50). Try not to be over-ambitious about what you can achieve, and don't feel too proud to accept support.

Don't expect too much from your toddler during the early days, either. It will be quite normal for her to experience some jealousy and resentment. She has probably imagined a picture-book infant, gurgling and smiling, and the reality of a crying baby who takes up so much of your time may come as something of a shock. She might have expected the baby to be her new best friend and playmate, and her initial interest may fade rapidly once she realises that little babies aren't interested in playing toddler games and don't really seem to be able to do much at all.

Encourage your toddler to understand that the baby is part of the whole family, and is her new baby as well as yours. Some toddlers feel a real sense of pride towards their younger siblings, and you might be able to interest her in helping out now that she is the 'big sister'. She may enjoy going to get clean nappies when you need them, or passing the baby wipes. You could even let her choose what the baby is going to wear. Make sure you tell her how much you appreciate all that she is doing for you. If she makes it clear she doesn't want to help, don't insist. The last thing you want is for her to resent having to do things for the new baby.

It is important to find some time to spend alone with your toddler when the baby is asleep, and to use it to do something she enjoys, such as playing a game or doing a jigsaw puzzle together. Tell her that this is your special time and make sure she realises that you enjoy being with her in just the same way you did before the baby came along. If the baby starts crying during this time, wait a moment before jumping up and leaving your toddler in the middle of whatever you were doing. Explain that you have to check the baby, but you will be back as soon as you can and will make sure you spend some extra time together later on. Also explain to her that she was just the same when she was a baby, and you spent lots of time feeding and changing her when she was very little.

When you start to have more visitors, you can involve your toddler in this by asking her to introduce people to her little sister or brother. People often like to bring gifts for the baby, but may not always think about bringing a small present for your toddler, too. It can help if you have a supply of little items stored away so that your toddler doesn't feel overlooked if the baby is showered with gifts.

If your partner has some time off when the baby is born, one of the difficult transitional stages will be the day that he first goes back to work. It is often a good idea to ask a friend or relative to spend at least part of the day with you. It can feel very lonely and overwhelming to be by yourself with a toddler and a baby for the first time.

Feeding the baby

It can take a while to feed a baby, and your toddler may find it extremely frustrating that you are unable to focus on her during this time. In the early days, when you have support in the house, it may not be so difficult, but once you are alone with your toddler and baby, you will want to make sure she is occupied before you start feeding the baby.

Consider letting your toddler do something special that she enjoys while you are feeding the baby, such as watching a favourite DVD or pretending to feed her toys. Try to make it feel as though it is a special treat that she gets when you feed the baby. Some children like to have a baby doll of their own that they can dress or feed with a little bottle while their mother is busy with the baby. If you can find something that works for your toddler, this will ensure she feels less resentment about the time you spend feeding the baby, and will keep her safely occupied.

Ideas for how to keep your toddler occupied, while you're feeding (or settling) your baby, include:

- Crayons and large sheets of paper for drawing

- Simple picture books and stories

- Talking books on CD or cassette tape

- Large two-, three- or four-piece jigsaws (depending on your toddler's age and abilities)

- 'Magic drawing' boards, such as Megasketcher, Aquadraw or Etch-a-sketch

- A bag of 'pocket money' toys all wrapped individually so that your toddler can choose one a day

- Homemade play dough or salt dough

- A child's tea set for a doll and teddy tea party (with or without water)

Eating well

I've come across mothers who get so overwhelmed by all that there is to do with a new baby that they simply forget to eat. As you will be even busier with two children, this is even more likely to happen, but I can't stress enough how important it is that you eat properly when your body is recovering from birth and when you are breast-feeding.

It is a good idea to stock up the freezer with some home-cooked meals for you and your partner when you are still pregnant (see page 30). You should also freeze some healthy meals for your toddler. This way, you can all eat good, nutritious food with the minimum effort in the early days after the birth. Try not to rely on ready-meals at this time, as most are full of additives and preservatives, which are not good for breast-feeding mothers. Eating properly will give you the energy you need.

Some mothers worry about the weight they have gained during pregnancy and want to try to lose it as quickly as possible, but this is not the time to start dieting. It is normal to eat more than usual when you are breast-feeding as your body is having to work harder than usual to provide food for your baby. Keep to a balanced diet with a good intake of protein, carbohydrates, vegetables and fruit and dairy products, and make sure that you are drinking plenty of water.

Shopping

You should get in some supplies before the birth (see page 29) – if you can stock up on non-perishable basics, it will be one less thing to worry about. You won't want to drag yourself around the supermarket with your baby and toddler during your first few weeks at home, and it should be possible to avoid this.

You will need to do food shopping at some point, and I suggest doing this online if you can. Try to arrange for your shopping to be delivered when you are going to have someone else at home with you; that way you won't be attempting to put the shopping away while looking after two children. If you can't get an online delivery, ask your partner, or a relative or friend, to get any shopping you need. If you have a local shop that sells groceries, this may be a good alternative for the first few weeks.

Getting out and about

You will probably feel too exhausted to go out much in the first week or so after the birth, but once you are sure you are up to it, try to get out of doors every day. Just a short walk to the park or the shops will make all the difference. If your toddler is at home with you all day, this becomes really essential as she will need some fresh air and exercise on a daily basis. You will find you both feel much better once you have been out.

I have worked with some mothers who found it could take them up to half an hour to get out of the door with their baby and toddler. There are a few things you can do to make the 'leaving the house' process quicker and easier:

- Always have a bag on the back of your pram and in your car containing everything you need. As well as spare nappies and wipes it should hold a change of clothes, warm tops for both children, a beaker of water, a healthy snack that you know your toddler will enjoy and a favourite book or toy.

- Make sure you always have your pram's rain cover with the pram.

- In the summer the bags should include suncream and sun hats for both children, as well as a light raincoat for your toddler.

- Check the content of the bags regularly to ensure you always have the right size nappies and clothes in them. I know of many mothers who discovered, too late, that the spare set of clothes they were carrying was too small!

- Keep coats and other outdoor clothes, including wellington boots for your toddler, near the pram.

- Ten minutes before you are due to go out make sure your toddler has been to the loo and, if your baby is awake, change his nappy. In the summer, allow an extra five minutes to put suncream on both children.

Things will get quicker with time as your baby grows and you adjust to life with two children, but the more prepared you are the easier you will find leaving the house.

Household chores

This is not the time to be too house-proud. Try to accept that you may need to lower your standards a little – no one expects the mother of a newborn baby to be spending all her time tidying. You won't want to be playing hostess, so during the first few weeks invite only those close friends and relatives who will make their own cup of tea and be happy to help out with your toddler if need be. Ask for help – find out if they would mind taking your older child for a walk to feed the ducks or play on the swings, so that you can give your baby a more relaxed feed or have a lie down if your baby is asleep.

Looking after yourself and your children should be your priority at this time. If you try to do too much, you will just end up exhausted and that won't help you or your children.

I know some mothers who find it difficult to live in a less-than-spotless home, but you need to try to ignore these feelings during the first few weeks at least.

I have always encouraged mothers 'to have less stuff, more staff' at this time. Parents spend an enormous amount of money on what they consider to be essential baby kit: new buggies, prams, cots and accessories. However, I would encourage any mother to borrow bits of equipment if it means they can spend a little money on some paid help (see page 34), even if it is just a couple of hours a week. It only takes a few hours for someone to clean the house and to do some laundry, and yet this can make an enormous difference to a new mother.

Getting help from family and friends

When you already have an older child, it is even more important to accept any offers of help during the first few weeks at home with a new baby, even if you have some paid help as well. I know many mothers believe they should be superwomen, able to cope with anything that life with a newborn and a toddler can throw at them, but it is usually tough going at first. In past generations, mothers usually had an extended family network close at hand, with grand-mothers and aunts to call on for help and advice when things got difficult. Nowadays, families often live long distances apart from one another, and it is quite rare to have this kind of help at hand.

If you are fortunate enough to have family members nearby, don't feel guilty about asking them for some support. If you have friends with children who may be happy to invite your toddler over to play now and again, make the most of it. You should never feel that accepting help is a sign that you aren't coping, and things will get easier far more quickly if you have some help at the start. If friends ask what they can do, don't be too embarrassed to ask if they could unload the washing machine, or heat up your toddler's lunch. People like to feel that they have been useful, and if you think of something they could do that would really help you out, you will both feel better afterwards.

Your toddler's reactions to the new baby

You are never going to avoid sibling rivalry entirely, no matter how well prepared your child is or how much she was looking forward to having a baby brother or sister. However, you can keep it to a minimum by making sure your toddler feels secure and loved, and that her life is not subject to too much change and disruption because of the new baby.

Explain that the baby is interested in her and proud to have such a lovely big sister. Once the baby can focus, show your toddler that her brother likes watching what she does. It is often hard for toddlers to be sufficiently gentle with newborns, but encourage her to interact with the baby as much as you can. Don't leave your toddler alone with the baby. If you have a playpen, put your toddler into it temporarily while you go to answer the phone or the front door.

Don't panic if your toddler seems to start to go back a few stages in her behaviour and skills at this time. It is not uncommon for toddlers to suddenly want to be treated as babies – to use a dummy, to be carried around and to sleep in a cot. It can be annoying, but do your best to remain patient. It may help if you try to explain that it is really not much fun being a baby. The baby can't tell you how he is feeling or what he wants, he can't go out and play or have fun. Most of the time he just lies about and sleeps. Tell your toddler that the baby can't wait until he is as big as his sister, so that he can do all the things she enjoys.

Your toddler is likely to get annoyed with the new baby at some point, and may show signs of jealousy. Try not to get angry with her, but instead work out why she may be feeling this way and whether there is anything you can do to improve the situation. When you are talking to her, don't blame the baby for the fact that you have less time and are tired. Try to focus on the one-to-one time you set aside to be with your toddler, making sure that she knows there will be some space for her every day, and that you look forward to this and appreciate being with her.

Perhaps the most important thing you can do at this stage is to ensure there is as much continuity as possible in your toddler's life. If her routines are firmly established, she will know what to expect each day, and this will help her feel more secure. Keep her busy, ensure she still has fun and you will make things easier for your entire family.

4
Establishing Routines

In this book I have created a set of routines and guidelines that will help you cope in the months ahead, and help you meet the needs of both your baby and toddler. At times you may find establishing the routines challenging, but by being consistent and persistent you will reap the rewards in the long-term of having two happy and contented children.

The main observations that I made from babies who settled quickly into a good feeding and sleeping pattern were:

- They did not go for long spells between feeds during the day.

- The parents had a positive approach, wanted a routine and tried to keep the first couple of weeks as calm as possible.

- Handling of the baby by visitors was kept to a minimum so that the baby felt relaxed and secure in his new surroundings.

- The baby was kept awake for a short spell after the daytime feeds.

- When he was awake, and had been well fed and winded, he was then stimulated and played with for short periods.

- A bedtime routine was established from day one. The baby would be bathed and fed at the same time every evening. If he did not settle, the parents would ensure that they kept things as quiet as possible and continued to comfort him in a dimly lit quiet room until he did eventually settle.

The above observations of my experience of working with hundreds of babies and their parents over the years became the basic principles of what are now known as the CLB routines.

Establishing the Contented Little Baby and Toddler Routine

There are many benefits for both babies and parents who follow the CLB routines, but one of the main ones I have observed is that the babies rarely cry, if at all. This is because the routines quickly help you learn the signs of hunger, tiredness, boredom or, indeed, many of the other reasons that young babies get upset. The fact that you are able to understand your baby's needs and meet them quickly and confidently will leave both of you calm and reassured, and avoid unnecessary crying. The common scenario of fretful baby and fraught parents, which you certainly won't want with a second baby, is avoided.

To get off to a good start with the routines, it is essential to establish a good milk supply. How to establish breast-feeding while coping with an energetic toddler is a major concern for many mothers who are pregnant with their second baby. If you breast-fed the first time around, you will no doubt remember that in the early days your baby spent a great deal of his waking time feeding. Given that feeds can take up to an hour, and that most babies will normally need to feed a minimum of between eight and 10 times a day, it may seem like an impossible task to successfully breast-feed your second baby and look after your lively toddler. I will not pretend that it is easy, but I know, from the many mothers I have worked with personally, and the thousands of posts on my forums from mothers of two and three children, that it can be done. By using the same CLB principles on breast-feeding as you did with your first baby, you can avoid excessive night-time feeding. Looking after a newborn baby and toddler during the day is exhausting enough without being woken every couple of hours to feed during the night. To avoid a pattern of several night-time wakings, how you approach feeding your baby in the first week is critical.

The key to successful breast-feeding is getting off to the right start. Breast milk is produced on a supply-and-demand basis, and feeding your baby 'little and often' after the birth is essential to help establish a good milk supply. All of my mothers who established three-hourly feeding in the hospital found that by the end of the first week a pattern had emerged. They were then very quickly able to move on to the first routine, and by structuring daytime feeding from the very beginning, excessive night-time feeding was avoided.

Establishing CLB breast-feeding

The following guidelines will help to ensure the best possible start to establishing breast-feeding. For information on bottle-feeding see page 64.

- Feeding your baby three-hourly will help to build up your milk supply much faster, and if he is fed enough during the day, he will be much more likely to go to sleep for longer periods between feeds in the night. The three hours is calculated from the beginning of one feed to the beginning of the next feed.

- A newborn baby's tummy is tiny and his needs can only be satisfied by feeding little and often. If you feed your baby three-hourly between 6am and midnight, the 'feeding all night syndrome' should never occur. Even if a very small baby is capable of going one longer spell in between feeds, following my advice ensures that this will happen to all babies at night and not during the day.

- During the first few days, between 6am and midnight, wake your baby every three hours for short feeds. This will ensure that the feeding gets off to the best possible start in time for when the milk comes in.

- Start off by offering five minutes on each breast every three hours, increasing the time by a few minutes each day until the milk comes in.

- Once your milk is in, you should have increased the baby's sucking time on the breast to around 15–20 minutes. Many babies will get enough milk from the first breast, and be content to go three hours before demanding a feed again. However, if you find your baby is demanding food long before three hours have passed, he should of course be fed, and offered both breasts at each feed, if he still remains unsettled.

- It is important to ensure that your baby has emptied the first breast totally before putting him to the second breast. In my experience, mothers who change breasts too soon end up feeding their baby too much fore milk, which I believe is one of the main causes of babies never seeming satisfied and suffering from colic (see page

263). It can take a sleepy baby 20–25 minutes to reach the very important hind milk (which is at least three times fattier than the fore milk). But other babies may reach the hind milk much quicker. Be guided by your baby as to how long he needs to get a good feed and learn to spot the signs that he has reached the hind milk (see below). If your baby feeds well, within the times I suggest, is happy and contented between feeds and is producing lots of wet nappies, he is obviously getting enough milk in the time he is on the breast.

Fore milk and hind milk

Nowadays, many breast-feeding counsellors advise that mothers should not concern themselves too much about the difference between fore milk and hind milk, and that getting the balance right bears no relevance to how well a baby settles. I totally disagree with this advice, and still firmly believe what I advised in my first book – that the amount of hind milk a baby gets at each feed plays a large part in how well he settles between feeds. At the beginning of the feed, your baby gets the fore milk, which is high in volume and low in fat. As the feed progresses, your baby's sucking will slow down and he will pause for longer between sucks. This is a sign that he is reaching the hind milk. Although he only gets a small amount of hind milk, I believe that it is very important that he is left on the breast long enough to reach it. It is this hind milk that will help your baby go longer between feeds.

During the last 10 years I have advised over 5,000 mothers, and a large number of these women were experiencing problems with their baby's sleeping and feeding. With some of these women, one of the main causes was that their baby was not being allowed long enough on the first breast to reach the hind milk. If you transfer your baby to the second breast before he has totally emptied the first breast, he will be more likely to get two lots of fore milk. This will have a knock-on effect and leave him feeling hungry again in a couple of hours. Another feed of fore milk will quickly lead to your baby becoming very 'colicky' (see page 263).

Gradually increase the time that your baby is on the breast, and by the end of the first week, if you are giving at least 25 minutes on the first breast, and then offer the second breast for 5–15 minutes, you can be fairly sure that your baby is getting the right balance of fore milk and hind milk. This will also ensure that your baby will be content to go at least three hours between most of his daytime feeds. If your baby is feeding from both breasts at each feed, always remember to start the next feed on the breast you last fed from, so that you can be sure that each breast is totally emptied every second feed.

In order to encourage a quick and easy let-down of milk, and ensure that your baby gets the right balance of fore milk and hind milk, the following guidelines should be followed:

- Prepare in advance everything needed for the feed: a comfortable chair with arms and a straight back, and perhaps a footstool; cushions to support both you and the baby; a drink of water and some soothing music will all help towards achieving a relaxing, enjoyable feed for both of you.

- When your toddler is around for the feed, make sure that you have a plan of how to occupy her (see page 17), plus a backup plan if she starts to get bored.

● It is essential that you take your time to position the baby on the breast correctly as poor positioning can lead to painful and often cracked, bleeding nipples. This, in turn, can affect your let-down of milk and result in a poor feed.

● Always make sure your baby has completely emptied the first breast before putting him on the second. It is the small amount of high-fat hind milk at the end of a feed that will help your baby go longer between feeds.

● Not all babies need the second breast in the early days. If your baby has totally emptied the first breast, burp him and change his nappy, then offer him the second breast. If he needs more he will take it. If not, start him off on that breast at the next feed.

● If your baby does feed from the second breast, you should still start on that breast at the next feed. This will ensure that each breast is totally emptied every second feed, thus signalling the breasts to make more milk.

● Once the milk is in and you have built up the time your baby feeds from the breast, it is important that he is on the breast long enough to reach the hind milk. Some babies may need up to 30 minutes but efficient feeders may be satisfied at 15.

● Never, ever allow your baby to suck on an empty breast; this will only lead to very painful nipples.

● Some babies, especially in the couple of weeks after birth, are very sleepy feeders. I find the current advice for 'skin to skin' contact with newborns when feeding really helpful as it not only promotes bonding between mother and baby, but also keeps the baby nice and cool which helps stimulate him enough to take a good feed. In addition, although I recommend keeping night feeds as brief and low-key as possible (only changing his nappy if absolutely necessary), if you find he is very sleepy and it's difficult to keep him awake for a full feed it can help to take off his swaddling or sleeping bag, maybe even unbutton his Babygro, give one breast, change his nappy and then re-swaddle him to finish the feed. Having fewer clothes on here, as well as changing his nappy, will promote good feeding and minimise chances of a second night waking.

Remembering which breast your baby has fed from

Some mothers I have worked with use an elastic band round their wrist on the side of the breast they have to feed from next, others prefer to use a safety pin on their bra strap. To start with, you need to find a method to help you remember which breast you should offer first at the next feed. Once you get into a good pattern of feeding, though, you will instantly know that you always feed, for example, from the right breast at the mid-morning feed, the left one at the mid-afternoon feed, etc. This is yet another benefit of following my routine.

Expressing breast milk

In my first book I said that I believed that expressing milk in the early days plays a huge part in determining how successful a mother will be in combining breast-feeding while following a routine. I know that some mothers do find it difficult to fit in the expressing times with a second baby, and choose not to do so. Some still manage to establish the routines by simply putting the baby to the breast more often and for longer during growth spurts, but I have observed from reading many of the messages on the forums that this can lead to other problems, such as excessive night-time waking, or the introduction of formula sooner than the mother had wished. When time is so precious in the early days, it may seem unrealistic to spend 10–20 minutes twice a day expressing. However, this is not really very long and should not be difficult as long as you have a plan for occupying your toddler. I would urge you to weigh up the time spent expressing against all the time you may have to spend giving extra night-time feeds and extended daytime feeds during growth spurts.

I have listed below the reasons why I believe that expressing is important to help establish the routines in the very early days:

- Breast milk is produced on a supply-and-demand basis. During the very early days, most babies will empty the first breast and some may take a small amount from the second breast. Very few will empty both breasts at this stage. By the end of the second week, the milk production balances out and most mothers are producing exactly the amount their baby is demanding.

- During the third and fourth week, the baby goes through a growth spurt and demands more milk. This is when a problem often sets in if you are attempting to put your baby into a routine and have taken advice not to express before six weeks.

- In order to meet the increased demand for more food, you would more than likely have to go back to feeding two- or three-hourly and often twice in the night. This feeding pattern is repeated each time the baby goes through a growth spurt and often results in the baby being continually fed just prior to sleep time. This can create the problem of the wrong sleep association, making it even more difficult to get the baby back into the routine.

● Mothers who express the extra milk they produce in the very early days will always be producing more milk than their baby needs. When their baby goes through a growth spurt, the routine stays intact, because simply expressing less milk at the early-morning feeds can immediately satisfy any increased appetite. Expressing from the very early days can also help to avoid the problem of a low milk supply.

● If you have previously experienced difficulties with expressing, do not be disheartened. Expressing at the times suggested in my routines along with the following guidelines should help make it easier:

○ The best time to express is in the morning as the breasts are usually fuller. Expressing will also be easier if it is done at the beginning of a feed. Express one breast just prior to feeding your baby, or feed your baby from one breast, then express from the second breast before offering him the remainder of his feed.

○ Some mothers actually find that it is easier to express while they are feeding the baby on the other breast. It is also important to note that expressing at the beginning of a feed allows slightly longer for that breast to make more milk for the next feed.

○ In my routines I suggest that the mother expresses at 6.45am; however, if you are producing a lot of milk and can't face the early-morning slot, or your toddler needs your attention at this time, you could, instead, express from the second breast at around 7.30am, after the baby has fed from the first breast.

A mother who is concerned about her milk supply, or who is following the plan for increasing the milk supply (on page 285), should try to stick to the recommended times.

○ In the early days, you may need to allow at least 15 minutes to express 60–90ml (2–3oz) at the morning feeds, and up to 30 minutes in the evenings. Try to keep expressing times quiet and relaxed. The more you practise, the easier it will become. I usually find that by the end of the first month, the majority of my mothers can easily express 60–90ml (2–3oz) within 10 minutes if they use a double pumping system (see below) at the 10pm feed.

○ If you can manage to get up 15 minutes earlier and express prior to the 7am feed, before your toddler is up and about, it will be a lot easier.

○ If you cannot manage the 9.30am expressing, try to express a couple of ounces when things are quieter after lunch. I would not recommend expressing any later than 1.30pm as the majority of mothers produce less milk as the day goes on, and it is important that you have enough in the evening so that your baby settles well at 7pm.

● An electrical, heavy-duty pumping machine – the type used in hospitals – is by far the best way to express milk in the early days. The suction of these machines is designed to simulate a baby's sucking rhythm, encouraging the milk flow. If you are expressing both breasts at 10pm, it is worthwhile investing in an attachment that enables both breasts to be expressed at once, therefore saving time.

● Sometimes, the let-down is slower in the evening when the breasts are producing less milk; a relaxing warm bath or shower will often help encourage the milk to flow more easily. Also, gently massaging the breasts before and during expressing will help.

● Some mothers find that expressing is easier if their baby, or a photograph of their baby, is close by for them to look at, while others find it better to watch a favourite television programme or to chat to their partners or husbands. Experiment with different approaches to see which one works best for you.

Establishing bottle-feeding

If you have decided to bottle-feed your second baby, follow the same routines as for breast-feeding (see page 55). The only difference is that you may find your baby is happy to go longer than three hours after the 7am feed; otherwise the timing is exactly the same. In the instances where a breast-feed is being split, e.g. one breast before the bath and one after, the same pattern applies to bottle-feeding. I would normally make up two separate smaller feeds for this time.

When your baby is born, the hospital will provide you with ready-made formula. You may be given a choice of two different brands; both are approved by the health authorities and there is very little difference in the composition of either milk. The bottles of formula will come with pre-packed sterilised teats, which are used once and then thrown away.

Unless the bottles have been stored in the fridge, they do not need to be heated; they can be given at room temperature. However, if for some reason you decide to heat the formula, do so by using either an electric bottle-warmer or by standing it in a jug of boiling water. Never heat the formula in a microwave, as the heat may not be evenly distributed and you could scald your

649.123 FORD

649.12 FORD

baby's mouth. Whichever form of heating you use, always test the temperature before giving the bottle to your baby. This can be done by shaking a few drops on the inside of your wrist; it should feel lukewarm, never hot. Once milk is heated, it should never be reheated as this very rapidly increases the bacteria levels, which is a common cause of upset tummies in formula-fed babies.

The advice given in hospital for formula-fed babies seems to be much the same as for breast-fed babies: 'Feed on demand whenever the baby wants and give him however much he wants.' While you do not have the problem of establishing a milk supply as in breast-feeding, many of the other problems are likely to occur. A bottle-fed baby weighing 3.2kg (7lb) or more at birth could go straight on to the two- to four-week routine (see page 109). A smaller baby might not manage to last quite as long between feeds and will need feeding nearer three-hourly.

How much and how often?

Health authorities advise that a baby under four months would need 70ml (2½oz) of milk for each pound of his body weight; a baby weighing around 3.2kg (7lb) would need approximately 510ml (18oz) a day. This is only a guideline; hungrier babies may need an extra ounce at some feeds. If your baby is one of these, try to ensure that you structure your feeds so he is taking the bigger feeds at the right times, i.e. 7am, 10.30am or 10.30pm. If you allow him to get into the habit of having bigger feeds in the middle of the night, it will eventually have the knock-on effect of him not being as hungry when he wakes in the morning. A vicious circle then emerges where he needs to feed in the night because he does not feed enough during the day.

The same guidelines apply as for breast-feeding: aim to get the baby to take most of his daily milk requirements between 6 and 7am and 11pm. This way he will only need a small feed in the middle of the night, and will eventually drop it altogether.

Guidelines for establishing bottle-feeding

Prepare everything in advance: chair, cushions, bib and muslin. As with breast-feeding, it is important that you are sitting comfortably (see page 58). In the early days, I advise all mothers to support the arm in which they are holding the baby with a pillow, which enables you to keep the baby on a slight slope with his back straight. By holding the baby as shown in diagram A (below), you will lessen the likelihood of your baby getting air trapped in his tummy if fed as shown in diagram B.

When your toddler is there for the feed make sure you have a plan of how to occupy her (see page 17), plus a backup plan if she starts to get bored.

Before starting to feed your baby, loosen and screw the teat back on; it should be very slightly loose. If it is screwed on too

Diagram A: Correct

Diagram B: Incorrect

tightly, it will not allow air into the bottle, and your baby will end up sucking and not getting any milk.

Check also that the milk is not too hot; it should be just slightly warm. If you get your baby used to very warm milk, you will find that as the feed progresses and the milk cools down he will refuse to feed. In this case, as it is dangerous to reheat the milk or keep the milk standing in hot water for any length of time, you could end up having to heat up two bottles for every feed.

Once feeding, make sure that the bottle is kept tilted up far enough to ensure that the teat is always filled with milk, to prevent your baby taking in too much air. Allow your baby to drink as much as he wants before stopping to burp him. If you try to burp him before he is ready, he will only get upset.

Some babies will take most of their feed, burp and then want a break of 10–15 minutes before finishing the remainder of the milk. In the early days, allowing for a break midway, it can take up to 40 minutes to give the bottle. Once your baby is six to eight weeks old, he will most likely finish his feed in about 20 minutes.

If you find your baby is taking a very long time to feed or keeps falling asleep halfway through a feed, it could be because the hole in the teat is too small. I find that many of my babies have to go straight on to a medium-flow teat as the slow-flow one isn't fast enough (see page 263).

Occasionally there are babies who will drink a full feed in 10–15 minutes and look for more. These babies are often referred to as 'hungrier babies'; the reality is that these babies are usually 'sucky' babies, not hungrier ones. Because they have such a strong suck, they are able to finish the bottle very quickly. As well as being a means of feeding, in the early days sucking is one of a baby's natural pleasures. If your baby is taking the required amount of formula at each feed very quickly and looking for more, it may be worthwhile trying a teat with a smaller hole. Offering him a dummy after feeds may also help to satisfy his 'sucking needs'.

It is very easy for bottle-fed babies to gain weight too quickly if they are allowed to have feeds well in excess of the amounts recommended for their weight. While a few ounces a day should not create a problem, a baby who is overeating and regularly putting on more than 226g (8oz) each week will eventually reach a stage where milk alone is not enough to satisfy his hunger. If this happens before the recommended age for giving solids (see page 175), it can create a real problem.

While it is normal for some babies to need an additional 30ml (1oz) at some feeds, special attention should be given if a baby is taking in excess of 150ml (5oz) every day, and is regularly gaining more than 226g (8oz) each week. When my formula-fed babies show signs of being particularly 'sucky', I have found that offering some cool boiled water between feeds and a dummy afterwards helps to satisfy their sucking needs.

If you are concerned that your baby is overfeeding, it is essential that you discuss the problem with your health visitor or doctor.

Sleep

All babies are different and, when establishing a sleeping routine with your second baby, it is unrealistic to expect him to follow exactly the same pattern of sleeping through as your first. It is important to remember that the aim of the CLB routines in the early days is to achieve a regular sleeping pattern where the baby settles well for daytime naps and in the evening, and then only wakes up once in the night after the late feed. One of the biggest mistakes I see many mothers of second babies making is trying to eliminate the middle-of-the-night feed at a certain age, because their first baby dropped the night feed at that age. They often spend weeks trying to settle the baby in the middle of the night with water or a cuddle, which more often than not leads to a regular pattern of night waking, and a fractious, overtired baby during the day.

When this happens, my advice is always the same – instead of trying to force the baby to go through the night without a feed, go back to night-time feeding, and pay more attention to structuring daytime feeds and sleeps. The majority of babies will sleep through the night when they are ready, provided of course that you establish the right sleep associations, structure daytime feeds and sleep, and ensure that the baby is not sleeping too much during the day.

The key to succeeding with the CLB routines is to ensure the baby feeds and settles quickly in the night. If he is awake for lengthy periods during the night, he will become irritable and overtired during the day. A baby who is constantly tired during the day will not sleep or feed so well, and a vicious circle soon emerges of poor daytime sleep and poor night-time sleep.

Swaddling

I firmly believe that during the first few weeks all babies sleep better when swaddled. The swaddle should always be made of lightweight pure cotton that has a slight stretch to it. To avoid overheating, always swaddle your baby in a single layer, and, when sleeping swaddled, reduce the number of blankets on the cot. It is, however, important that by six weeks you start to get your baby used to being half-swaddled, under the arms. Cot death rates peak between two and four months and overheating is thought to be a major factor. Always check that you are not putting too many layers on and that the temperature of the room remains between 16 and 20°C (61–68°F), as recommended by the Foundation for the Study of Infant Deaths (FSID). For further FSID advice see page 323.

How to swaddle your baby

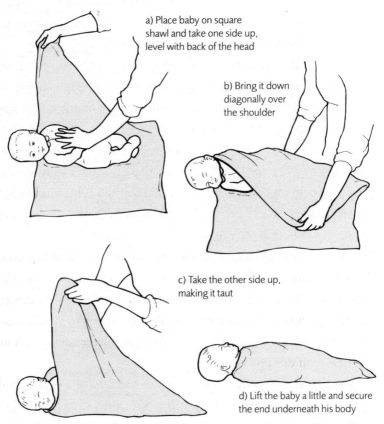

a) Place baby on square shawl and take one side up, level with back of the head

b) Bring it down diagonally over the shoulder

c) Take the other side up, making it taut

d) Lift the baby a little and secure the end underneath his body

Structuring daytime sleep

It is often the case that with a first baby it is easier to follow the routines to the letter, but that does not mean that with your second baby you cannot also achieve a routine and good sleeping habits early on. The key to getting the routine right for your second baby is to learn how to adapt the routines, so that your second baby's feeding and sleeping needs are met, but that they also fit in with your toddler's feeding and sleeping needs.

By following the basic CLB principles to establishing healthy sleep habits early on, and adapting the routines when necessary, you will achieve your ultimate aim: to have a happy and contented baby who sleeps well during the day and at night.

One of the most important things to remember is that I say that most babies in the early days can stay awake happily for up to two hours before needing a nap. I do not say that they *must* stay awake for the full two hours. It is, however, important that they do not stay awake longer than two hours to avoid overtiredness. So if, during the early days, you find that your baby is only staying awake for an hour or an hour and a half at a time, you do not need to worry as he is obviously a baby that needs more sleep, and as he grows he will start to stay awake for longer.

Of course if you have a baby who is only staying awake an hour at a time during the day, and partying for several hours in the night, this is a different matter. You may have to try harder to encourage him to stay awake longer during the day to avoid excessive night-time waking. Please refer to page 302 for advice on how to deal with this problem.

With a second baby, because of your toddler's school runs and play dates, you will probably find that you will have to make more adjustments to the routines during the first six months. On page

87 I suggest lots of ways to adapt the routines for feeding and sleeping, so that you can juggle the needs of two children. Try not to get stressed if you find yourself doing lots of adapting and juggling in the early days; the most important thing that you are trying to achieve is the right sleep associations and a baby who settles and sleeps well at nap times and in the night. Sometimes, the nap times will not be exactly as the routine suggests, and you may find yourself doing far more split feeds and naps than you did with your first baby. But, remember, the ultimate aim is to avoid your baby becoming overtired, for him to sleep well between 7pm and 10pm and to wake only once during the night.

The importance of nap times

In my first book I stress the importance of structuring naps so that the longest nap of the day is at midday, with two shorter ones in the morning and late afternoon. I advise that a longer nap in the morning followed by a shorter nap in the afternoon should be avoided as it can lead to early-morning waking during the second part of the first year.

It can be really tempting to allow a second baby to sleep longer in the morning, as it gives you more time for household chores and your toddler's play dates, etc. However, I can't stress enough how important it is to try to keep the morning nap shorter. At around four to six months, when your baby reduces his daytime sleep naturally, he is most likely to cut back on his late afternoon nap. His longest nap of the day would then be in the morning. By late afternoon he will be exhausted and need to go to bed by 6.30pm. This has a knock-on effect, which results in him waking up at 6am. Even if you do manage to get him to have a nap in the late afternoon, you could then be faced with the problem of him not settling well at 7/7.30pm. A fretful baby at this time could cause your toddler to become fretful too, and having two fretful children at bedtime is a scenario that you definitely want to avoid.

Below are some guidelines to help ensure that your baby sleeps for the right amount of time during the day and settles well in the evening:

- Very young babies can only stay awake for *up to two hours*, before becoming tired. If your baby stays awake for longer than two hours, he could become so exhausted that he will need a much longer sleep at his next nap time. This will have a knock-on effect, altering the rest of his routine, resulting in poor evening and night-time sleep. Therefore, it is essential that you structure the awake period properly, so that the feeding and sleeping plan works well.

- To determine whether your baby is a sleepy baby or not, look at his night-time sleep. If he can only stay awake for an hour at a time during the day, but settles well in the evening, and feeds and settles quickly during the night, he is a baby who needs more sleep. He will eventually manage to stay awake longer provided you give him the opportunity. You can do this by trying, whenever possible, to settle him in a quieter environment for naps, and during his waking time have him in a bright, social and noisier environment.

   However, if your baby can only stay awake for an hour at a time during the day, but stays awake for several hours during the night, it is possible that he has got his day and night muddled up, and it is worthwhile encouraging him to stay awake more during the day. Refer to page 302 for advice on how to deal with this particular problem.

● Babies learn by association. It is very important that from day one your baby learns the right associations, and to differentiate between feeding, playing, cuddling and sleeping.

● There will be some times of the day when your baby will stay awake for *up to two hours* quite happily, then other times when he will be tired after an hour. This is perfectly normal in the early days, which is why I say that babies can stay awake for up to two hours – *not that they must stay awake for two hours.*

Along with the routines, the following guidelines will help your baby to develop healthy sleeping habits:

● Try to keep him awake for a short spell after his day feeds.

● Do not let him sleep too long for the morning nap or in the late afternoon.

● Do not feed him after 3.15pm, as it will put him off his next feed.

● Follow the same routine every evening and do not allow visitors during wind-down time.

● Do not let your baby get overtired; allow at least one hour for the bath, feed and wind-down time.

● Do not overstimulate him or play with him after his bath.

● Do not rock him to sleep in your arms; try to settle him in his cot before he goes into a deep sleep.

- If you use a dummy (see page 270) to wind him down, ensure he is well tucked in according to FSID guidelines.

- If he falls asleep on the breast or bottle, rouse him slightly before settling him in his cot.

Managing sleep

It is crucial that you progress through the routines at a steady pace. All too often I work with parents who say that their babies used to sleep perfectly but now they are struggling with early-morning waking. Assuming feeding is going well the cause is almost always that the parents have failed to move on and cut down the naps quickly enough. It is true, some babies will naturally cut down on the amount of daytime sleep they take as soon as they are physically able to stay awake for longer periods in the day, but many do not. For these babies, it's absolutely essential that parents gradually move on and cut down naps before problems arise rather than waiting until their baby starts waking earlier in the morning or in the night. You can cut down naps easily and painlessly by gradually putting your baby down a few minutes later every few days. Being proactive in cutting down your baby's naps means that you can prevent any potential problems from arising and you can all continue to enjoy 12 hours of sleep a night.

The bedtime routine

Once your baby has regained his birth weight and has a good weekly weight gain, you can look at establishing a regular bedtime of 6.30/7pm. You can also allow him to sleep past the 9pm feeding, and feed him at around 10pm instead. It is at this stage that he should manage to sleep for slightly longer in the night. If he feeds well here, and settles at around 11/11.30pm, he will hopefully manage to sleep until 2/3am. If he feeds well then, and settles back within an hour, he should manage to sleep until around 6/7am. During the early days, how soon your baby wakes up after midnight will be very much dependent on how awake he was at the late feed, and how much milk he took. It is worthwhile spending a little longer giving this feed to ensure that your baby does start to sleep a longer stretch in the night.

Establishing a good bedtime routine and getting your baby to sleep well between 7pm and 10pm is a major factor in how quickly he will sleep through the night. A baby who feeds well at 6pm and settles to sleep well between 7pm and 10pm will wake up refreshed and ready to take a full feed. However, there are other factors that affect this bedtime routine: your baby needs a structured feeding and sleeping pattern during the day, so that he is hungry enough to take a full feed at 5/6.15pm; he also needs to have been awake enough during the day, so that he is ready to sleep at 7pm.

The thought of establishing a bedtime routine for your baby and toddler can be very daunting, but it is achievable provided your baby is well fed and ready to sleep at 6.30/7pm. For example, if you allow your baby to sleep for lengthy periods late afternoon, he is unlikely to settle well at 7pm, even if he has fed well.

The key to encouraging your baby to sleep well at night is very dependent on what happens during the day. Below is a summary of a typical day for a contented little baby and toddler, along with two different options for how to deal with the bathtime routine. The exact timings of the routine will vary depending on the age of your baby. These are laid out under the age-specific routines in chapters 5–13.

A typical routine for a Contented Little Baby and Toddler

6am–8am

- Baby needs to be fed and either settled back to sleep, depending on the time he awoke, or encouraged to sit in his chair while your toddler has her breakfast.

- If the baby fed from one breast at 6am, it would be best to wake him and give him the second breast while your toddler is having breakfast.

- Try to get both children fed by 8am, so that you allow plenty of time for washing and dressing.

8am–10am

- Get both children washed and dressed.

- Baby will be ready for a nap around 8.30/9am. If you need to drop your toddler at pre-school or nursery, this nap will have to take place in the car or the pram or pushchair.

- Once you have dropped your toddler off at nursery, time permitting, you can probably fit in the daily shopping. This will ensure that the baby sleeps well during his morning nap.

10am–12 noon

- Baby will need a feed at some point between 10am and 11am, and will probably be ready for a nap between 11.30am and 12 noon.

- Once he has been fed, encourage him to go on his play mat for a short spell so that you can fit in a few chores and prepare lunch for you and your toddler.

11.30am/12 noon

- Baby will be ready for a nap around now. If you have to pick your toddler up from pre-school or nursery, your baby will have to take the first part of the nap in the car or in his pram.

- Try to prepare his bed before you go out, so that he can go straight down the minute you get home. Offer a top-up feed first if necessary.

12.30pm–2pm

- Have lunch with your toddler. During this stage of development, your toddler will benefit greatly if you make time to eat with her. It will also help her realise that, although she now has to share you with her baby brother, she still gets special time with Mummy.

- Even if your toddler has dropped her lunchtime nap, I would try to encourage her to have some quiet time after lunch and discourage noisy games and running around. This will allow time for both you and her to recharge your batteries and ensure that the baby has a really good sleep at lunchtime.

2pm–5pm

- Aim to have baby awake and feeding no later than 2pm, so that he has had at least half of his feed during your toddler's nap or quiet time.

- By 2.30pm your toddler will probably be starting to get a bit restless, and it will become very difficult if she has to sit through nearly an hour of you feeding the baby. She will probably be happy to play with some of her toys while you finish off the baby's feed. This is also a good time to offer her a drink and a snack. If she is demanding your attention, try reading her a story while you finish off the feed. Also see page 17 for ways to occupy your toddler while you're feeding the baby.

- Your toddler will most certainly be getting bored by 3pm, so try to arrange in advance different activities each afternoon, such as a trip to the park or an arranged activity or play date with some of her friends. Alternate the activities so that she does not have really hectic ones two or three days in a row. If she is at nursery school every morning, afternoon activities should most certainly be more relaxed ones to avoid overtiredness becoming a real problem at bedtime.

- Baby will need a short nap between 4pm and 5pm. This can be taken in his pram or pushchair during a trip to the park or, if you're at home, with you in the garden or a quiet room downstairs.

- If a play date is taking place at your home, I would advise that you ask the other mothers to help you put the bulk of the toys away at 4.30pm. The fewer toys there are, the easier it will be to get the toddlers to co-operate in clearing them away, at a time when they are beginning to get tired and hungry.

5pm–6pm

- Baby will need to have a half of his breast-feed or bottle at around 5pm.

- Depending on what you have been doing that afternoon, aim to give your toddler her tea at 5pm. It is a good idea to feed your toddler before she gets really hungry as it can be stressful breast-feeding your baby if your toddler is irritable. Aim to breastfeed your baby while your toddler is having her tea.

- It is important that if you are feeding the baby at the same time as your toddler is having her tea, you do so in a seat very close to your toddler. A young child should never be left alone while eating; not only is it dangerous, but it will also make her feel very abandoned if you go off to another room to feed the baby.

- If your toddler has friends to play, she may be content until 5.30pm, which will give you time to feed the baby.

- The baby, having been fed, should be happy to sit in his bouncy chair or go under the play gym while you prepare and give tea to your toddler.

6pm–7.30pm

This is usually one of the most difficult times of the day for parents with a young baby and toddler, especially when you are coping with everything by yourself. If you have a partner who can help out when he gets home, that's wonderful, but for many mothers this time is one they have to manage alone. The guide below will enable you to manage on your own:

- The majority of young babies and toddlers are getting tired and irritable by this time, so trying to get them both bathed and settled happily in their beds at a reasonable time requires a huge amount of patience and discipline.

- Try to get both children upstairs no later than 6pm. It is essential during the early days that the baby does not become overtired. Remember that, during the early days, he will be ready to sleep two hours from the time he last woke. You will also need to take into consideration how long he slept during the late afternoon. If it was only a short nap, I would aim to get him into bed by 6.30pm.

- Try to create a calm, quiet atmosphere at this time so that neither of the children gets overstimulated or overexcited. Make sure that there are not too many toys lying around that could encourage your toddler to get hyped up.

- Whether you attempt to bath both your toddler and baby together will depend very much on the age of your toddler and how active she tends to be in the bath. You may want to invest in a towelling apron to prevent you getting very wet.

Bathtime

It is impossible for me to predict the temperament of your toddler and how she may react to sharing her bath. As with all interactions between your two children it is crucial to always try and pre-empt any conflict, particularly where this could occur in a confined space. If your toddler is gentle and kind to your baby in every other way then it is not unreasonable to expect that she will be happy to share her bath with her baby brother. It's a good idea to channel her energy into a bit of gentle washing of baby's feet, or another part of the body away from the head, if she seems keen, but, again, don't push her on this. If you find that your toddler seems resentful of sharing her bath then it's probably best to bath them separately for the time being. As I have said before, this is the most taxing part of any mother's day and whatever you can do to make it easier for yourself is a good thing.

The following describes two approaches to bathtime. I suggest that you try both to work out which one works best for you.

Bathtime: approach 1

- Bath both children together, putting the baby in one of the specially designed, moulded plastic bath seats that he can lie back in. Although this will free up both your hands you should *never* leave your baby unattended in the bath.

- Wash your toddler first, so that she can play while you quickly wash the baby. Have a changing mat on the bathroom floor so that you can transfer the baby to it to be dried, massaged and dressed while you keep an eye on your toddler.

- Having been fed at 5pm, your baby will hopefully be happy to lie on his changing mat once dressed, long enough for you to get your toddler out of the bath and dried and creamed.

- Encourage your toddler to dress herself while you give your baby the second breast or the remainder of his bottle-feed.

- Once your toddler is dressed, she should be encouraged to sit next to you and drink her milk, which you will have prepared earlier, while you read her a story, or she watches a DVD.

- Avoid telling your toddler that she must not shout or run around because you are trying to get the baby to sleep. This is the fastest way to ensure that she will start running around screaming at the top of her voice. Instead, explain that it is quiet time now and once baby is asleep she can have some special time with Mummy. When a toddler was active and not the type to sit still, I found that giving her several little 'beds' (painted shoe boxes, with makeshift blankets, etc) in which to put her special toys to sleep would occupy her for quite a while. She would then, in turn, give each toy a drink from a special bottle or beaker before tucking them in and kissing them goodnight. You could also have a special toy with its own bed near the baby's, so that when you settle the baby in his bed your toddler can quietly tuck in her special toy for the night.

- A few minutes prior to settling your baby in his bed, make a point of using a very low, quiet voice to tell baby that he must be very quiet now as it is time to go in his bed so that you can read his big sister a very special story. Emphasise to the baby what a good girl his big sister is and how quiet she is. Of course this must all be done within earshot of your toddler!

- Once your baby is settled in his bed, you can then read your toddler her special story. You will have to be strict about how long you spend reading to her, otherwise a situation could arise where she will want just one more story and the bedtime settling begins to take longer and longer. I would suggest that you allow no longer than 10–15 minutes of reading.

Bathtime: approach 2

If bathing both children at the same time is too daunting in the early days, establish a separate bathtime routine for each child. It would be advisable to start earlier, if you still want both children in bed by 7.30pm, as it will obviously take longer to bath and settle each child separately.

● Allow baby a good kick without his nappy while you prepare things needed for bath and bedtime. Get your toddler to help you with bathing, drying and massaging the baby, if she is willing. I always used to encourage an older child to wash, dry and cream the feet, counting the baby's toes. It will hopefully distract your toddler from the more delicate parts of the baby's body such as the head, eyes and mouth and genitals.

● Once your baby is ready to feed, you can adopt the same routine, but omit the toddler's milk at this stage. You should manage to settle the baby in bed by 6.30pm. Even if he has fed and winded well but does not seem ready to sleep, you can still lay him in his bed, but leave a dim light on and prop a cot mirror or baby cot book along the side for him to look at. I used to have to do this when I was settling twins in the evening and they very quickly got into the habit of going in the cot while wide awake, gazing happily at their books or mirror before drifting off to sleep.

● This will allow you or your partner to start your toddler's bathtime at around 6.30/7pm, aiming to be reading her story and give her some milk at around 7/7.15pm. This will ensure that she is still in bed by 7.30pm.

Night waking/early-morning waking in toddlers

After the arrival of a new baby, it is not uncommon for toddlers who have always slept really well to go through a phase of waking in the night or waking early in the morning. I have found the best way to deal with this is to go to the toddler very quickly and give her the reassurance that she needs, but not to get into lengthy conversations with her. Once she is settling back to sleep fairly quickly you can start a form of gradual withdrawal, where you stand further and further away from the bed when you go into the room, then eventually not go into the room at all and reassure her from the doorway. Once you reach this stage, I have often found that the use of a two-way baby monitor means that you can reassure your toddler without getting out of bed. I would also suggest, once you reach the stage of not having to go into your toddler's room, that you introduce a star chart to encourage your toddler to settle herself back to sleep without calling out for you.

For toddlers waking around 6am, consider using a bunny alarm clock, CD or light on a digital timer, to encourage them to stay in their bed slightly longer. The star chart can also be useful for encouraging your toddler to stay in bed until 7am. See *The Contented Toddler Years* for more information.

If you find that your toddler is constantly getting out of her bed and coming to your room, it can be worthwhile fitting a stair gate across her door. This can act as a deterrent to her getting out of bed in the first place, and is also an important safety consideration, especially with a new baby in the house.

It is often around the time of the new arrival that a toddler develops a fear of the dark. If this happens, I do not believe that a toddler should be forced to sleep in complete darkness, and I usually advise the use of a plug-in low voltage night light to help her feel more secure in preference to keeping the door open, as the latter can encourage your toddler to get up, expecting to start the day. You may also want to introduce a 'special' toy for your toddler to take to bed with her. A toddler who wakes up before 6am expecting to start the day should be told simply and firmly, 'It's not time to get up yet.' It is important not to get into discussions of any sort. If you are consistent enough and follow it through, no matter how often she wakes, this method should eventually work.

It is also really important to look at the amount of sleep that your toddler is having. I have noticed that the cause of disruptive sleep for many toddlers is in fact the need to reduce daytime sleep rather than the arrival of a newborn baby. An 18-month-old can need anywhere between just half an hour and two hours sleep between 7am and 7pm (although the average is two hours) but I have known some 18-month-olds who have dropped their daytime nap altogether. If your toddler is still having a long nap in the day and waking at night it is important that you cut this nap back, otherwise you risk a cycle developing where she needs more sleep in the day to make up for lost night sleep. Although overtiredness can also be a problem that can cause night-time waking this tends to be easier to spot (with a child waking scream-ing in the night or early morning and being near impossible to settle). In these cases, an earlier bedtime will solve the problem immediately and your toddler will start to sleep through soundly to 7am again. However, if this does not happen and her sleeping is still erratic, then it is essential that you keep reducing her daytime sleep every few days, until she is sleeping through soundly to nearer 7am.

Adjusting the routines

As I have mentioned earlier, with a second baby, depending on the age of your first baby, you may have to adjust the routines more in the early days. However, I would stress that these adjustments should ideally be made within the guidelines of the 7am to 7pm routine.

I have tried many different routines over the years and, without exception, I have found the 7am to 7pm routine to be the one that makes tiny babies the happiest and most contented. It fits in with their natural sleep rhythms and their need to feed little and often. I urge parents to try to stick to the original routine whenever possible. Once your baby is past the age of six months, is on four feeds a day and needs less sleep, it is possible to change the routine without affecting your baby's natural need for the right amount of sleep and number of feeds.

Up to the age of six months, the following points should be noted when planning a routine:

- In the very early weeks, to avoid more than one night-time feed, you must fit in at least between five to six feeds before midnight. This can only be done if your baby starts his day at 6am or 7am.

- An 8am to 8pm routine in the first few weeks would mean your baby would end up feeding twice between midnight and 7am.

Adjusting the routines to accommodate nursery drop-offs and pick-ups

I find that many parents expecting their second baby worry about whether they can follow my routines if they have to drop off and pick up their toddler from nursery or school. All of my routines can be adapted to suit the nursery or school run by following the suggestions below.

If your toddler goes to school in the morning, your baby will have to have part of his nap in the car or pram while he is under four weeks old. Once he has reached four weeks you can split the morning nap to suit your drop-off time (see page 301).

If you have to go out during the lunchtime nap then you will have to settle your baby in the car or pram. If it is still naptime when you get home you should quickly move him to his bed and settle him back down. Offer a top-up feed, if necessary.

It is very common for babies to fall asleep on their way to a 3–3.30pm pick-up even if they do not need the sleep. If this happens, do not try to keep him awake. Instead allow him just a short nap at this time followed by another short nap just before 5pm. By effectively splitting the late afternoon nap in this way you will ensure he does not have too much sleep overall.

If your toddler's pick-up time coincides with your baby's feeding time then you will have to feed him before you leave the house and then offer a top-up feed when you get home. This will also help you to settle your baby if you get home in the middle of his lunchtime nap.

Six months onwards

From six months, when your baby has started solids (see page 175), and you have dropped the 10pm feed, it is easier to adjust the routine. If your baby has been sleeping regularly until 7am, it could be possible to change to a 7.30am or 8am start, and push the rest of the routine forward. Your baby would obviously need to go to sleep later in the evenings. If you want your baby to sleep later but still go to bed at 7pm, try the following:

- Cut right back on the morning nap, or eliminate it altogether, so that your baby is ready to go to bed at 12–12.30pm.

- Allow a nap of no longer than two hours at lunchtime. The late afternoon nap will have been dropped by now.

As I have already mentioned, I do think it is important to try to stick to the original routine for your baby's age as much as possible, but I do understand that it might be difficult when you have to take into consideration the needs of your toddler as well. The following suggestions should help, but please remember that they are guidelines. You know your baby best, so if you have to make further adaptations, please do so.

Adjusting the routines to allow your baby to sleep until 7.30/8am

In previous editions of the Contented Little Baby books I stated that, once your baby was over six months and sleeping regularly until you woke him at 7am, it may be possible to let him sleep until 7.30/8am and drop the morning nap. It is true that this was possible for a handful of the babies I helped care for; however, I have seen lots of parents on my website get into difficulty with this as the extra sleep in the mornings causes their babies to wake in the subsequent nights. If you are trying this and find that your baby is waking in the night then it is sensible to go back to a 7am start. The other problem that can arise with a later morning is that your baby will not be having breakfast until 8/8.30am. Without a morning nap you will find that he is too tired to wait much past 12 noon for his lunch but, having eaten such a late breakfast, he may not be hungry at this time. The way round this would be to ensure that breakfast is kept really small (maybe just some fruit and a small amount of yoghurt) but, again, if you find that your baby isn't eating well at lunchtime then you may have to return to my original timings.

Evening routine at a friend's house

If you are spending the whole day at a friend's house, try to keep the evening routine similar to home. Explain the routine to your friend, and ask if it would be okay to give your baby and toddler their baths there before you leave. This means your toddler can drink her milk and get into the car at 7pm already in her sleep suit/pyjamas and sleeping bag for the journey home. If she is not overtired from the day's activities she will probably enjoy having a bath somewhere different! Once at home, with luck you will be able to transfer your sleeping baby and toddler straight into their beds. If the baby doesn't settle, offer a top-up of milk. This may result in him taking less milk at breakfast, but don't worry as his milk intake will even out over the day once he is back in the routine.

Clearly it might be difficult to give your children a bath if you are somewhere other than a good friend's house. But, again, don't worry. It is unlikely that your toddler will be disturbed through having missed her bath. Just ensure that she has a good wash the next morning!

Fresh air and exercise

Wherever you may be on your day out, try to let your baby and toddler get some fresh air and exercise. If you are going to a friend's house or visiting family, it should still be possible for your baby to have a little kick on a blanket, or your toddler to have a run around. Fresh air often helps children to sleep better, so even if your child sleeps in the car, if she has had lots of fresh air and some exercise, she could still be shattered by bedtime. When out with a young baby, try to avoid passing him round too much, so he ends up being in someone's arms most of the time. I am sure family and friends will want a cuddle, but also explain how much your baby likes his little kick!

The next day

A child who finds busy social activities overwhelming might be more tired after a day out than a more naturally sociable child. If your baby or toddler seems exhausted after a busy day, make sure the following one is peaceful and predictable to restore their sense of security and avoid them becoming overtired. Let your child guide you on this, and remember that, although a quiet day at home might seem boring to you, it can be a great source of comfort to children who need routine in which to develop safely and at their own pace.

Important recommendations

The most recent advice from the Foundation for the Study of Infant Deaths (FSID) and the Department of Health is that, until they are six months old, babies should now be put to sleep in a room with you at all sleep times during the day and evening as well as during the night. They recommend that that the safest place for the baby to sleep is in a crib, cot or Moses basket, and that babies should be checked regularly when asleep. It is safest to only have bed clothes in the bed, and no objects like toys, muslins or tagging. They also advise that a car seat is not an ideal place for very young babies to sleep in the home, and that on long car journeys babies should be carefully observed while in the car seat, with regular stops for fresh air and feeding.

It is also important to remember that these recommendations are only for the first six months, and after that time you can start to settle your baby in his own room for naps and night-time sleep. Until your baby reaches six months, if you do not have help at bath time, you will have to alter the bedtime routine slightly, taking both the baby and toddler downstairs after the bath, so that you can finish off the remainder of the bedtime routine in the room where the baby is being settled to sleep for the evening. Try to replicate the same atmosphere downstairs as you would upstairs, by dimming the lights, drawing the curtains and keeping everything calm and quiet. It is unlikely that you will have a cot both in your bedroom and downstairs, therefore, according to FSID, a pram with a proper firm mattress would be an acceptable option, and, I personally feel, possibly the safest option when you have a boisterous toddler around. It is important to follow the same guidelines for settling your baby in the pram as those given for settling your baby in a cot. The baby should be placed in the pram with its feet at the bottom, and it is essential that any sheets and blankets used are tucked in securely that they cannot work their way loose. Please check the images on FSID's website (see page 325) or www.contented baby.com on how to do this properly.

FSID understands that, during the day and evening, there will be times when a baby is asleep downstairs and parents may have to leave the room for a short spell, i.e. to settle your toddler in his room for his nap or at bedtime. They say that this is acceptable as long as the baby is not left for lengthy periods on its own while asleep. If you have any concerns about this advice it is important that you contact FSID or discuss them with your health visitor or GP.

Although the new guidelines may mean that it will take a little longer to establish the routines, please take heart that your second baby will eventually get into a good sleep routine, and sleep right through the night.

5
Weeks One to Two

Starting the routine

When moving on through the routines, it is important to remember that your baby's feeding and sleeping needs may not automatically fit straight into the feeding and sleeping times of the next routine. Try not to start the next routine until your baby is following the routine he is in at present. However, some babies go through a stage of needing one routine for feeding but a different one for sleeping. The following checklist will help you decide if your baby is ready to move on from feeding three-hourly (see page 55) into the one- to two-week routine:

- Your baby has regained his birth weight.

- He is happily going three hours between feeds, the three hours being calculated from the beginning of one feed to the beginning of the next feed. This means that if a feed has been taking around one hour, there is only a two-hour gap between feeds.

- Your baby shows signs of wanting to go longer between some feeds – you have to wake him for some of his feeds.

- He is staying awake happily for a short time after day feeds.

If your baby is showing all of the above signs, you can confidently start to implement the one- to two-week routine. The one- to two-week routine is not so different to the three-hourly routine, except that it starts to establish proper nap times, in particular the lunch-time nap. It is also the beginning of you starting to introduce a proper bedtime routine, and a longer sleep after the bedtime bath.

Your baby will still need to be fed three-hourly at some parts of the day, but in the one- to two-week routine there is a split feed at 10/11am in the morning, which helps establish the lunchtime nap. Also a split feed at 5/6pm, which will help encourage a longer sleep between 7pm and 10pm.

Routine for Baby and Toddler – one to two weeks

Feed times	Nap times between 7am and 7pm
7am	8.30am–10am
10am–11.15am	11.30am–2pm
2pm	3.30pm–5pm
5pm	
6pm	
10pm–11.15pm	**Maximum daily sleep:** 5½ hours

Expressing times: 6.45am and 9.15/9.30am

7am

● Baby should be awake, nappy changed and feeding no later than 7am.

- He needs up to 25–35 minutes on the full breast, then offer 10–15 minutes on the breast that you have expressed 90ml (3oz) from.

- If he fed at 5am or 6am, offer 20–25 minutes from the second breast after expressing 90ml (3oz).

- Depending on when your toddler wakes up, she can be given breakfast while you feed the baby. If the baby fed from one breast at 6am, give him the second breast while your toddler is having breakfast.

- Do not feed baby after 8am, as it will put him off his next feed. He can stay awake for up to one and a half hours.

- Try to have some cereal, toast and a drink no later than 8am.

8am

- Encourage your toddler to wash and dress herself while baby has a kick on his play mat.

8.15am

- Baby should start to get a bit sleepy by this time. Even if he does not show signs, he will be getting tired, so change his nappy and start winding down now.

- If you have to take your toddler to playgroup or pre-school, this nap will have to take place in the car or pram.

8.30am

- Before he gets too sleepy, swaddle (see page 70) and settle baby wherever this nap is due to take place, no later than 9am. He needs a sleep of no longer than one and a half hours.

- This is a good time to wash and sterilise any bottles and expressing equipment.

- If you are out and about, having dropped your toddler at day care, time permitting, you can probably fit in the daily shopping to coincide with your baby's nap.

- If your toddler is at home in the morning she can do some colouring or drawing while you tidy up the breakfast things and prepare the lunch.

9.15/9.30am

- Express 90ml (3oz) from the breast you first fed with at 7am.

9.45am

- Unswaddle the baby so that he can wake up naturally.

10am

- Baby must be fully awake now, regardless of how long he slept.

- He should be given 25–35 minutes from the breast he last fed on, while you drink a large glass of water.

- Give your toddler a snack and a small drink of water or very well-diluted juice. Try not to offer snacks later than 10.30am as it may put her off lunch.

- Lay the baby down so he can have a good kick and doesn't become too sleepy.

10.45am

- Settle your toddler down with a favourite activity.

- Wash and dress baby, remembering to cream all his creases. If your toddler is interested do involve her and encourage gentle interaction.

11am

- Offer baby up to 15–20 minutes from the breast you expressed from at 9.15/9.30am.

11.20am

- Baby should start to get a bit sleepy by this time. Even if he does not show the signs, he will be getting tired, so change his nappy and start winding down now.

- Once he is drowsy, settle baby, fully swaddled in his bed, no later than 11.30am.

- If he doesn't settle within 10 minutes, offer him 10 minutes from the fuller breast. Do this with no talking or eye contact.

- If you have to pick your toddler up from day care, the baby will have to take the first part of his nap in the car or pram. Prepare his bed before you go out so that he can go straight down the minute you get home.

11.30am–2pm

- Baby needs a nap of no longer than two and a half hours from the time he went down.

- If he wakes up after 45 minutes, check the swaddle, but do not talk to him.

- Allow 10 minutes for him to resettle himself; if he's still unsettled, offer him half his 2pm feed and try to settle him back to sleep until 2pm.

12 noon

- Have lunch with your toddler – she can either have a light lunch now or a full meal, which includes protein, depending on her morning activities and how tired she is at midday.

- If your toddler has dropped her lunchtime nap, encourage her to have some quiet time in her room or lying on the sofa. A talking book or short DVD can be useful to encourage quiet time.

- If your toddler is still having a lunchtime nap, make the most of this time to rest and try to have a nap.

- Wash and sterilise expressing equipment.

2pm

- Baby must be awake and feeding no later than 2pm, regardless of how long he has slept.

- Unswaddle him and allow him to wake naturally. Change his nappy.

- Give him 25–35 minutes from the breast he last fed on. If he is still hungry, offer 10–15 minutes from the other breast while you drink a large glass of water.

- Once your toddler is awake or up from quiet time, offer her a drink and a small snack.

- Change baby's nappy.

- Do not feed the baby after 3.15pm, as it will put him off his next feed.

- It is very important that baby is fully awake now until 3.30pm, so he goes down well at 7pm; if he was very alert in the morning, he may be sleepier now. Do not overdress him, as extra warmth might make him drowsy.

3.30pm

- If your toddler has had a physical activity, or been to playgroup or pre-school in the morning, try to arrange a quieter activity for the afternoon. If she had a quieter morning, try to encourage something more physical in the afternoon. Weather permitting, a short walk to the park or a run around the garden to get some fresh air before teatime is always a good idea for both baby and toddler, regardless of earlier activities.

- Baby will need a nap of up to one and a half hours.

- Baby should not sleep after 5pm if you want him to go down well at 7pm.

5pm

● Teatime for your toddler – something easy to prepare and eat, such as soup and a sandwich, is fine if she had a full meal that included protein at lunchtime.

● Baby must be fully awake and feeding no later than 5pm.

● Give him a good 25–30 minutes on the breast he last fed on.

● It is very important that he is not dozy while feeding (see page 224) and that he waits for the other breast until after his bath.

5.45pm

● Allow baby a good kick without his nappy while you prepare things needed for his bath and bedtime. Your toddler might enjoy helping but, if she doesn't want to, try to engage her in a peaceful activity.

● Give baby a quick bath. Dry and cream him paying particular attention to his creases.

6pm

● Baby must be feeding no later than 6pm; this should be done in a quiet room with care taken not to over stimulate him with talking and eye contact.

● If he did not finish the first breast at 5pm, give him 5–10 minutes on it before putting him on the full breast. Allow a good 20–25 minutes on the full breast.

- Encourage your toddler to enjoy a story, DVD or talking book while sitting next to you.

- Settle baby in his bed, fully swaddled, by 6.30pm. Leave a dim light on and prop a cot mirror or book along the side for him to look at.

6.30/7pm

- Bathtime for your toddler. This should take no longer than 10–15 minutes for you or your partner.

- Encourage your toddler to dry and dress herself.

- She can then have a beaker of milk and a story.

7/7.30pm

- Settle your toddler in bed after a bedtime story.

- If baby hasn't settled well, offer him 10 minutes from the fuller breast. Do this without stimulating him by talking or eye contact.

8pm

- It is very important to have a healthy meal and a good drink of water before the next feed.

9.45pm

- Turn the lights on fully and unswaddle baby so that he can wake up naturally.

- Allow at least 10 minutes before feeding to ensure that he is fully awake and can feed well.

- Lay out things for the nappy change, plus a spare draw sheet, muslin and swaddle blanket in case they are needed in the middle of the night.

- Give baby up to 25–35 minutes from the breast he last fed on or most of his bottle-feed, change his nappy and re-swaddle him.

- Dim the lights and, with no talking or eye contact, give him 20–25 minutes on the second breast or the remainder of his bottle-feed.

In the night

- During the first week, it is important that breast-fed babies are not allowed to go too long in the night between feeds.

- A baby weighing less than 3.2kg (7lb) at birth should be woken at around 2.30am for a feed, and a baby weighing between 3.2–3.6kg (7–8lb) should be woken no later than 3.30am.

- A formula-fed baby who weighs more than 3.6kg (8lb) or a baby that weighed over 3.6kg (8lbs) at birth, who has fed well during the day, may be able to go slightly longer, but not longer than five hours.

- If you are in doubt as to how long to allow your baby to sleep between feeds in the night, please seek advice from your GP or health visitor.

Changes to be made during the one- to two-week routine

Sleeping

Depending on how long your baby sleeps after the 10pm feed, you can choose one of the following options.

- If your baby feeds well and settles well and then sleeps until after 2am, then feeds well in the night and sleeps until nearer 6am, following the routine and having him awake for an hour at the 10pm feed is fine.

- If your baby feeds well and settles well after being awake an hour at the 10pm feed, but then wakes up before 2am and then wakes up again before 6am, I would continue with a split feed at 10pm to try to eliminate the twice-a-night waking. It can take at least a week to establish this split feed so do not get disheartened if you do not see immediate results. For the split feed to work well, you should start to wake your baby at around 9.45pm, and by 10pm start the feed. Give him as much of this feed as he wants, then allow him to have a good kick on his play mat. At nearer 11pm take him to the bedroom, change his nappy then offer him the second part of his feed. If he is formula-fed, I would advise that you make up two bottles.

Feeding

When your baby wakes in the night, it is really important that he takes a big enough feed, so that he sleeps well until nearer 6/7am. You should not restrict the amount he wants to feed at this stage; by doing so you could risk him waking at 5am looking for another feed. At this stage you are aiming to feed your baby well enough so that he only needs to feed twice between 7pm and 6/7am.

Depending on what time he fed in the night, your baby will probably wake up between 6am and 7am, but he should always be woken at 7am regardless. If he wakes up at 6am, this means that you can give him most of his first morning feed before your toddler gets up (treat this as a night feed), and then offer him a top-up feed while your toddler is eating breakfast. If the baby sleeps until 7am, then your toddler can drink her milk cuddled up next to you in bed while you give the baby his feed. Allowing the baby 20/25 minutes on the breast, then changing his nappy and taking him downstairs for the remainder of the feed, while your toddler eats breakfast usually works quite well. It not only stops the toddler getting bored, but also stimulates the baby who is often getting sleepy on the breast at this time.

The next feed will usually be at around 10am. I know that, with an energetic toddler to cope with, it might be tempting to let the baby sleep longer, but the aim is to ensure that your baby feeds regularly during the day so that he only needs to wake once for a feed between 11pm and 6/7am. Hopefully you still have some help at this stage and your toddler can be taken out for the morning, allowing you to spend some one-to-one time with your new baby. On the mornings that your toddler is at home with you, try to organise everything in advance for the baby's feed, and also a snack and drink for your toddler so that she is occupied for the first part of the feed. You will have to be realistic about how long she will sit happily before getting bored. If you get 10–15 minutes of her sitting quietly having her drink and snack, then she is doing exceptionally well! When she shows signs of boredom, be quick to suggest activities (see page 17), while you continue with the feed.

When following the routines, remember that they are guidelines to help you decide just how long your baby can stay awake before he needs to nap. Most babies in the early days can stay awake happily for up to two hours before needing a nap. This does not mean they *must* stay awake for the full two hours, only that it is important that they do not stay awake for longer if overtiredness is to be avoided. So if, during the early days, you find that your baby is only staying awake for an hour or an hour and a half at a time, you do not need to worry as he is obviously a baby that needs more sleep, and as he grows he will start to stay awake longer (see page 73).

During this routine I suggest that you always offer the baby a top-up feed at 11.15am, or just prior to the midday nap. This will hopefully avoid him waking up hungry during the middle of the nap. However, should he wake up before 2pm, I would assume that hunger is the genuine cause and offer him a feed before trying to settle him back to sleep. If he will not settle back to sleep, then it is best just to get him up, and then offer him two shorter naps at around 2.30pm and 4pm.

If your toddler is still having a nap, depending on how long she sleeps, try to adapt it so that you manage to get at least part of the baby's 2pm feed finished before you need to get your toddler up. If she has dropped this nap and only has quiet time after lunch, try to move any DVD watching that she may have had over the lunchtime to during the baby's 2pm feed. DVDs and TV can be a life-saver in the early days when breast-feeding is taking an hour or so, but try to hold off using them until as late in the day as possible.

Try to time your toddler's tea so that it coincides with the baby's 5pm feed. Choose something that is quick and easy, and can be prepared within 10 minutes or so at around 4.45pm. Once your toddler is seated at the table, you can then offer the baby his 5pm feed while she is eating. Check pages 252–5 for advice on what to do if your toddler plays up at this time.

As daunting as it may seem, this is a good time to start to implement a joint bedtime. Check page 81 for options on how to cope with the bathing and bedtime routine for a baby and toddler.

Advancing to the two- to four-week routine

By the end of the second week, you should be able to advance on to the two- to four-week routine.

The following signs will help you decide whether you can advance on to the two- to four-week routine:

- Your baby should weigh over 3.2kg (7lb), have regained his birth weight and show signs of gaining some weight each day.

- He is sleeping well at nap times and more often than not you have to wake him from his naps for him to be fed.

- He is feeding more efficiently and often emptying a breast within 25–30 minutes.

- He is showing signs of being more alert and managing to stay awake easily for an hour and a half at a time.

If you find that your baby is happy to go longer between feeds, but still needs to sleep more than the two- to four-week routine suggests, then you can still follow this routine for feeding, and continue to follow the one- to two-week routine for sleep until he shows signs of needing less sleep. Remember that a baby who needs more sleep will be sleeping well at night as well as during the day. If your baby is sleeping well during the day, but starting to be more wakeful in the middle of the night, it is possibly a sign he needs to be awake more during the day.

6

Weeks Two to Four

Routine for Baby and Toddler – two to four weeks

Feed times	Nap times between 7am and 7pm
7am	8.30/9am–10am
10/10.30am	11.30am/12 noon–2pm
2pm	4pm–5pm
5pm	
6pm	
10/10.30pm	**Maximum daily sleep:** 5 hours

Expressing times: 6.45am, 9.15/9.30am and 9.30pm

7am

- Baby should be awake, nappy changed and feeding no later than 7am.

- He needs up to 20–25 minutes on the full breast, then offer up to 10–15 minutes on the breast that you have expressed 60–90ml (2–3oz) from.

- If he fed at 5am or 6am, offer 20–25 minutes from the second breast after expressing 60–90ml (2–3oz).

- Depending on when your toddler wakes up, she can be given breakfast while you feed the baby. If the baby fed from one breast at 6am, give him the second breast while the toddler is having breakfast.

- Do not feed baby after 7.45am, as it will put him off his next feed. He can stay awake for up to two hours.

- Try to have some cereal, toast and a drink no later than 8am.

8am

- Encourage your toddler to wash and dress herself while baby has a kick on his play mat.

8.30/8.45am

- Baby should start to get a bit sleepy by this time. Even if he does not show the signs, he will be getting tired, so change his nappy and begin winding down now.

- If you have to take the toddler to playgroup or pre-school, the baby's nap will have to take place in the car or pram. He will need a sleep of no longer than one and a half hours.

9am

- If you are at home for this nap, wash and sterilise bottles and expressing equipment while your toddler engages in some quiet play or drawing activity. Or she could 'help' you wash some bottles in a bowl of warm water.

9.15/9.30am

- Express 60ml (2oz) from the breast you first fed with at 7am.

9.45am

- Unswaddle baby so that he can wake up naturally.

- Prepare things for top-and-tailing and dressing.

- Prepare snack and drink for your toddler.

10am

- Baby must be fully awake now, regardless of how long he slept.

- He should be given 20–25 minutes from the breast he last fed on, while you drink a large glass of water.

- Snack time for your toddler. It is important that her snack is finished by 10.30am to avoid taking the edge off her appetite for lunch.

- Wash and dress baby, remembering to cream all his creases – involve your toddler in this if she is keen to help.

10.30am

- Lay him on his play mat so that he can have a good kick before he gets too tired. Make sure there is no danger of the toddler accidentally falling over the baby by staying very close by or by putting the baby in a playpen or travel cot.

- Offer 10–15 minutes on the breast you last expressed from.

11.30am

- If baby was very alert and awake during the previous two hours, he may start to get tired by 11.30am and would need to be in bed by 11.45am.

11.45am

- Regardless of what he has done earlier, baby should now be winding down for his nap.

- Check the draw sheet and change his nappy.

- If you have to pick your toddler up from day care, then the baby will have to take the first part of this nap in the car or pram. Prepare his bed before you go out so that he can go straight down the minute you get home.

- If you are home for this nap, settle baby once he is drowsy, fully swaddled in his bed, no later than 12 noon.

11.30am/12 noon–2pm

- Baby needs a nap of no longer than two and a half hours from the time he went down.

- If he slept one and a half hours earlier, only allow him two hours this nap time.

- If he wakes up after 45 minutes, check the swaddle, but do not overstimulate him by talking.

- Allow 10–20 minutes for him to resettle himself; if he's still unsettled, offer him half his 2pm feed and try to settle him back to sleep until 2pm.

12/12.30pm

- Have lunch and then rest/nap with your toddler before the next feed.

- Wash and sterilise expressing equipment.

2pm

- Baby must be awake and feeding no later than 2pm, regardless of how long he has slept.

- Unswaddle him and allow him to wake naturally. Change his nappy.

- Give 20–25 minutes from the breast he last fed on. If he is still hungry, offer 10–15 minutes from the other breast, while you drink a large glass of water.

- Snack time for your toddler.

- Do not feed baby after 3.15pm as it will put him off his next feed and try to keep him awake.

- It is very important that he is fully awake now until 4pm, so he goes down well at 7pm; if he was very alert in the morning, he may be sleepier now. Do not overdress him, as extra warmth will make him drowsy.

- Lay him on his play mat in a safe place and encourage him to have a good kick.

3.30–4pm

- Change baby's nappy.

- This is a good time to take him for a walk to ensure that he sleeps well, and is refreshed for his bath and next feed. Your toddler will also benefit from some fresh air at this time.

- Baby should not sleep after 5pm, if you want him to go down well at 7pm.

5pm

- Teatime for your toddler.

- Baby must be fully awake and feeding no later than 5pm.

- Give him a good 20 minutes on the breast he last fed on.

- It is very important that he waits for the other breast until after his bath.

5.45pm

- Allow baby a good kick without his nappy on while you prepare things needed for his bath and bedtime. Your toddler might enjoy helping but, if she doesn't want to, try to engage her in a quiet activity.

- Give baby a quick bath. Dry and cream him paying particular attention to his creases.

6pm

- Baby must be feeding no later than 6pm; this should be done in a quiet room with care not to overstimulate him with talking or eye contact.

- If he did not finish the first breast at 5pm, give him 5–10 minutes on it before putting him on the full breast. Allow a good 20–25 minutes on the full breast.

- Encourage your toddler to enjoy a story, DVD or talking book while sitting next to you.

- Settle baby in his bed, fully swaddled, by 6.30pm. Leave a dim light on and prop a cot mirror or book along the side for him to look at.

6.30/7pm

- Bathtime for your toddler. This should take no longer than 10–15 minutes for you or your partner.

- Encourage your toddler to dry and dress herself.

- She can then have a beaker of milk and a story.

7/7.30pm

- Settle your toddler in bed after a bedtime story.

- If your baby hasn't settled well, offer him 10 minutes from the fuller breast. Do this without stimulating him by talking or eye contact.

8pm

- It is very important that you have a really good meal and a rest before the next feed or expressing.

9.30pm

- Express full feed from both breasts if offering a bottle at the late feed.

10/10.30pm

- Turn up the lights fully and unswaddle baby so that he can wake up naturally.

- Allow at least 10 minutes before feeding to ensure he is fully awake, so that he can feed well.

- Lay out things for the nappy change, plus a spare draw sheet, muslin and swaddle blanket in case they are needed in the middle of the night.

- Give him 20 minutes from the breast he last fed on or most of his bottle-feed, change his nappy and re-swaddle him.

- Dim the lights and, with no talking or eye contact, give him 20 minutes on the second breast or the remainder of the formula- feed.

In the night

- If baby wakes before 4am, give him a full feed.

- If he wakes between 4am and 5am, give him one breast, then the second at 7am after expressing.

- If he wakes at 6am, give him one breast, then the second at 7.30am after expressing.

- Make sure that you keep the lights dim and avoid eye contact or talking. Only change his nappy if absolutely necessary.

Around the two- to four-week routine is usually the time that you have to take over the full care of both children, and it also coincides with your baby's first growth spurt. Many babies become a bit fretful or unsettled during growth spurts, so even if your partner has gone back to work full-time, try to arrange for him to get home earlier than usual, if possible, so that he can help out with the bedtime routine. The majority of babies and toddlers get a bit irritable around 5pm and it is probably the most challenging time of the day for all mothers, so do not take it as a failure on your part if things get fraught at this time of the day. It is certainly a time that many toddlers tend to throw their biggest tantrums. I recall times when it seemed that climbing Mount Everest would have been easier than attempting to get a crying baby and screaming toddler upstairs for a bath.

Tempting as it may be, do not put off getting out and about, in order to establish the routine. I sometimes hear mothers saying that they are putting off taking their toddlers to play dates until the baby is more settled in the routine. Remember that there are over eight routines in the first year, and you could end up delaying going out for weeks and weeks if you wait until the baby is following the routine exactly. It is also unfair to expect your toddler to sit around the house for hours on end while you feed the baby, and it is exactly this scenario that can lead to jealousy and tantrums.

On pages 250–1 I give advice on how to adapt the routines for outings, in particular how to fit in play dates for your toddler.

Certainly, there may be days when it feels as if the whole routine has gone wrong, but as long as you manage to get both children settled in bed by 7/7.30pm in the evening, I think you should give yourself a pat on the back and remember that tomorrow is another day.

If the worst comes to the worst and both children are not settling well at bedtime, concentrate on settling one. As long as the baby is reasonably happy sitting in his bouncy chair or lying in his pram, I would choose to settle your toddler. At least that way you will be keeping one of them in a routine, which is preferable to ending up trying to get the routine right for both, and failing both.

On the occasions you have to have a later bedtime for the baby, you can easily get his routine back on track by pushing his 10pm feed slightly later.

Changes to be made during the two- to four-week routine

Sleeping

By three to four weeks, your baby should start to show signs of being more wakeful and for longer periods. Ensure that you encourage the wakefulness during the day so that his night-time sleep is not affected. By four weeks the morning nap should be no more than one hour, to ensure that he sleeps well at lunchtime.

Gradually, aim to keep him awake longer in the morning, until he is going down for his sleep at 9am. If you find that he is going to sleep at 8.30am and waking up between 9.15am–9.30am, which has an adverse effect on the rest of the day, topping-and-tailing him around 8.20am should be enough to revive him enough to last until 9am. If school runs prevent you from doing this and he is awake from 9.15am, you could try allowing him a short catnap of 10 minutes around 10.45am–11am. This means he would go down for his lunchtime nap somewhere between 12.15pm–12.30pm, avoiding the much earlier time of 11.15am if he had been awake since 9.15am. The afternoon nap should be no more than one hour in total; this nap is sometimes broken into a couple of catnaps between 4pm and 5pm.

By five weeks he should be half-swaddled, under the arms (see page 70), for the 9am and 12 noon nap, and for the late afternoon nap. Around four weeks it becomes more obvious when the baby comes into his light sleep: normally every 45 minutes, although it can be every 30 minutes with some babies. If a feed is not due, most babies, given the opportunity, settle themselves back to sleep. Rushing too quickly to your baby and assisting him back to sleep by rocking or patting could result in a long-term sleep association problem. This means that in the night when your baby comes into his light sleep, you could end up getting up several times to help him back to sleep, long after the time he no longer needs night feeds.

Feeding

Most babies go through a growth spurt around the third week. When your baby goes through a growth spurt, reduce the amount you express at 6.45am by 30ml (1oz) and by the end of the fourth week reduce the 10.30am expressing by 30ml (1oz). This will ensure that your baby immediately receives the extra milk he needs. If you have not been expressing, you will need to allow your baby to feed more often on the breast and for longer periods, in order for him to get the amounts he needs. During this time, try to get extra rest so that your baby's increased feeding demands do not have the opposite effect on you, causing you to become so exhausted that your milk supply decreases even further. If you do not wish to lose his sleeping routine, you could try using the plan on page 285, which increases your milk supply without losing the sleep routine. Once your milk supply has increased, you can then go back to following the routine suitable for your baby's age.

If you are breast-feeding and have decided to give one bottle-feed a day, this is a good age to introduce it. If you leave it any later than this age, it is very possible that your baby will refuse a bottle altogether, which can cause enormous problems later on, particularly if you are going back to work. It is advisable to express between 9.30pm and 10pm, extracting as much milk as possible. This milk can either be used for the 10.30pm feed, or frozen and used on the occasions when you need to leave your baby with a babysitter. Introducing a bottle of expressed milk at 10.30pm also allows the father to get involved and enables you to get to bed earlier, giving you the extra sleep that all mothers need during the early weeks.

Bottle-fed babies should have their 7am, 10.30am and 10.30pm feeds increased first during growth spurts. Some bottle-fed babies are ready to go from using a newborn teat to a slow flow teat (see below).

Low weight gain in breast-fed babies is usually caused by a low milk supply or poor positioning at the breast; the two usually go hand in hand. It would be worthwhile following the plan for increasing your milk supply on page 285. I would also advise that you arrange a home visit from a breast-feeding counsellor to check that you are positioning your baby on the breast correctly.

If your baby is formula-fed and not gaining sufficient weight, try moving him from the newborn teat with one hole to the slow flow teat with two holes. Always discuss any concerns you have regarding your baby's low weight gain with your health visitor or GP.

If you find your baby is still waking at around 2am then again at 5am, I would suggest that you start to wake him up at 9.45pm, so that he is wide awake by 10pm. Give him most of his feed and keep him awake for longer than the recommended one hour. At 11.15pm his nappy should be changed and the lights dimmed while you give him a small top-up feed. By giving him a split feed and having him awake slightly longer at this time, he will more than likely sleep well past 3am, provided he is not getting out of his swaddle.

Once your baby reaches four weeks, he will probably show signs of being happy to go slightly longer between feeds, and you should be able to move him on to the four- to six-week feeding routine, provided he is regularly gaining weight each week. Babies who are not gaining sufficient weight should remain on the two- to four-week routine until their weight gain improves.

In my experience, babies who regularly gain between 170–226g (6–8oz) a week in the first few months are usually more content and sleep better than those who are putting on less than 170g (6oz) a week. On saying this, I have cared for some very happy and content babies who would thrive well on a weight gain of only 113–142g (4–5oz) a week. However, if you find your baby is constantly irritable between feeds, not sleeping well at night and gaining less than 170g (6oz) a week, it may be that he is not getting enough to eat and it would be advisable to discuss his weight gain with your health visitor or GP.

7

Weeks Four to Six

Routine for Baby and Toddler – four to to six weeks

Feed times	Nap times between 7am and 7pm
7am	9am–10am
10/10.30am	11.30am/12 noon–2/2.30pm
2/2.30pm	4.15pm/5pm
5pm	
6pm	
10/10.30pm	**Maximum daily sleep:** $4^{3}/_{4}$ hours

Expressing times: 6.45am, 9.15/9.30am and 9.30pm

7am

- Baby should be awake, nappy changed and feeding no later than 7am.

- If he fed at 3am or 4am, he needs up to 20–25 minutes on the full breast. If he's still hungry, offer 10–15 minutes on the breast that you have expressed 60ml (2oz) from.

- If he fed at 5am or 6am, offer 20–25 minutes from the second breast after expressing 60ml (2oz).

- Depending on when your toddler wakes up, she can be given breakfast while you feed the baby. If the baby fed from one breast at 6am, give him the second breast while your toddler is having breakfast.

- Do not feed baby after 7.45am, as it will put him off his next feed. He can stay awake for up to two hours.

- Try to have some cereal, toast and a drink no later than 8am.

8am

- Encourage your toddler to wash and dress herself while your baby has a kick on his play mat.

8.45am

- Baby should start to get a bit sleepy by this time. Even if he does not show the signs, he will be getting tired, so change his nappy and begin winding down now.

- If you have to take your toddler to playgroup or pre-school, the baby's nap will have to take place in the car or pram.

9am

- When he is drowsy, settle baby, fully or half-swaddled (see page 70), wherever this nap is due to take place, no later than 9am.

- He needs a sleep of no longer than one hour.

- If you are at home for this nap, wash and sterilise bottles and expressing equipment. Your toddler may enjoy helping with this but must not be forced to if she's not keen.

9.15/9.30am

- Express 30ml (1oz) from the breast you first fed with at 7am.

9.45am

- Unswaddle baby so that he can wake up naturally.

- Prepare things for top-and-tailing and dressing.

- Prepare snack and drink for your toddler.

10am

- Baby must be fully awake now, regardless of how long he slept.

- Wash and dress him, remembering to cream all his creases and dry skin.

- Snack time for your toddler. It is important that her snack is finished by 10.30am to avoid taking the edge off her appetite for lunch.

10.30am

- Baby should be given 20–25 minutes from the breast he last fed on.

- Lay him on his play mat so that he can have a good kick. Then offer him 10–15 minutes from the breast you last expressed from.

- Do not feed baby after 11.30am, as it will put him off his next feed.

- Prepare lunch for you and your toddler.

11.30am

- If baby was very alert and awake during the previous two hours, he may start to get tired by 11.30am and would need to be in bed by 11.45am.

- If you have to pick your toddler up from day care, then the baby will have to take the first part of this nap in the car or pram. Prepare his bed before you go out so that he can go straight down the minute you get home.

11.45am

- Regardless of what baby has done earlier, he should now be winding down for his nap.

- Check the draw sheet and change his nappy.

- Close the curtains and when he is drowsy settle him fully swaddled wherever this nap is due to take place, no later than 12 noon.

11.30am/12 noon–2/2.30pm

- Baby needs a nap of no longer than two and a half hours from the time he went down.

- If he wakes up after 45 minutes, check the swaddle, but do over-stimulate him by talking.

- Allow 10–20 minutes for him to resettle himself; if he's still unsettled, offer him half his 2pm feed.

- Try to settle him back to sleep until 2.30pm.

12 noon

- Have lunch and a well-earned rest/nap with your toddler before the next feed.

- Wash and sterilise expressing equipment.

2/2.30pm

- Baby must be awake and feeding no later than 2.30pm, regardless of how long he has slept.

- Unswaddle him and allow him to wake naturally. Change his nappy.

- Give him 20–25 minutes from the breast he last fed on, then offer him 10–15 minutes from the other breast, while you drink a large glass of water.

- Snack time for your toddler.

- Do not feed baby after 3.15pm as it will put him off his next feed.

- It is very important that baby is fully awake now until 4.15pm, so he goes down well at 7pm; if he was very alert in the morning, he may be sleepier now. Do not overdress him, as extra warmth may make him drowsy.

- Lay baby on his play mat and encourage him to have a good kick.

3–4pm

- It is a good idea to prepare your toddler's tea now so that there is less to do when you return from your walk.

- If your toddler has had a physical activity or been to playgroup/pre-school in the morning, try to arrange a quieter activity for the afternoon. If she had a quieter morning, try to encourage something more physical in the afternoon. Weather permitting, a short walk to the park or a run around the garden to get some fresh air before teatime is always a good idea, regardless of earlier activities.

- Change baby's nappy. This is a good time to take him for a walk to ensure that he sleeps well, and is refreshed for his bath and next feed. He may start to cut right back on this nap.

- Baby should not sleep after 5pm if you want him to go down well at 7pm.

5pm

- Baby must be fully awake and feeding no later than 5pm.

- Give him a good 20 minutes on the breast he last fed on while your toddler is eating tea.

- It is very important that baby waits for the other breast until after his bath.

5.45pm

- Allow baby a good kick without his nappy while you prepare things needed for his bath and bedtime. Your toddler might enjoy helping but, if she doesn't want to, try to engage her in a quiet activity.

- Give baby a quick bath. Dry and cream him paying particular attention to his creases.

6pm

- Baby must be feeding no later than 6pm; this should be done in a quiet room with care not to overstimulate him with talking or eye contact.

- If he did not finish the first breast at 5pm, give him 5–10 minutes on it before putting him on the full breast. Allow a good 20–25 minutes on the full breast.

- Encourage your toddler to enjoy a story, DVD or talking book while sitting next to you.

- Settle baby in his bed, fully swaddled, by 6.30pm. Leave a dim light on and prop a cot mirror or book along the side for him to look at.

6.30/7pm

- Bathtime for your toddler. This should take no longer than 10–15 minutes for you or your partner.

- Encourage your toddler to dry and dress herself.

- She can then have a beaker of milk and a story.

7/7.30pm

- Settle your toddler in her bed after a bedtime story.

- If your baby hasn't settled well, offer him 10 minutes on the fuller breast. Do this without stimulating him by talking or eye contact.

8pm

- It is very important for you to have a really good meal and a rest before feeding or expressing.

9.30pm

- Express from both breasts if offering a bottle at the late feed.

10/10.30pm

- Turn up the lights fully and unswaddle baby so that he can wake up naturally.

- Allow at least 10 minutes before feeding to ensure that he is fully awake and can feed well.

- Lay out things for the nappy change, plus a spare draw sheet, muslin and swaddle blanket in case they are needed in the middle of the night.

- Give baby 20 minutes from the first breast or most of his bottle-feed, change his nappy and re-swaddle him.

- Dim the lights and, with no talking or eye contact, give him 20 minutes on the second breast or the remainder of the bottle-feed.

In the night

- If baby wakes up before 4am, give him a full feed.

- If he wakes between 4am and 5am, give one breast, then the second at 7.30am after expressing.

- If he wakes up at 6am, give him one breast, then the second at 7.30am after expressing.

- Always avoid eye contact and talking, and keep the lights low. Do not change his nappy unless absolutely necessary.

Changes to be made during the four- to six-week routine

Sleeping

By the age of six weeks, the majority of babies that I cared for were sleeping for a much longer spell during the night, and many were sleeping through to nearer 7am. Parents who are struggling to get their babies to sleep longer often ask me how I achieved this. My response has always been that, by following the routines, it just happened naturally, and that the babies themselves started to sleep longer and longer in the night. Certainly from reading the forums on my website, this seems to be true for the majority of parents. But what has also become obvious from reading thousands of posts over the last few years is that many of the parents whose babies do not manage to sleep a longer stretch during the night by six weeks appear to have much more sleep during the day than I recommend at this age. They believe that they have sleepy babies that need more daytime sleep. While I do believe that some babies need more sleep, from my own personal experience those babies who genuinely needed more sleep would also begin to sleep longer in the night. If your baby is not showing signs of sleeping longer during the night, perhaps look more closely at his daytime sleep, and gradually start to reduce the amount he is having. By putting him down for his first nap of the day five minutes later every three or four days, it will avoid the problem of him becoming overtired and not settling, but also reduce the amount of daytime sleep he is having.

I recommend that at this stage the daily nap time between 7am and 7pm should be reduced to a strict four and a half hours: the morning nap should be no more than one hour, the afternoon nap no more than 30 minutes between 4.15pm and 5pm. With second babies a problem that often occurs at this stage is that the baby falls asleep on the school run at around 8.30am, and then sleeps until nearer 10am; this results in too much daytime sleep and can affect how long the baby sleeps at night. If you find this is happening, I would suggest that you wake your baby up at 9am, so that he only sleeps 30 minutes, then allow him a further 15-minute catnap around 9.45am. He should be fully awake by 10am. This will keep his total morning sleep to just under an hour, and by allowing only a 15-minute nap or catnap between 9.45am and 10.15am his lunchtime nap should not be affected.

It is very important that by the end of six weeks you start to get your baby used to being half-swaddled (under the arms) for the 9am and the 7pm sleeps. Cot death rates peak between two and four months and overheating is considered to be a major factor in this. When you start to half-swaddle your baby, it is important to tuck him in securely. If he is waking earlier than the time the routine suggests, check if he has kicked his covers off; babies become more active at this age and this is another cause of them waking up earlier in the night.

It should now take less time to settle your baby to sleep. The cuddling time should gradually be reduced and now is a good time to get him used to going down when he is more awake. Often a lullaby light, which plays a tune and casts images on the ceiling for 10 minutes or so, will help a baby to settle himself.

Another important factor in helping your baby sleep longer in the night is to ensure that he is getting most of his daily milk intake between 6am–7am and 11.30pm. A good indicator of this will be his weight gain; he should regularly be gaining weight each week.

Once he has done this stretch several nights in a row, try not to feed him if he suddenly goes back to waking earlier again. The hours after the 10.30pm feed are sometimes referred to as the 'core night' (see pages 280–2 for a full explanation of the 'core night method'). On waking at this time, he should initially be left for a few minutes to settle himself back to sleep. If that doesn't work, then other methods apart from feeding should be used to settle him. I would try settling him with some cool boiled water or a cuddle; others recommend a dummy. Attention should be kept to the minimum, while reassuring your baby that you are there. This teaches the baby one of the most important sleep skills: how to go back to sleep after surfacing from a non-REM sleep. Obviously, if he refuses to settle you would need to feed him. The core night method could also be used to encourage an older baby who has got into the habit of waking at the same time in the night, to sleep longer.

Before embarking on this method, the following points should be read carefully to make sure that your baby really is capable of going for a longer spell in the night:

- These methods should never be used with a very small baby or a baby who is not gaining weight.

- The above methods should only be used if your baby is regularly gaining weight each week, and if you are sure that his last feed is substantial enough to help him sleep for the longer stretch in the night.

- The main sign that a baby is ready to cut down on a night feed is regular weight gain and the reluctance to feed, or taking less at the 7am feed.

- The aim of this method is gradually to increase the length of time your baby can go from his last feed and not to eliminate the night feed in one go. The core night method can be used if, over three or four nights, a baby has shown signs that he is capable of sleeping for a longer stretch. However, I cannot stress enough the importance of not using this method if your baby is not settling quickly in the night. If it is not working within three or four nights, you should abandon it and continue to feed your baby. If you persist with this method and your baby is not settling back quickly, you will actually create a sleep association problem that could mean your baby will continue to be unsettled in the night for many weeks.

Feeding

If your baby is feeding between 3am and 4am, you have to wake him up at 7am every morning for at least 10 days, and he is starting to show less interest in his morning feed, then you can very gradually, and by a small amount, cut back the amount of milk he is taking in the night. This will have the knock-on effect of him drinking more during the day and less in the night, and eventually he will drop the middle-of-the-night feed altogether. It is important not to cut back too much or too fast as the baby could then start to wake up hungry long before 7am; this will defeat the whole purpose of getting him to sleep through from 11pm to 7am.

At around six weeks, your baby will go through another growth spurt, and you will need to reduce the amount you are expressing first thing in the morning by a further 30ml (1oz), and cut out the mid-morning expressing altogether. If your baby woke and fed well between 3am and 4am, then slept until 7am, then woke and fed well again, he should be happy to go a stretch after the 7am feed. You can gradually start to push the 10am feed to nearer 10.30am. The exception to this would be a baby who is getting to nearer 5am in the morning and having a top-up at 7.30am. It is unlikely that he would get through to 10.30am if he's only had a top-up feed at 7.30am, so continue to feed him at 10am until he is feeding at between 6am and 7am.

On the days that you are taking your baby and toddler to a playgroup, parent and toddler group or other activity, you may find it easier to do a split feed at 10am with a top-up on your return home and just prior to the lunchtime nap.

During growth spurts, your baby will probably need to spend longer on the breast at some feeds, especially if you have not been expressing at the suggested times. It is important to allow the baby this extra time on the breast and, if need be, extra top-ups. While it may feel as if you are backtracking with the routines, the extra feeding during the day will only be short term, and will avoid the problem of your baby starting to wake up earlier or more in the night because he has not fed well enough during the day. For a plan to increase your milk supply see page 285.

Bottle-fed babies should have the 7am, the 10.30am and the 6.15pm feeds increased first during growth spurts. If your baby is happily waiting until 10.30am for his feed, and during this growth spurt you find that he starts to wake up during his lunchtime nap or earlier than usual, it would be worthwhile giving him a small top-up prior to him going down for his nap. Once he has done a week of uninterrupted midday naps, you can gradually cut back on the top-up until you have eliminated it altogether and he is back to having a full feed at 10.30am. However, should you find that your baby is more unsettled at the lunchtime nap without a top-up, there is no reason why you should not continue to offer it. The most important thing at this stage is that your baby sleeps well at the lunchtime nap.

8

Weeks Six to Eight

Routine for Baby and Toddler – six to eight weeks

Feed times	Nap times between 7am and 7pm
7am	9am–9.45am
10.45am	11.45am/12 noon–2/2.30pm
2/2.30pm	4.30pm–5pm
5pm	
6.15pm	
10/10.30pm	**Maximum daily sleep:** 4 hours

Expressing times: 6.45am and 9.30pm

7am

- Baby should be awake, nappy changed and feeding no later than 7am.

- If he fed at 4am or 5am, offer him 20–25 minutes on the full breast. If he's still hungry, offer 10–15 minutes from the breast that you have expressed 30–60ml (1–2oz) from.

- If he fed at 6am, offer him 20–25 minutes from the second breast after you have expressed 30–60ml (1–2oz).

- Depending on when your toddler wakes up, she can be given breakfast while you feed the baby. If the baby fed from one breast at 6am, give him the second breast while your toddler is having breakfast.

- Do not feed baby after 7.45am, as it will put him off his next feed. He can stay awake for up to two hours.

- Try to have some cereal, toast and a drink no later than 8am.

8am

- Wash and dress baby, remembering to cream all his creases and dry skin.

- Encourage your toddler to wash and dress herself.

8.50am

- Check baby's nappy and begin winding down.

9am

- Settle the drowsy baby, half-swaddled, wherever this nap is due to take place, no later than 9am.

- He needs a sleep of no longer than 45 minutes.

- If you are at home, wash and sterilise bottles and expressing equipment, involving your toddler if she is keen to help.

9.45am

- Unswaddle baby so that he can wake up naturally.

- Prepare your toddler's snack.

10am

- Baby must be fully awake now, regardless of how long he slept.

- If your baby had a full feed at 7am, he should last until 10.45am for his next feed. If he fed earlier, followed by a top-up at 7.30am, he may need to start this feed slightly earlier.

- Snack time for your toddler.

- Encourage baby to have a good kick under his play gym.

10.45am

- Baby should be given 20–25 minutes from the breast he last fed on, then offered 10-15 minutes from the second breast, while you have a large glass of water.

11.30am

- If baby was very alert and awake during the previous two hours, he may start to get tired by 11.30am and would need to be in bed by 11.45am.

11.45am

- Regardless of what your baby has done earlier, he should now be winding down for his nap.

- Check the draw sheet and change his nappy.

- Close the curtains and settle baby, half- or fully swaddled, in his bed no later than 12 noon.

11.45am/12 noon–2/2.30pm

- Baby needs a nap of no longer than two and a half hours from the time he went down.

12 noon

- Have lunch and a rest/nap while your toddler sleeps.

- Wash and sterilise the expressing equipment.

2/2.30pm

- Baby must be awake and feeding no later than 2.30pm, regardless of how long he has slept.

- Unswaddle him and allow him to wake naturally. Change his nappy.

- Give 20–25 minutes from the breast he last fed on, then offer him 10–15 minutes from the other breast, while you drink a large glass of water.

- Snack time for your toddler.

- Do not feed baby after 3.15pm as it will put him off his next feed.

- It is very important that baby is fully awake now until 4.30pm, so he goes down well at 7pm.

- If he was very alert in the morning, he may be sleepier now. Do not put too many clothes on him, as extra warmth will make him drowsy.

- Lay him on his play mat and encourage him to have a good kick.

3pm

- It is a good idea to prepare your toddler's tea now so that there is less to do when you return from your walk.

- If your toddler has had a physical activity or been to playgroup or pre-school in the morning, try to arrange a quieter activity for the afternoon. If she had a quieter morning, try to encourage something more physical in the afternoon.

4.15pm

- Change baby's nappy, and offer him a drink of cool boiled water no later than 4.30pm.

- This is a good time to take him for a walk to ensure that he sleeps well, and is refreshed for his bath and next feed.

5pm

- Teatime for your toddler.

- Baby must be fully awake now if you want him to go down well at 7pm.

- Offer him up to 10–15 minutes on the breast he last fed on; otherwise try to get him to wait until after his bath for a full feed. By eight weeks, he should be happy to wait until after the bath.

5.30pm

- Allow baby a good kick without his nappy, while preparing things needed for his bath and bedtime.

- Encourage your toddler to undress herself.

5.45pm

- Bath baby and toddler together. See page 81 for further advice on bath and bedtime routines.

6.15pm

- Your baby must be feeding no later than 6.15pm and this should be done in a quiet room with no talking or eye contact.

- If he did not feed at 5pm, he should start on the breast he last fed on. Give him 20 minutes on each breast.

- If he fed at 5pm, allow him up to 10–15 minutes to empty that breast completely, before putting him on the second breast.

- Your toddler should have a drink of milk from a beaker while you feed baby.

- It is very important that your baby is in bed two hours from when he last woke up.

7pm

- Settle baby, half-swaddled, no later than 7pm.

- Settle toddler in her bed at around 7–7.30pm after a bedtime story.

8pm

- It is very important to have a really good meal and a rest before the next feed or expressing.

9.30pm

- Express from both breasts if offering a bottle at the late feed.

10/10.30pm

- Turn on the lights fully and unswaddle baby so that he can wake up naturally.

- Allow at least 10 minutes before feeding to ensure that he is fully awake, so that he can feed well.

- Lay out things for the nappy change, plus a spare draw sheet, muslin and swaddle blanket in case they are needed in the middle of the night.

- Give baby 20 minutes from the first breast, or most of his bottle-feed, change his nappy and re-swaddle him.

● Dim the lights and, with no talking or eye contact, give him 20 minutes on the second breast or the remainder of the bottle-feed.

In the night

● If your baby is feeding before 4am, feeding well and losing interest in his 7am feed, it would be wise to try settling him with some cool boiled water. If he even takes an ounce or two before going on the breast, it should have the knock-on effect of him feeding better at 7am. The aim is to get him to take all his daily requirements between 7am and 11pm. As long as he is gaining weight regularly you can encourage him to cut down and eventually drop the night feed. (See core night method on page 280.)

● If he wakes at between 4am and 5am, give one breast, then the second at 7am after expressing.

● If he wakes up at 6am give him one breast, then the second at 7.30am after expressing.

● As before, keep the lights low and any stimulation to a minimum. Do not change his nappy, unless absolutely necessary.

Changes to be made during the six- to eight-week routine

Sleeping

Most babies who weigh over 4kg (9lb) should be sleeping longer in the night now, provided they are getting most of their daily nutritional needs between 6am–7am and 11pm. They should also be sleeping no more than four hours between 7am and 7pm. Once he has lasted longer for several nights in a row, try not to feed your baby before his latest time again. The morning nap should be no more than 45 minutes, the lunchtime nap should be 2¼–2½ hours – no longer – and the afternoon nap should be no more than 30 minutes. He may catnap on and off during this nap and some babies cut out this nap altogether. Do not allow him to cut out this nap if he is not managing to stay awake until 7pm. If you want him to sleep until 7am, it is important that he goes to sleep nearer 7pm. Between six and eight weeks, you should ensure that your baby's morning nap is no longer than 45 minutes, as allowing longer than this could result in a shorter lunchtime nap. If you notice that your baby has already become more unsettled at lunchtime, despite offering a top-up prior to his nap, I would suggest cutting this nap to 30 minutes, even if it means bringing the time of the lunchtime nap forward slightly.

Lunchtime nap

From six weeks onwards, if your baby is sleeping the full 45 minutes in the morning, he should be woken after two and a quarter hours. If for some reason his morning nap was much shorter, then you could allow him two and a half hours. If your baby develops a problem with his night-time sleep, do not make the mistake of letting him sleep longer during the day. Keep his morning nap to no more than 30 minutes, and his lunchtime nap no more than 2 hours.

It is at around eight weeks that the lunchtime nap may sometimes go wrong: you may find that your baby wakes up 30 to 40 minutes after falling asleep and is unsettled. This is due to your baby taking on a more adult sleep cycle as he drifts from light sleep into a dream-like sleep (known as REM), then back into a deep sleep. While some babies only stir when they come into light sleep, others will wake up fully. If the baby has not learned to settle himself and is consistently assisted back to sleep, then a real problem can develop. If your baby is waking during his lunchtime nap (and you are already offering a top-up prior to settling him), allow him 10–15 minutes to see if he will resettle himself. If he is unable to return to sleep, or he becomes distressed at any point, go straight to him and offer him half of his 2pm feed (treat as a night feed) before returning him to his cot. If, even after this, he is still unsettled, just get him up for the afternoon.

Obviously, if his lunchtime nap was cut short, he cannot make it through from 1pm to 4pm happily. I find the best way to deal with this is to allow 30 minutes after the 2.30pm feed, then a further 20/30 minutes at 4.30pm. This should stop him getting overtired and irritable and get things back on track so that he goes to sleep well at 7pm. See page 296 for more in-depth problem-solving.

He should now be half-swaddled at the 9am and 7pm sleeps, and at 12 noon and from 11pm to 7am by the end of eight weeks. Some babies may start to wake up earlier in the night again once they are out of the swaddle; try to settle without feeding or re-swaddling.

Feeding

During growth spurts, breast-fed babies should be given longer on the breast to ensure that their increased needs are met. If you have been expressing, you can reduce this by 30ml (1oz) to ensure that his needs are immediately met. If you have not expressed, you can still follow the feeding times from the routine for your baby's age, but you will have to top him up with a short breast-feed before his daytime naps. If you do this for a week or so, this should help increase your milk supply. A sign that this has happened is that your baby will sleep well at the naps, and not be so interested in the next feed. Once this happens you can gradually decrease the length of time that you top-up for, until you are back on your original feeding schedule. A formula-fed baby should have his feeds increased by 30ml (1oz) when he is regularly draining his bottle, starting with the morning feed.

Between the ages of six to eight weeks, a baby who is gaining a regular amount and weighs over 4kg (9lb) should manage to go a longer spell in the night from his late feed, provided he is feeding well during the day and not sleeping more than the recommended amounts. If your baby is still waking between 2am and 3am, despite taking a good feed between 10pm and 11pm, I would advise, if you are not already doing so, that you give a split feed at 10/11.15pm. The extra milk and time awake is often enough to help the baby sleep longer in the night. For this to work it is important that you start to wake your baby no later than 9.45pm, so that he is fully awake and feeding by 10pm. Allow him to drink as much of the feed as he would want, then allow him a good kick on the floor under his play gym. At 11pm you should then take him to the bedroom and change his nappy, then offer him a further feed. If you are formula-feeding, I would advise that you make a fresh feed up for the second feed.

If your baby then wakes in the night, check that he has not kicked off his covers as this is another cause of night-time waking in babies of this age. You should then try to settle him with some cool boiled water. If he refuses to settle, then you will have to feed him, but it would be advisable to refer to chapters 14 and 15 to check for possible reasons why he is not sleeping for longer in the night. If he does settle, he will probably wake up again at around 5am, at which time you can give him a full feed, followed by a top-up at 7–7.30am. This will help keep him on track with his feeding and sleeping pattern for the rest of the day.

Within a week, babies usually sleep until nearer 5am, gradually increasing their sleep time until 7am. During this stage, when your baby is taking a top-up at 7–7.30am instead of a full feed, he may not manage to get through to 10.45am for his next feed. You may need to give him a full feed at 10–10.15am, followed by a top-up just before he goes down for his lunchtime nap, to ensure that he does not wake up early from the nap.

If your baby starts to wake up earlier again, wait 10 minutes or so before going to him. If he will not settle back to sleep, try settling him with some cool boiled water or a cuddle before feeding.

Keep increasing day feeds, not night feeds. Most babies are happy to wait longer after the 7am feed, so keep pushing this feed forward until your baby is feeding at 10.45am. However, if your baby is still feeding at 5–6am with a top-up at 7–7.30am he may not manage to go longer and will need to have at least half of his next feed at 10am. Most babies go through a second growth spurt at six weeks. Cut back on the first expressing of the day by a further 30ml (1oz) and by the end of eight weeks cut out the 6.45am expressing so your baby gets the extra milk he needs. He may also need to spend longer on the breast at some feeds during growth spurts.

Bottle-fed babies should have the 7am, 10.45am and 6.15pm feeds increased first during growth spurts. The 10.30pm feed should only be increased if all the other feeds have been increased, and he is not going a longer spell in the night. Try not to give more than 180ml (6oz) at this feed unless your baby weighed over 4.6kg (10lb) at birth. Some babies will need to move to a medium-flow teat with three holes at this stage.

9
Weeks Eight to Twelve

Routine for Baby and Toddler – eight to twelve weeks

Feed times	Nap times between 7am and 7pm
7am	9am–9.45am
10.45/11am	12 noon–2/2.15pm
2/2.15pm	4.45pm–5pm
5pm	
6.15pm	
10/10.30pm	**Maximum daily sleep:** 3½ hours

Expressing time: 9.30pm

7am

- Baby should be awake, nappy changed and feeding no later than 7am.

- He should be given 20 minutes from the first breast, then offered 10–15 minutes from the second breast.

- Your toddler can be given breakfast while you feed the baby.

- Do not feed baby after 7.45am, as it will put him off his next feed.

- He can stay awake for up to two hours.

- Try to have some cereal, toast and a drink no later than 8am.

8am

- Wash and dress baby, remembering to cream all his creases and dry skin.

- Encourage your toddler to wash and dress herself.

8.50am

- Check baby's nappy and draw sheet.

9am

- Settle the drowsy baby, half-swaddled wherever this nap is due to take place, no later than 9am.

- He needs a sleep of no longer than 45 minutes.

- If you are at home, wash and sterilise bottles and expressing equipment.

9.45am

- Unswaddle baby so that he can wake up naturally.

10am

- Baby must be fully awake now, regardless of how long he slept.

- Encourage him to have a good kick under his play gym.

- Snack time for your toddler.

10.45/11am

- Baby should be given 20 minutes from the breast he last fed on, then offered 10–15 minutes from the second breast, while you have a large glass of water.

- Prepare lunch for you and your toddler.

11.45am

- Regardless of what your baby has done earlier, he should now be winding down for his nap.

- Check the draw sheet and change his nappy.

- Settle baby, half-swaddled in his bed no later than 12 noon.

12 noon–2/2.15pm

- Baby needs a nap of no longer than two and a quarter hours from the time he went down.

- Wash and sterilise bottles and expressing equipment if you didn't do this earlier.

- Lunchtime for you and your toddler.

- Nap time/quiet time for your toddler while you have a rest.

2/2.15pm

- Baby must be awake two and a quarter hours from the time he went down, regardless of how long he has slept and he must be feeding no later than 2.30pm.

- Unswaddle him and allow him to wake naturally. Change his nappy.

- Give him 20 minutes from the breast he last fed on, then offer him 10–15 minutes from the other breast, while you drink a large glass of water.

- Snack time for your toddler.

- Do not feed baby after 3.15pm as it will put him off his next feed.

- It is very important that baby is fully awake now until 4.45pm, so he goes down well at 7pm.

3pm

- If your toddler has had a physical activity or been to playgroup or pre-school in the morning, try to arrange a quieter activity for the afternoon. If she had a quieter morning, try to encourage something more physical in the afternoon.

4.15pm

- Change baby's nappy, and offer him a drink of cool boiled water no later than 4.30pm.

- He may have a short nap between 4.45pm and 5pm.

5pm

- Teatime for your toddler.

- Baby must be fully awake if you want him to sleep at 7pm.

- He should be happy to wait until after his bath for his feed.

- Feed baby for up to 15 minutes from one breast, if needed.

5.30pm

- Allow baby a good kick without his nappy, while preparing things needed for his bath and bedtime.

5.45pm

- Bathtime for your baby and toddler. See page 81 for further advice on bath and bedtime routines.

6.15pm

- Baby must be feeding no later than 6.15pm and this should be done in a quiet room with no talking or eye contact.

- He should be given 20 minutes on each breast, while you drink a large glass of water.

- Your toddler should have a drink of milk from a beaker while you feed baby.

- It is very important that your baby is in bed two hours from when he last awoke.

7pm

- Settle your drowsy baby, half-swaddled, no later than 7pm.

- Settle your toddler in her bed around 7/7.30pm after a story.

8pm

- It is very important for you to have a really good meal and a rest before the next feed or expressing.

9.30pm

- Express full feed from both breasts if offering a bottle at the late feed.

10/10.30pm

- Turn on the lights fully and unswaddle baby so that he can wake up naturally.

- Allow at least 10 minutes before feeding to ensure that he is fully awake, so that he can feed well.

● Lay out things for the nappy change, plus a spare draw sheet, muslin and swaddle blanket in case they are needed in the middle of the night.

● Give him 20 minutes on the first breast or most of his bottle-feed, change his nappy and re-swaddle him using a half swaddle.

● Dim the lights and, with no talking or eye contact, give him 20 minutes on the second breast or the remainder of the bottle-feed.

In the night

● If your baby is feeding before 5am, feeding well and losing interest in his 7am feed, it would be wise to try settling him with some cool boiled water. Remember, the aim is to get him to take all his daily requirements between 7am and 11pm. As long as he is gaining weight regularly, he can be encouraged to go through to 7am without a milk feed (see core night method on page 280).

● If he wakes up at 5am, give him the first breast and, if needed, 5–10 minutes on the second breast.

● If he wakes up at 6am, give the first breast, then the second at 7.30am.

● Avoid night-time stimulation; only change his nappy if necessary.

Changes to be made during the eight- to twelve-week routine

Sleeping

Most babies who are nearer 5.4kg (12lb) in weight can manage to go through the night from the 10–11pm feed at this age, provided they are taking all their daily nutritional needs between 7am and 11pm. They should also be sleeping no more than three and a half hours between 7am and 7pm. A totally breast-fed baby may still be waking up once in the night, hopefully nearer 5am or 6am.

Cut back your baby's daily nap time by a further 30 minutes, to a total of three hours. The morning nap should be no more than 45 minutes, but if he is not sleeping so well at lunchtime, it can be cut back to 30 minutes. The lunchtime nap should be no more than two and a quarter hours. It is around this stage that the lunchtime nap can sometimes go wrong. The baby comes into a light sleep usually 30–45 minutes after he has gone to sleep. Some babies will wake up fully and it is important that they learn how to settle themselves back to sleep to avoid the wrong sleep associations. For more details on this problem, refer to chapter 15.

Most babies have cut out their late afternoon nap by now. If your baby hasn't, do not allow him to sleep for more than 15 minutes, unless for some reason the lunchtime nap has gone wrong and then it would be slightly longer. All babies should only be half-swaddled and particular attention should be paid when tucking the baby in.

One reason many babies of this age still wake up is because they move around the cot. If this is happening with your baby, I would advise that you purchase a 0.5 tog light summer-weight sleeping bag. They are so lightweight that you can still use a sheet to tuck your baby in, without the worry of overheating. (See page 23 for further details on cots and bedding.)

Feeding

Your baby should be well established on five feeds a day now. If he is totally breast-fed and has started waking up earlier in the morning, it may be worth trying a top-up from a bottle of expressed milk after you feed him at 10/10.30pm. If he is sleeping regularly until 7am, gradually bring the 10.30pm feed forward by five minutes every three nights until he is feeding at 10pm. As long as he continues to sleep through to 7am and takes a full feed, you can keep pushing the 10.45am feed forward until he is feeding at 11am.

Once your baby has slept through the night for two weeks, the 5pm feed can be dropped. I would not recommend dropping the split feed until this happens, as a larger feed at 6.15pm could result in your baby taking even less at the last feed, resulting in an earlier waking time. With many of the babies that I cared for, I kept giving them a split feed until solids were introduced to ensure that they were getting enough milk during the day. Once you eliminate the 5pm feed and your baby is taking a full feed after his bath, he could cut down dramatically on his last feed of the day, which could result in an early waking.

If you are considering introducing a further bottle-feed, the best time to introduce it is at the 11am feed. Gradually reduce the time of the feed by two or three minutes each day and top up with formula. By the end of the first week, if your baby is taking a bottle-feed of 150–180ml (5–6oz), you should be able to drop the breast-feed easily without the risk of serious engorgement. Bottle-fed babies should continue to have their 7am, 11am and 6.15pm feeds increased first during the next growth spurt at around nine weeks. Increase the bottle-feed to suit your baby's needs.

Moving on to the three- to four-month routine

You may still have to adjust the daytime routine slightly to fit in with your toddler's routine. As long as you are not exceeding your baby's daytime sleep, and he is following the eight- to twelve-week routine at night, then you can move on to the next routine. However if, despite following all the advice, your baby is not sleeping as long in the night as the routine suggests, stick with this routine and try to improve the night sleeping. On pages 235–7 and 302 there is a question and answer that gives advice on how to deal with night-time waking at this age, as well as some additional information that may help. Both involve dropping the 10pm feed for a short period, to try to establish a longer period of sleep from 7pm onwards. Once a longer period of sleep becomes established, the 10pm feed can be reinstated, and hopefully the baby's longer spell of sleep will then happen between 11pm and 6/7am. Once this happens, you can then move on to the three- to four-month routine.

10

Months Three to Four

Routine for Baby and Toddler – three to four months

Feed times	Nap times between 7am and 7pm
7am	9am–9.45am
11am	12 noon–2/2.15 pm
2.15/2.30pm	
6.15pm	
10/10.30pm	**Maximum daily sleep:** 3 hours

Expressing time: 9.30pm

7am

- Baby should be awake, nappy changed and feeding no later than 7am.

- He should feed from both breasts or take a full bottle-feed and then should stay awake for two hours.

- Your toddler can have breakfast while you feed the baby.

- Try to have some cereal, toast and a drink no later than 8am.

8am

- Your baby should be encouraged to have a good kick on his play mat for 20–30 minutes.

- Wash and dress baby, remembering to cream all his creases and dry skin.

- Encourage your toddler to wash and dress herself.

9am

- Settle the drowsy baby, half-swaddled, no later than 9am.

- He needs a sleep of no longer than 45 minutes.

- Wash and sterilise bottles and expressing equipment.

9.45am

- Unswaddle baby so that he can wake up naturally.

10am

- Baby must be fully awake now, regardless of how long he slept.

- Encourage him to have a good kick under his play gym.

- Snack time for your toddler.

11am

● Your baby should be given a feed from both breasts or a full bottle-feed.

11.50am

● Check the draw sheet and change his nappy.

● Close the curtains and settle the drowsy baby, half-swaddled, no later than 12 noon.

12 noon–2/2.15pm

● Baby needs a nap of no longer than two and a quarter hours from the time he went down.

● Wash and sterilise bottles and expressing equipment if you didn't do this earlier.

12 noon

● Have lunch with your toddler, followed by a nap or some quiet time.

2/2.15pm

● Baby must be awake two and a quarter hours from the time he was put to bed, regardless of how long he has slept, and he must be feeding no later than 2.30pm.

● Unswaddle him and allow him to wake naturally. Change his nappy.

- He needs a feed from both breasts or a bottle-feed.

- Do not feed baby after 3.15pm as it will put him off his next feed.

- If he has slept well at both naps, he should manage to get through the rest of the afternoon without a further sleep.

- Snack time for your toddler.

- Spend some time outside with your baby and toddler.

- Change baby's nappy and offer him a drink of cool boiled water no later than 4.30pm.

5pm

- Teatime for your toddler.

5.30pm

- Put baby on the changing mat on the floor without his nappy, so that he can have a good kick, while you prepare his bath.

5.45pm

- Bathtime for baby and toddler. See page 81 for further advice on bath and bedtime routines.

6.15pm

- Baby must be feeding no later than 6.15pm.

- He should feed from both breasts or have 210–240ml (7–8oz) of formula milk.

- Give your toddler a drink of milk.

- Dim the lights and sit your baby in his chair for 10 minutes while you tidy up.

7pm

- Settle the drowsy baby, half-swaddled, no later than 7pm.

- Settle your toddler in her bed around 7/7.30pm after her story.

9.30pm

- Express full feed from both breasts if offering a bottle at the late feed.

10/10.30pm

- Turn the lights on low and wake your baby enough to feed.

- Give him most of his breast-feed or 180ml (6oz) bottle-feed, change his nappy and half-swaddle him.

- Dim the lights and, with no talking or eye contact, give him the remainder of his feed.

Changes to be made during the three- to four-month routine

Sleeping

If you have structured the milk feeds and nap times according to the routine, your baby should manage to sleep through the night from his last feed to nearer 6am–7am in the morning. If he shows signs of starting to wake up earlier, assume that it may be due to hunger. Increase his 10pm feed and, if need be, go back to having him awake for longer at that feed. You should also ensure that his maximum daily sleep between 7am and 7pm totals no more than three hours. Some babies may need less sleep than this, and you may have to look at cutting his total daytime sleep back to around two and a half hours, with a 30-minute nap in the morning, and a two-hour nap at lunchtime.

If your baby is following the routine well, he will have cut right back on his late afternoon sleep and some days may manage to get through the afternoon without the nap, but may need to go to bed five to 10 minutes earlier on those days. Should your baby have slept less than two hours at lunchtime, he should certainly be encouraged to have a short nap of no longer than 30 minutes between 4pm and 5pm, otherwise he may become so overtired at bedtime that he doesn't settle to sleep easily.

Between three and four months, the time that your baby is awake at the late feed should be gradually reduced to 30 minutes, provided he has been sleeping through regularly to 7am, for at least two weeks. This should be very quiet and treated like a middle-of-the-night feed. Bring it forward by 10 minutes every three nights until it becomes a very quick, sleepy feed at 10pm. However, if your baby is still waking up at between 5am and 6am, it would be advisable to continue to try and keep him awake for at least an hour at the last feed, following the suggestions for the split feed – see page 153.

Even if he is not getting out of his half-swaddle, I would suggest that now is a good time to get him used to a 100 per cent cotton, very lightweight sleeping bag. He will still need to be tucked in firmly, with one sheet, and perhaps one blanket, depending on the room temperature; therefore it is important that you purchase a 0.5tog bag to avoid the risk of overheating.

Feeding

Between three to four months, if your baby has slept through the night until 7am for at least two weeks, you should try to ensure that any extra milk needed during growth spurts is increased at daytime feeds to prevent him backtracking on his night-time waking. If your baby is totally breast-fed and is still waking up in the night, despite being topped up with expressed milk at the late feed, it could be that he will need a bigger feed at this time. If you are unable to express extra milk earlier in the day, some mothers find that topping up with a small amount of formula at this feed helps. You should discuss this with your health visitor.

If your baby is formula-fed 210–240ml (7–8oz) four times a day, he may only need a small feed of 120–180ml (4–6oz) at the late feed. However, if your baby is not sleeping through the night at this age, it may be because he needs a little extra at this feed. Even if it means he cuts back on his morning feed, I would suggest offering him a full feed of 210–240ml (7–8oz) for several nights to see if that will help him sleep for longer in the night.

There are some babies who simply refuse the late feed at

three to four months. However, if you find that he starts to wake earlier again and will not settle back to sleep within 10 minutes or so, you would have to assume that it could be hunger and feed him. You may then have to consider reintroducing the 10pm feed until he is weaned and established on solids.

If you find that your baby keeps on waking before 4/5am in the night, refuses cool boiled water and will not settle without feeding, keep a very detailed diary listing exact times and amounts of feeding and times of daytime naps, to try to determine whether the waking is habit or actual hunger. Some breast-fed babies may still genuinely need to feed in the night if they are not getting enough at their last feed. If you are not already doing so, it is worth considering a top-up feed of expressed milk or formula, or a replacement formula-feed at the 10–11pm feed. Again, you should discuss this with your health visitor.

Whether you are breast-feeding or bottle-feeding, if your baby's weight gain is good, you are convinced he is waking up from habit and he refuses cool boiled water, try waiting 15–20 minutes before going to him. Some babies will actually settle themselves back to sleep. A baby of this age may still be waking up in the night because he is getting out of his covers. Tuck him in securely.

If your baby is formula-fed and is taking 995–1130ml (35–40oz) of formula between 7am and 11pm, he should not really need to feed in the night. However, some very big babies who weigh over 6.8kg (15lb) at this stage may still need to feed between 5am–6am, followed by a top-up at 7am–7.30am until they reach six months and are weaned. Current guidelines are that babies are not weaned before six months. If you are concerned that your baby is showing all the signs of needing to be weaned (see page 176), it is important that you discuss this with your health visitor or GP.

It is better to keep feeding in the night for a slightly longer time than take the risk of weaning your baby before he is ready. A totally breast-fed baby may also need to feed at around 5am–6am as he may not be getting enough to eat at the last feed. Regardless of whether they are breast- or bottle-fed, a good indicator of whether your baby is ready to drop the night feed is how he takes his top-up at 7–7.30am. If he takes it greedily, he is probably genuinely hungry at 5–6am. If he fusses and frets and refuses the top-up, I would assume the early wake-up was more habit than hunger and try to settle him back with some cool boiled water or a cuddle.

If your baby continues to sleep through to 7am once his waking time at the late feed has been reduced to 30 minutes, plus he is cutting back on his 7am feed, start very slowly reducing the amount he is drinking at 10–10.30pm. Only continue with this if he is sleeping well until 7am. However, I would not advise dropping this feed altogether until he reaches six months and solids have been established. If you abandon the 10pm feed before solids are introduced, and your baby goes through a growth spurt, you may find that you have to go back to feeding him in the middle of the night again.

If your baby is exclusively breast-fed and is over 6.3kg (14lb) in weight, you may find that during growth spurts you have to go back to feeding him in the middle of the night anyway, until solids are introduced. If you feel that your milk supply is too low, follow the plan for increasing milk supply on page 285.

11

Months Four to Six

Routine for Baby and Toddler – four to six months

Feed times	Nap times between 7am and 7pm
7am	9am–9.45am
11am	12 noon–2/2.15 pm
2.15/2.30pm	
6.15pm	
10pm	**Maximum daily sleep:** 2½–3 hours

Expressing time: 9.30pm

7am

● Baby should be awake, nappy changed and feeding no later than 7am.

● He should feed from both breasts or have a full bottle-feed and should then stay awake for two hours.

● Your toddler can have breakfast while you feed the baby.

- Try to have some cereal, toast and a drink no later than 8am.

8am

- He should be encouraged to have a good kick on his play mat for 20–30 minutes.

- Wash and dress baby, remembering to cream all his creases and dry skin.

- Encourage your toddler to wash and dress herself.

9/9.15am

- Settle the drowsy baby, securely tucked in, no later than 9.15am.

- He needs a sleep of no longer than 45 minutes.

- Wash and sterilise bottles and expressing equipment.

9.45am

- Untuck him so that he can wake up naturally.

10am

- Baby must be fully awake now, regardless of how long he slept.

- Encourage him to have a good kick under his play gym or take him on an outing.

- Snack time for your toddler.

11am

- If you have been advised to wean your baby early (see page 177), give him a full breast-feed or a full bottle-feed before offering solids.

- Encourage him to sit in his chair while you prepare lunch.

11.50am

- Check the draw sheet and change his nappy.

- Settle the drowsy baby, securely tucked in, no later than 12 noon.

- He will need a nap now of no longer than two and a quarter hours from the time he went down.

12 noon

- Have lunch with your toddler followed by a nap or some quiet time.

2/2.15pm

- Untuck your baby and allow him to wake naturally.

- Change his nappy.

- Give him a feed from both breasts or a full bottle-feed.

- Snack time for your toddler.

- Do not feed baby after 3.15pm as it will put him off his next feed.

- If he has slept well at both naps, he should manage to get through the rest of the afternoon without a further sleep.

4.15pm

- Change baby's nappy and offer him a drink of cool boiled water no later than 4.30pm.

- If he did not sleep so well at lunchtime, he may need a short nap some time between now and 5pm.

5pm

- Teatime for your toddler.

- Your baby should be content to wait until after his bath for his feed, but if he is showing signs of hunger, offer a small feed now.

- Put baby on the changing mat on the floor without his nappy, so that he can have a good kick while you prepare his bath.

5.45pm

- Bathtime for baby and toddler. See page 81 for further advice on bath and bedtime routines.

6pm

- Baby should start his feed between 6pm and 6.15pm, depending on his tiredness levels.

- He should feed from both breasts or have a full bottle-feed while your toddler has a drink of milk from a beaker.

7pm

- Settle the drowsy baby, securely tucked in or in his sleeping bag, no later than 7pm.

- Settle your toddler in her bed around 7/7.30pm after reading her a story.

9.30pm

- Express full feed from both breasts if offering a bottle at the late feed.

10pm

- Turn the lights on fully and wake your baby enough to feed.

- Give him most of his breast- or bottle-feed, change his nappy and securely tuck him in.

- Dim the lights and, with no talking or eye contact, give him the remainder of the feed. If he does not want the remainder, do not force it; he could start to cut back on this feed now.

- This feed should take no longer than 30 minutes.

Changes to be made during the four- to six-month routine

Sleeping

Between four and six months, your baby should manage to sleep from his last feed at 10pm until 6/7am in the morning, provided he is taking four to five full milk feeds a day, and not sleeping more than three hours between 7am and 7pm.

If he is still waking in the night and you are confident that it is not due to hunger, I would advise trying the 'core night method', as described on pages 280–2. If this does not work, it could be that he is a baby who needs less sleep, and I would suggest gradually cutting back on his daytime sleep to two and a half hours. If after a couple of weeks this has not improved things, then I would suggest dropping the 10pm feed to see how long he will sleep. The time he wakes up will help you decide whether to continue with the 10pm feed. For example, if he sleeps until 5am, then feeds and settles back to sleep until 7am, he will at least be sleeping one longer spell between 7pm and 7am, and this would be preferable to him waking and feeding at both 10pm and 5am.

However, if you drop the feed and he wakes at something like 1am and 5am, then it would make sense to continue with the 10pm feed so that he doesn't wake and feed twice between midnight and 5am.

If your baby weighs over 6.8kg (15lb) genuine hunger could be the cause of night waking, particularly if he is fully breast-fed. If this is the case, then you may have to accept that he will need a breast-feed in the night until he is established on solids at six months. If you feel that he is showing signs that he is ready to be weaned, consult your health visitor or GP for advice as to whether he should begin earlier than the recommended six months. If you decide to continue to feed him in the middle of the night, it is crucial to ensure that feeds are given quickly and quietly and that he settles back to sleep quickly and sleeps soundly until 7am.

If you have not already introduced a sleeping bag, it would be advisable to do so at this stage. If you leave it any later, he may be unhappy about being put into one.

Until your baby is able to crawl and manoeuvre himself around the cot, he still needs to be tucked in firmly. In very hot weather he can be put into a 0.5tog bag, with just a nappy on, and tucked in with a very thin cotton sheet.

If he is not sleeping the full two hours at lunchtime, cut back his morning nap to 20–30 minutes, and then bring the 11am feed forward to 10.30am. Top him up with some milk just before he goes down for his lunchtime nap.

Feeding

I recommend that you still continue to feed your baby at 10pm until solids are introduced. The current guidelines are that solids should now be introduced at six months, rather than at four months as previously recommended. As your baby will continue to go through growth spurts between four and six months, his nutritional needs will still need to be met. In my experience this can rarely be done on four milk feeds a day. If you decide to drop the 10pm feed and he starts to wake earlier and not settle back to sleep quickly, then you should assume that it is hunger and feed him. It would then be worth considering reintroducing the 10pm feed until solids are established. If you find that he refuses a 10pm feed, but wakes up at 5am hungry, then you should feed him and settle him back to sleep until 7am, then offer him a top-up feed before 8am. If this happens, you may then have to feed him earlier, between 10am and 10.30am, but then I would suggest that you offer him a further top-up before he goes down for his lunchtime nap, to ensure that he does sleep well.

During growth spurts, you may find that your baby is not content on five feeds a day. If this is the case, you may have to offer a split feed (see pages 64 and 97) in the morning and reintroduce the 5pm feed.

If your baby becomes very discontented between feeds, despite being offered extra milk, and you think that he is showing signs of needing to be weaned, then it is important to discuss this with your health visitor or GP. If weaning your baby before six months is recommended, then it is important to introduce solids very carefully. Solids should only be seen as tasters at this stage and given in addition to milk; they should not be a replacement for milk feeds (see page 177).

If you find that your baby is too tired to take all of his milk at 6pm followed by the solids, give him two-thirds of the milk at 5.15/5.30pm, followed by the solids, followed by the remainder of his milk feed after bathtime. If you are formula-feeding, it is advisable to make up two separate bottles to ensure that the milk is fresh.

Once solids are introduced at this feed, and as they increase, your baby should automatically cut back on his last feed at 10pm. Once he is down to taking only a very short breast-feed or just a couple of ounces of formula at 10pm, and continuing to sleep well through to 7am, you should be able to drop the 10pm feed without risking that he will wake earlier in the morning.

A breast-fed baby who has reached five months, is weaned, and is now starting to wake up before 10pm, may not be getting enough at this time. Try giving a full breast-feed at 5.30pm followed by the solids, with a bath at 6.15pm, followed by a top-up of expressed milk or formula after the bath. A baby who is not weaned would more than likely need to continue to have a split milk feed at 5/6.15pm until solids are introduced.

Early weaning

If you have been advised that your baby is ready for weaning before the recommended age of six months, it is important to remember that milk is still the most important food for him. It provides him with the right balance of vitamins and minerals. Solids given before six months are classed as first tastes and fillers, which should be increased very slowly over several weeks, gradually preparing your baby for three solid meals a day. By offering the milk first you will ensure that your baby's daily milk intake does not decrease too rapidly before he reaches six months.

Remember that, as soon as your baby has teeth, he will need his teeth cleaned twice a day, preferably after each solid food meal.

How to begin weaning

- Introduce solids after the 11am feed. Prepare everything you need for giving the solids in advance: a baby chair, bib, spoon, bowl and a clean, fresh damp cloth.

- Start by offering your baby a teaspoonful of pure organic baby rice mixed to a very smooth consistency using either expressed milk, formula or cool, filtered freshly boiled water.

- Make sure the baby rice is cooled enough before feeding it to your baby. Use a shallow plastic spoon for him – never a metal one as this will be too sharp and get too hot.

- Some babies need help in learning how to feed from the spoon. By placing the spoon just far enough into your baby's mouth, and bringing the spoon up and out against the roof of his mouth, his upper gums will take the food off, encouraging him to feed.

● Once your baby is established on baby rice at 11am and is toler-
ating it, give the rice after the 6pm feed instead. When he finishes
the one teaspoonful and shows signs of looking for more food,
the amount of solids can be increased, provided he continues to
take the required amount of milk at 6pm.

● Once your baby is happily taking one to two teaspoonfuls of baby
rice mixed with milk or water after the 6pm feed, a small amount
of pear purée can be introduced after the 11am feed. For babies
who are weaned before six months of age, this usually happens
between the fourth and sixth day; with babies over six months, it
will probably happen between the second and fourth day.

● Be guided by your baby as to when to increase the amounts. He
will turn his head away and get fussy when he has had enough.

● If your baby tolerates the pear purée, transfer it to the 6pm feed.
Mixing the purée with baby rice in the evening will make it more
palatable and prevent your baby from getting constipated.

● Small amounts of various organic vegetables and fruit can now be
introduced, one by one, after the 11am feed. To prevent your
baby from developing a sweet tooth, try to give more vegetables
than fruit. At this stage, avoid the stronger-tasting ones, like
spinach or broccoli, and concentrate on root vegetables, such as
carrot, sweet potato and swede.

● With babies under six months, it is important to introduce new
foods in small amounts every three to four days. Increasing one to
two teaspoonfuls a week between the two meals is a good
guideline. Babies over six months will probably need their meals
increased by larger amounts every couple of days, and as long as
you stick to the foods listed in first-stage weaning (see page 188),

you can introduce new foods closer together. Keeping a food diary will help you see how your baby reacts to each new food.

- Always be very positive and smile when offering new foods. If your baby spits a food out, it may not mean he dislikes it. Remember, this is all very new to him and different foods will get a different reaction. If he positively refuses a food, however, leave it and try again in a week's time.

- Always offer milk first, as this is still the most important food at this stage in nutritional terms. While appetites do vary, in my experience the majority of babies will be taking four to five full feeds of formula or breast milk a day. Provided your baby is happy and thriving, the minimum daily recommended amount of milk required at this age, once solids are established, is 600ml (20oz) a day.

For more comprehensive advice on weaning, including daily plans and recipes you can prepare for your baby, see *The Contented Little Baby Book of Weaning*.

12
Months Six to Nine

Once your baby reaches six months, things really do get easier. At six months the introduction of solids will help move your baby's mealtimes closer to that of your toddler, and by the time he reaches seven to eight months you should be able to feed both children the same food and at the same time.

You can also get your baby used to sleeping in his own room once he reaches six months. Because he will have been used to always having people around him during nap times and in the evening, it is best to do this gradually. Start off with settling him at either the morning or lunchtime nap in his own room. Once he is sleeping well at either of these times, you can then move on to settling him in his own room from 7pm. As your baby will not have been used to sleeping in the dark for daytime naps, I would suggest that you allow him a small night light for naps and in the evening, until he is used to sleeping in his own room. Gradually phase this out once he is settling and sleeping well at these times.

Routine for Baby and Toddler – six to nine months

Feed times	Nap times between 7am and 7pm
7am	9am–9.30/45am
11.45am	12.30pm–2.30pm
2.30pm	
5pm	
6.30pm	**Maximum daily sleep:** $2^{1}/_{2}$–$2^{3}/_{4}$ hours

7am

- Baby should be awake, nappy changed and feeding no later than 7am.

- He should feed from both breasts or have a full bottle-feed, followed by breakfast cereal mixed with either expressed milk or formula and fruit, once weaning is established.

- Your baby should stay awake for two hours.

- Your toddler can have breakfast while you feed the baby.

- Try to have some cereal, toast and a drink no later than 8am.

8am

- Baby should be encouraged to have a good kick on his play mat for 20–30 minutes.

- Wash and dress baby, remembering to cream all his creases and dry skin.

● Encourage your toddler to wash and dress herself.

9.15/9.30am

● Settle the drowsy baby, in his sleeping bag in the dark, with the door shut, no later than 9.30am.

● He needs a sleep of up to 30 minutes.

10am

● Open the curtains and undo his sleeping bag so that he can wake up naturally.

● Baby must be fully awake now, regardless of how long he slept.

● Encourage him to have a good kick under his play gym or take him on an outing.

● Snack time for your toddler.

11.45am

● By seven months baby should be given most of his solids before being offered a drink of water or well-diluted juice from a beaker, then alternate between solids and a drink.

● Encourage him to sit in his chair with some finger foods (see page 195), while you and your toddler have lunch.

● Keep pushing the time of your baby's lunch forward until he is eating at the same time as your toddler.

12.20pm

● Check the draw sheet and change his nappy.

● Close the curtains and settle the drowsy baby, in his sleeping bag in the dark, with the door shut, no later than 12.30pm.

12.30pm–2.30pm

● Your baby will need a nap of no longer than two hours from the time he went down.

● Your toddler will need a nap or her quiet time now.

2.30pm

● Baby must be awake and feeding no later than 2.30pm, regardless of how long he has slept.

● Open the curtains and undo his sleeping bag to allow him to wake up naturally. Change his nappy.

● He needs a feed from both breasts or a full bottle-feed.

● Snack time for your toddler.

● Do not feed baby after 3.15pm as it will put him off his next feed.

4.15pm

● Change baby's nappy and offer him a drink of cool boiled water or well-diluted juice no later than 4.30pm.

5pm

- Teatime for your toddler.

- Baby should be given most of his solids before being offered a small drink of water from a beaker. It is important that he still has a good milk feed at bedtime, so keep this drink to a minimum.

6pm

- Bathtime for baby and toddler. See page 81 for further advice on bath and bedtime routines.

6.30pm

- Baby must be feeding no later than 6.30pm. He should feed from both breasts or be given a full bottle-feed while your toddler has a drink of milk from a beaker.

- Dim the lights and sit baby in his chair for 10 minutes while you read both baby and toddler a story.

7pm

- Settle the drowsy baby in his cot and in the dark with the door shut, no later than 7pm.

- Settle your toddler in her bed around 7/7.30pm.

Changes to be made during the six- to nine-month routine

Sleeping

Once your baby is established on three meals a day, he should manage to sleep from around 7pm to 7am. If you have followed the most recent guidelines on weaning and started weaning your baby on to solids at six months, he will probably need a small feed at 10pm until he is nearer seven months. If you were advised to wean him before six months and solids were well established when he reached six months, you should be able to drop the 10pm feed sooner.

If your baby is not cutting down on his 10pm feed once solids are established, it may be that he is not getting the right quantities of solids for his age or weight, or needs a bigger feed at 6.30pm. Keep a diary of all food and milk consumed over a period of four days to help pinpoint why he is not cutting out that last feed. If you are confident that he is getting the right amounts and is taking the 10pm feed from habit rather than genuine hunger, I would suggest that you gradually start to reduce it. If you reduce it by an ounce every three to four days, provided he does not start to wake up early, you should continue to do this until he is taking only a couple of ounces. Once he is taking a couple of ounces, you can then drop it altogether.

Once he reaches six months you should aim to keep pushing the 9am nap forward to 9.30am. This will encourage him to go down for his lunchtime nap nearer to 12.30pm. This is important once solids are established and he is having three proper meals a day, with lunch coming around 11.45am/12 noon.

Some babies are happy to sleep later in the morning once they are established on three solid meals a day. If your baby sleeps until nearer 8am in the morning, he will not need a morning nap, but may not manage to get through until 12.30pm for his lunchtime nap; therefore, he may need to have lunch around 11.30am so he can go down at 12.15pm for his lunchtime nap.

Between six and nine months your baby will start to roll on to his front and may prefer to sleep on his tummy. When this happens, it would be advisable to remove the sheet and blanket to avoid him getting into a tangle with them. In the winter months, the lightweight sleeping bag will need to be replaced with a warmer one to make up for the loss of blankets.

By the end of six months, your baby will probably be ready to sit in a high chair for his meals. Always ensure that he is properly strapped in and never left unattended.

Feeding your baby and toddler together

Mealtimes with a baby and toddler can sometimes be fraught. I have already recommended that, depending on the age of your older child, when you find out you are expecting a baby you work towards ensuring that your toddler can feed herself. Once your baby reaches weaning age, however, some toddlers might regress a little. She may ask to be fed by you or start playing up at mealtimes in other ways. As a parent, your challenge is to be firm yet fair – maybe help her to get some food on her spoon or fork but try to resist feeding her (even though it may seem easier than waiting for her to do it). If she is throwing food then I would always suggest removing it with a firm 'no' and not offering her anything else to eat. She will soon learn that it is not acceptable behaviour. As I have said on page 44, concentrate on spending short periods of 'mummy and me' time with her doing things that the baby cannot do (such as drawing and jigsaws). Emphasise the benefits of being a 'big girl' and also express to her that you know things are a bit hard for her at the moment. She will appreciate your kindness and understanding at this time, even if she can't express her emotions with words.

Feeding

If you were advised to wean your baby early, you will probably have worked your way through the list of first-stage weaning foods (see below) by the time he reaches six months. Once he is taking around six tablespoonfuls of mixed vegetables at lunchtime, you can then introduce the second-stage foods, which include protein. For details of how to introduce protein, see page 191.

If you have waited until six months to introduce solids, it is important that you work through the different foods fairly quickly and keep increasing the amounts every couple of days or when your baby shows signs of wanting more. Start off by introducing baby rice after the 11am feed (see page 177), and then every couple of days introduce a new food, from the first-stage foods. Once your baby is taking a reasonable amount of solids at lunch and teatime, you can introduce solids at breakfast. As your baby reaches nearer seven months, he should be ready to drop his 11am milk-feed and have protein introduced at lunchtime.

Foods to introduce from six months

Pure organic baby rice, pear, apple, carrot, sweet potato, potatoes, green beans, courgettes and swede are ideal first weaning foods. Once your baby is happily taking these foods, you can introduce parsnips, mango, peaches, broccoli, avocados, barley, peas and cauliflower. Protein in the form of meat, poultry, fish and lentils should be introduced between six and seven months, once your baby is taking a reasonable amount of other solids. Check that all the bones are removed and trim off any fat and the skin. Some babies find the flavour of protein cooked on its own too strong. Try cooking chicken or meat in a casserole with familiar root vegetables, and fish in a milk sauce, until your baby becomes accustomed to the different texture and taste. Pulse casseroles in a food processor.

Introducing breakfast

A baby is ready to start having breakfast once he shows signs of hunger long before his 11am feed. This usually happens between the ages of six and seven months. Once your baby is eating breakfast, you can gradually start to move the 11am feed until later, eventually settling somewhere between 11.30am and 12 noon. By seven months, if your baby is eating a full breakfast of cereal, fruit and perhaps small pieces of toast, you should aim to cut back the amount offered to him from the bottle. Try to give part of the milk as a drink and the remainder with the cereal. Always try to encourage your baby to take at least 150–180ml (5–6 oz) before he is given his solids.

If you are still breast-feeding, gradually reduce the time your baby is on the first breast, then give him his solids and, finally, a further short feed from the second breast. Be very careful not to increase his solids so much that he cuts back too much on his breast-feed.

If your baby reaches seven months and is refusing breakfast, you can always cut back his milk slightly to encourage him to take small amounts of solids.

Regardless of whether you introduced solids before six months or at six months, aim to have a feeding plan similar to the one below before introducing protein. This will ensure that your baby's system is used to digesting reasonable amounts of solids, and can cope with the introduction of protein.

7/7.30am

- Breast-feed or give 180–240 ml (6–8oz) of formula milk.

- 2–3 tablespoons of oat cereal mixed with breast milk or formula, plus 1–2 tablespoons of fruit purée.

11.15/11.30am

- Breast-feed or give 60–90ml (2–3oz) of formula milk.

- 2–3 tablespoons of sweet potato purée and 2–3 tablespoons of root vegetable purée plus 1–2 tablespoons of cauliflower or green vegetable purée mixed with some chicken stock.

2/2.30pm

- Breast-feed or give 150–210ml (5–7oz) formula milk.

6pm

- Breast-feed or give 180–240ml (6–8oz) of formula milk.

- 5–6 tablespoons of baby rice mixed with breast milk, formula milk or cool boiled water, then mixed with 2 tablespoons of fruit purée.

Introducing protein at lunchtime

If you were advised to wean your baby earlier than normally recommended (see page 177), and if he is eating around six cubes or tablespoons of mixed vegetables, you should be able to introduce protein foods as soon as he reaches six months. If you started weaning your baby at six months, it could take between two to three weeks for him to be taking that amount.

The best way to introduce the protein is to start off by replacing two of the vegetable cubes with two of the simple chicken, red lentil or fish recipes in *The Contented Little Baby Book of Weaning*, *The Gina Ford Baby and Toddler Cook Book* and *Feeding Made Easy*. Introduce new protein foods slowly at this stage – one every three days is about right. If your baby has no reaction, then keep replacing one or two cubes of vegetables every day until the six cubes of vegetables are replaced with a complete protein recipe.

Once your baby is taking a full protein meal at lunchtime, it is important to introduce him to a beaker at lunchtime. Between the ages of six and seven months, you should start to use the tier system of feeding at lunchtime. When your baby is only taking a couple of ounces of milk at lunchtime, replace it with a drink of water or well-diluted juice from a beaker. Once the lunchtime milk is dropped, he may need to increase the 2.30pm feed. However, if you notice that he is cutting back too much on his teatime solids or bedtime feed, continue to keep this feed smaller.

Between six and seven months, once protein meals are established at lunchtime, evening solids should be transferred and changed to a proper tea at 5pm, with only a small drink of water from a beaker. You would then give your baby a full milk feed around 6.30pm.

Once protein is well established, your baby's milk feed should be replaced at lunchtime by a drink of cool boiled water or well-diluted juice from a beaker. Most babies are capable of sipping and swallowing at this age, and this should be encouraged by being consistent and always offering the lunchtime drink from a beaker. Do not worry if your baby only drinks a small amount at this meal. You will probably find that he makes up for it at his 2.30pm feed or takes an increase of cool boiled water later in the day. If you find that your baby's sleeping becomes unsettled at lunchtime when you drop the milk feed, you may for a short time have to go back to offering him a small top-up of milk prior to the lunchtime nap, but it is important that you keep persevering with offering him fluids from his beaker at lunchtime.

Tea

Once you feel confident that the lunchtime solids are going well, you can then look to replace the cereal and fruit given after 6pm with a proper tea with your toddler. If you always make sure that your baby has a well-balanced breakfast and lunch, you can be more relaxed about this meal. Both babies and toddlers can get fractious around this time, so offer foods that are easy to prepare – thick vegetable soups and vegetable bakes, prepared and frozen in advance, are always a good standby. Pasta or a baked potato served with vegetables are also nutritious and easy. If you offer a pudding, make sure that it is something quick and easy such as a milk pudding or yoghurt.

Daily requirements

Between six and seven months, it is important that you work towards establishing your baby on three proper meals a day. These should include three servings of carbohydrates, such as cereals, bread and pasta, plus at least three servings of vegetables and fruit, and one serving of puréed meat, fish or pulses. By six months a baby has used up most of the iron stores he was born with. As their iron requirements between six and 12 months are particularly high, it is important that their diet provides the right amount of this mineral. To help iron absorption in cereals and meat, always serve with fruit or vegetables rich in vitamin C.

Your baby still needs a minimum of 500–600ml (18–20oz) of breast or formula milk a day, inclusive of milk used for mixing food.

A very hungry baby who is taking three full milk feeds a day, plus three solid meals, may need a small drink and a piece of fruit mid-morning and afternoon.

Second stage: seven to nine months

During the second stage of weaning, the amount of milk your baby drinks will gradually reduce as his intake of solids increases. It is, however, important that he still receives a minimum of 500–600ml (18–20oz) a day of breast or formula milk. This is usually divided between three milk feeds and milk used in food and cooking as sauces are introduced. At this stage of weaning, you should be aiming to establish three good solid meals a day, so that by the time your baby reaches nine months of age he is getting most of his nourishment from solids. During this time, it is important to keep introducing a wide variety of foods from the different food groups (carbohydrate, protein, dairy, vegetables and fruit) so that your baby's nutritional needs are met.

Most babies are ready to accept stronger-tasting foods at this age. They also take pleasure from different textures, colours and presentation. Foods should be mashed or 'pulsed' and kept separate so that they avoid mixing everything up. Fruit need not be cooked; it can be grated or mashed. It is also at around this age that your baby will begin to put food in his mouth. Raw soft fruit, lightly cooked vegetables and toast can be used as finger foods. They will be sucked and squeezed more than eaten at this stage, but allowing your baby the opportunity to feed himself encourages good feeding habits later on. Once your baby is having finger foods, always wash his hands before a meal and *never* leave him alone while he is eating.

Between eight and nine months, your baby may show signs of wanting to use his spoon. To encourage this, use two spoons when you feed him. Load one for him to try and get the food into his mouth, and use the other one to actually get the food in! You can help your baby's co-ordination by holding his wrist gently and guiding the spoon into his mouth. Finger foods should be offered at every meal at this stage.

Foods to introduce

Dairy products, pasta and wheat can be introduced at this stage. Full-fat cow's milk can also be used in cooking, but should not be given as a drink until one year. Small amounts of unsalted butter can also be used in cooking. Egg yolks can be introduced, but must be hard-boiled. Cheese should be full fat, pasteurised and grated, and preferably organic. Olive oil can be used when cooking casseroles.

Tinned fish such as tuna may also be included, but choose fish in vegetable oil or spring water, as fish canned in brine has a higher salt content. A greater variety of vegetables can also be introduced such as coloured peppers, Brussels sprouts, pumpkin, cabbage and spinach.

Tomatoes and well-diluted unsweetened pure fruit juices can be included if there is no history of allergies. All these foods should be introduced gradually and careful notes made of any reactions.

Once your baby is used to taking food from a spoon, vegetables can be mashed rather than puréed. Once he is happy taking mashed food, you can start to introduce small amounts of finger food. Vegetables should be cooked until soft then offered in cube-sized pieces or steamed and then mixed to the right consistency. Once your baby is managing softly cooked pieces of vegetables and soft pieces of raw fruit, you can try him with toast or a low-sugar rusk. By nine months, if your baby has several teeth he should be able to manage some chopped raw vegetables. Dried fruit can also be given now but it should be washed first and soaked overnight. See the Baby and Toddler Menu Planner appendix on pages 313–321 for more suggestions.

Breakfast

Low-sugar, unrefined wheat cereals can now be introduced; choose ones fortified with iron and B vitamins. You may want to delay introducing these if you have a family history of allergies – check with your health visitor, doctor or a dietitian. Try adding a little mashed or grated fruit if your baby refuses them. Try to alternate the cereals between oat-based and wheat-based, even if your baby shows a preference for one over the other. You can encourage your baby with finger foods by offering him a little buttered toast at this stage. Once your baby is finger feeding, you can offer a selection of finger foods including fruits and lightly buttered toast.

Most babies are still desperate for their milk first thing in the morning, so still allow your baby two-thirds of his milk before solids. Once he is nearer nine months of age, he will most likely show signs of not being hungry for milk and this is the time to try offering formula or expressed breast milk from a beaker.

Lunch

If your baby is eating a proper breakfast, you will be able to push lunch to somewhere between 11.45am and 12 noon, and eventually you should plan so that you can feed both your toddler and baby at the same time. However, should he be eating only a small amount of breakfast, lunch will need to come slightly earlier. Likewise, babies who are having only a very short nap in the morning may also need to have lunch as early as 11am. It's important to remember that overtired, over-hungry babies will not feed as well, so when timing lunch take your cue from your baby.

During this stage of weaning, you will have established protein at lunchtime. Whenever possible, try to buy organic meat as this is free from additives and growth stimulators. Pork, bacon and processed hams should not be introduced until 18 months as they have a high salt content. You should still continue to cook without additional salt or sugar (see page 198 for foods to be avoided), although a small amount of herbs can be introduced at around nine months of age.

If you are introducing your baby to a vegetarian diet, it is important to seek expert advice on getting the right balance of amino acids. Vegetables are incomplete sources of amino acids when cooked separately and need to be combined correctly to provide your baby with a complete source of protein.

Once protein is well established, your baby's milk feed should be replaced at lunchtime by a drink of cool boiled water or well-diluted juice from a beaker. You might find that your baby only drinks a small amount from the beaker and looks for an increase of milk at the 2.30pm feed or an increase of cool boiled water later in the day.

If your baby is still hungry after his main meal, offer a piece of cheese, a breadstick, chopped fruit or yoghurt.

Tea

Once your baby is eating finger foods, tea can be a selection of mini sandwiches possibly served with soup. A baked potato or pasta served with vegetables and a sauce are also suitable, although he will need help eating these. Some babies get very tired and fussy by teatime. If your baby does not eat much, try offering some rice pudding, cereal or carrot or banana cake. A small drink of water from a cup can be offered after the tea. Do not allow too large a drink at this time as it will put your baby off his last milk feed. His bedtime milk feed is still important at this stage. If he starts cutting back too much on this feed, check you are not overfeeding him on solids or giving him too much to drink.

Daily requirements

At this second stage of weaning, it is important that you work towards establishing your baby on three proper meals a day. These should include three servings of carbohydrates, such as cereals, bread and pasta, plus at least three servings of vegetables and fruit, and one serving of puréed meat, fish or pulses.

Your baby still needs a minimum of 500–600ml (18–20oz) of breast or formula milk a day, inclusive of milk used for mixing food. If your baby starts to reject his milk, try reducing the amount of solids you give him at teatime. By the end of nine months, apart from his bedtime milk, all other milk feeds and drinks should ideally be from a beaker.

A very hungry baby who is taking three full milk feeds a day, plus three solid meals, may need a small drink and a piece of fruit mid-morning.

Foods to be avoided

During the first two years of your baby's and toddler's life, certain foods are best used sparingly, or avoided altogether, as they may be harmful. The two worst culprits in this regard are sugar and salt.

Sugar

During the first year of weaning, it is best to avoid adding sugar to any of your baby's food, as it may lead to him developing a taste for sweet things. A baby's appetite for savoury foods can be seriously affected if he is allowed lots of food containing sugar or sugar substitutes. But when buying commercial foods these ingredients can be hard to avoid. A survey by the Consumers' Association magazine, *Which?*, tested 420 baby products and reported that 40 per cent contained sugar or fruit juice or both. When choosing baby cereals or commercial foods, check the labels carefully; sugar may be listed as dextrose, fructose, glucose or sucrose. Watch out, too, for syrup or concentrated fruit juice, which are also sometimes used as sweeteners.

Too much sugar in the diet may not only cause your baby to refuse savoury food, but can lead to serious problems such as tooth decay and obesity. Because sugar converts very quickly into energy, babies and children who have too much may become hyperactive. Products such as baked beans, spaghetti hoops, corn-flakes, fish fingers, jam, tomato ketchup, tinned soups and some yoghurts are just a few of the everyday foods that contain hidden sugars, so care should be taken that, when your baby reaches toddlerhood, he does not eat these foods in excess. It is also important to check the labels of fruit juices and squashes.

Salt

Children under two years of age should not have salt added to their food – they get all the salt they need from natural sources such as vegetables. Adding salt to a young baby's food can be very dangerous as it can put a strain on his immature kidneys. Research also shows that an excessive salt intake may make children more prone to heart disease later in life. When your baby reaches the stage of joining in with family meals, it is important that you do not add salt to the food during cooking. Remove your baby's and toddler's portions, then add salt for you and your partner.

As with sugar, many processed goods and commercially prepared food, including packaged bread and breakfast cereal, contain high levels of salt. It is important to check the labels on these foods carefully before giving them to your toddler.

During the second stage of weaning, when your baby increases the types of foods that he eats, you can start to plan meals that are suitable for both your baby and toddler. When giving your baby casseroles, you will still have to purée or pulse the meat: simply remove a portion of the meat, along with a little of the liquid, and purée or pulse to a texture that your baby will accept. Then serve with the appropriate amount of vegetables in the casserole. At this stage you may still have to chop or slice the vegetables smaller, but it is important that you start to move away from serving whole meals pulsed or puréed.

See pages 317–321 for examples of the types of meals that you can plan for your toddler and baby during the second stage of weaning.

13

Months Nine to Twelve

Routine for Baby and Toddler – nine to twelve months

Feed times	Nap times between 7am and 7pm
7am	9.30am–10am
11.45am/12 noon	12.30pm–2.30 pm
2.30pm	
5pm	
6.30pm	**Maximum daily sleep:** 2–2½ hours

7am

- Baby should be awake, nappy changed and feeding no later than 7am.

- He should feed from both breasts or have a drink of formula from a beaker, followed by breakfast cereal mixed with either expressed milk or formula, fruit and finger foods.

- Your baby should stay awake for two to two and a half hours.

- Your toddler can have breakfast while you feed the baby.

- Try to have some cereal, toast and a drink no later than 8am.

8am

- Baby should be encouraged to play on the floor for 20–30 minutes.

- Wash and dress baby, remembering to cream all his creases and dry skin.

- Encourage your toddler to wash and dress herself.

9.30am

- Settle the drowsy baby in the dark, with the door shut, at around 9.30am.

- He needs a maximum of 30 minutes' sleep.

9.45am–10am

- Open the curtains so that he can wake up naturally.

10am

- Baby must be fully awake now, regardless of how long he slept.

- If you are not going out, get some toys out that both children can play with together.

- Snack time for your toddler.

11.45am/12 noon

- Baby should be given most of his solids before being offered a drink of water or well-diluted juice from a beaker, then alternate between solids and a drink.

- Encourage him to sit in his chair with some finger foods, while you and your toddler have lunch.

12.20pm

- Check the draw sheet and change his nappy.

- Close the curtains and settle baby in the dark, with the door shut, no later than 12.30pm.

- He will need a nap of no longer than two hours from the time he went down.

- Your toddler will need a nap or her quiet time now.

2.30pm

- Baby must be awake and feeding no later than 2.30pm, regardless of how long he has slept.

- Open the curtains, and allow him to wake up naturally. Change his nappy.

- He needs a breast-feed or formula milk, water or well-diluted juice from a beaker while your toddler has a drink and a small snack.

● Do not feed baby after 3.15pm as it will put him off his tea.

4.15pm

● Change baby's nappy and offer him a drink of cool boiled water or well-diluted juice no later than 4.30pm.

5pm

● Teatime for your baby and toddler.

● Baby should be given most of his solids before being offered a small drink of water or milk from a beaker. It is important that he still has a good milk feed at bedtime, so keep this drink to a minimum.

6pm

● Bathtime for your baby and toddler. See page 81 for further advice on bath and bedtime routines.

6.30pm

● Baby should be feeding no later than 6.30pm.

● He should feed from both breasts or have a full bottle-feed; this will eventually reduce when a beaker is introduced at one year.

● Give your toddler a beaker of milk.

● Dim the lights and read a story to baby and toddler.

7pm

- Settle baby in his cot, in the dark with the door shut, no later than 7pm.

- Settle your toddler in her bed around 7/7.30pm after a story.

Changes to be made during the nine- to twelve-month routine

Sleeping

The majority of babies cut right back on their daily sleep at this stage. If you notice that your baby is starting to wake in the night or earlier in the morning, it is important that you cut back on his total daily sleep.

The first nap to cut back on is the morning one. If he has been having 30 minutes, then cut it back to 10–15 minutes. Some babies may also cut back their lunchtime nap to one and a half hours, which can lead to them becoming very tired and irritable late afternoon. If this happens to your baby, try cutting out the morning nap altogether to see if it improves his lunchtime sleep. You may have to bring lunchtime forward slightly if he can't make it through to 12.30pm for his nap.

Your baby may also start to pull himself up in the cot, but get very upset when he can't get himself back down. If this happens, it would be advisable to encourage him to practise lying himself down when you put him down for his naps. Until he is able to manoeuvre himself up and down, you will need to go in and help him settle back down. It is important that this is done with the least fuss and talking. If this is happening, it is also worth taking a look at his daytime sleep total as waking up and standing up in the night can be a product of too much daytime sleep, which is easily rectified by cutting down, or cutting out, the morning nap.

Feeding

Your baby should be well established on three meals a day, and should also be able to feed himself some of the time. It is very important that your baby learns to chew properly at this stage. Food should be chopped or diced, although meat still needs to be pulsed or very finely chopped. By the end of his first year, he should be able to manage chopped meat. This is also a good time to introduce raw vegetables and salads. Try to include some finger foods at every meal and if he shows an interest in holding his own spoon, do not discourage these attempts. When he repeatedly puts it in his mouth, load up another spoon and let him try to get it into his mouth, quickly popping in any food that falls out with your spoon. With a little help and guidance, from 12 months most babies are capable of feeding themselves with part of their meal. It is important that he enjoys his meals even if a certain amount of it lands on the floor.

At nine months, a formula-fed baby should be taking all of his breakfast milk and 2.30pm feed from a beaker. By the age of one year, he should be drinking all his milk and other fluids from a beaker.

Breakfast

Aim to get your baby to have 240ml (8oz) of milk at this meal, divided between a drink and his breakfast cereal. Scrambled egg can be offered once or twice a week as a change.

Ensure that you still offer milk at the start of the meal. Once he has taken 150–180ml (5–6oz) of his milk, offer him some cereal. Then offer him the remainder of his milk again. It is important that he has at least 180–240ml (6–8oz) of milk divided between the beaker and the breakfast cereal. If you are still breast-feeding, offer him the first breast then the solids, then offer him the breast again.

Between nine and 12 months, a baby needs a minimum of 500ml (18oz) a day (inclusive of milk used in cooking or on cereal) divided between two or three milk feeds. This total also includes yoghurt and cheese – as a guide, a 125g (4.5oz) pot of yoghurt or a 30g (1oz) piece of cheese is the equivalent of approximately 210ml (7oz) of milk.

Lunch

Lunch should consist of a wide selection of lightly steamed, chopped vegetables served with a daily serving of protein. Babies of this age are very active and can become quite tired and irritable by 5pm. By giving your baby a well-balanced lunch, you will not need to worry if tea is more relaxed. By the end of the first year your baby's lunch can be integrated with the family lunch. Prepare the meal without salt, sugar or spices and reserve portions for your baby and toddler, and then add the desired flavourings for you and your partner.

Try to ensure that your baby's meals are attractively presented, with a variety of different coloured vegetables and fruit. Do not overload his plate; serve up a small amount and, when he finishes that, replenish his plate. This also helps to avoid the game of throwing food on the floor, which often occurs at this stage. If your baby does start to play up with his main course, refusing to eat and throwing food on the floor, quietly and firmly say 'no' and remove the plate. Do *not* offer him a biscuit or yoghurt half an hour later, as a pattern will soon emerge where he will refuse lunch knowing he will get something sweet if he plays up enough. A piece of fruit can be offered mid-afternoon to see him through to tea, at which time he will probably eat very well.

A drink of well-diluted, pure unsweetened orange juice in a beaker will help the absorption of iron at this meal, but make sure your baby has most of his meal before you allow him to finish the drink.

The 2.30pm feed

By 9–12 months, bottle-fed babies should be given their milk from a beaker, which should automatically result in a decrease in the amount they drink.

If your baby starts to cut back on his last milk feed, reduce, or cut out altogether, the 2.30pm feed. Many babies cut out the 2.30pm feed by one year. At 12 months, as long as your baby is getting a minimum of 350ml (12oz) of milk a day, inclusive of milk used in cereal and cooking, he will be getting enough. If he is getting 540ml (18oz) of milk a day (inclusive of milk used in cooking, on cereal and in cheese and yoghurt), plus a full balanced diet of solids, you could cut this feed altogether.

Once your baby has dropped this feed, it can be replaced by a small snack (for example a rice cake/unsweetened biscuit or small piece of fruit) and a drink of water or very well-diluted juice from a beaker.

Tea

If your baby has dropped the 2.30pm milk feed and you are worried that his daily milk intake is too low, try giving him foods such as pasta and vegetables with a milk sauce, baked potatoes with grated cheese, cheesy vegetable bake or mini quiches at teatime. Teatime is usually the meal when I would give small helpings of milk pudding or yoghurt, which are also good alternatives if milk is being rejected. Try to include some finger foods at teatime.

The bedtime bottle should be discouraged after one year, so during this stage get your baby gradually used to less milk at bedtime. This can be done by offering him a small drink of milk with his teatime meal, then a drink of 150–180ml (5–6oz) of milk from a beaker at bedtime.

The 6pm–7pm feed

By 10–12 months, bottle-fed babies should be taking all of their milk from a beaker. Babies who continue to feed from a bottle after one year are more prone to feeding problems, as they continue to take large amounts of milk, which takes the edge off their appetite for solids.

Start encouraging your baby to take some of his milk from a cup at 10 months, so that by one year he is happy to give up his bottles.

Daily requirements

By one year, it is important that large volumes of milk are discouraged; no more than 600ml (20oz), inclusive of milk used in food or on cereal, should be allowed. More than this can adversely affect your toddler's appetite for solid food. After one year, your baby needs a minimum of 350ml (11¼ oz) a day. This is usually divided between two or three drinks and is inclusive of milk used in cooking or on cereals, and in cheese and yoghurt.

Full-fat, pasteurised cow's milk can be given to drink after one year. If your baby refuses cow's milk, try gradually diluting his formula with it until he is happy to take full cow's milk. If possible try to give your baby organic milk as it comes from cows fed exclusively on grass, unlike non-organic milk. All bottles or beakers used for formula milk should still be sterilised until your baby is 12 months old.

Aim to give your baby three well-balanced meals a day and avoid snacks of biscuits, cakes and crisps. Every day aim for him to have three to four servings of carbohydrate, three to four servings of fruit and vegetables and one portion of animal protein or two of vegetable protein.

14
Problem-Solving

Myths, misconceptions and questions surrounding the Contented Little Baby routines

Q I was fairly laid-back with my first child, who just happened to fall naturally into a routine similar to the CLB one. I am aware that I may not be as lucky with my second baby and am keen to implement some sort of routine from the beginning. But I have been told by some friends that I must be prepared for lots of crying if I follow your routines. I do want to encourage a routine, but am concerned about leaving my baby to cry.

A The whole aim of the CLB routines is to ensure that the baby's needs are being met from the very beginning, so that he does not need to cry for any length of time. The guidelines I give are also to help mothers understand the different reasons why their baby may cry. If a baby is in a routine from a very early age, the mother will quickly learn to understand, and hence anticipate, his needs. I have found that this results in the baby crying very rarely – around 5–10 minutes a day. However, I do stress that some babies who get overtired may fight sleep, and should be allowed a 5–10-minute crying down period. They should never be left for any longer than this before they are checked again. I also stress that a baby should never be left crying for even 2–3 minutes if there is any doubt that he could be hungry or need winding.

In my book, *The Complete Sleep Guide for Contented Babies and Toddlers*, I do give advice on sleep training and controlled crying, for parents who have not followed my routines and whose older babies have learned the wrong sleep associations and are waking several times a night. But, I stress that these methods should only be used as a last resort, and only after having established a good feeding and sleeping routine during the day. I also advise that before commencing sleep training you should take your baby to see the doctor to check there are no medical problems.

I am confident you will find that if you follow my routines and advice properly you will have a very contented baby who settles well into a good feeding and sleeping routine with very little crying.

Q **My second baby is due in six weeks. We did not follow a routine with our first baby, and he did not sleep through until he was nine months old. I am not sure I can cope with a toddler and getting up several times in the night to feed the second baby. I am thinking of trying the CLB routines, but I have read that it is cruel to wake a sleeping baby and that he will wake up when he is ready to feed. Could I risk some sort of psychological or physical damage to my baby by waking him to feed?**

A During my many years of working with new mothers, the one thing that became apparent was that allowing newborn babies to sleep for long spells between feeds was not conducive to establishing a good milk supply. In the first few days after birth I observed that those babies who were very sleepy and allowed to sleep long spells of three to four hours between feeds were the ones that usually ended up being fully formula-fed within weeks of being born.

These early experiences in my career soon led me to advise mothers to feed their babies little and often during the early days to help establish a good milk supply, and avoid excessive night-time waking. The tummy of a newborn baby is tiny, and can only take small amounts of milk. Therefore, in my opinion, it is common sense that at least eight feeds would be needed during a 24-hour period. I advise that the baby should be encouraged to feed at least eight times a day, even if this means waking him.

On occasion, I was called in to care for babies who, before my arrival, had ended up seriously ill and dehydrated because they were allowed to go long spells between feeds, and this was proof enough to me that waking a baby to feed is not only essential for establishing a good milk supply, but also essential if the very serious problem of dehydration is to be avoided. I also stress in my books that some babies need to be fed more than eight times a day in the early days, and that, if a newborn baby is crying, the mother should always assume that hunger is the cause and the baby should be offered a feed.

During my career when I had to care for premature and sick babies, I was always advised by the hospital or doctors to wake and feed the babies on a regular basis, as this was the only way to ensure their survival. Over the years, watching these babies grow up into young children, I can assure you that I have never encountered any of them showing any psychological or physical damage.

Q I am seven months pregnant with my second baby. My daughter, who will be just over two years of age when her brother or sister is born, was fed on demand. She did eventually fall into a routine, but for the first six months I was feeding two or three times a night. I just know that it will be difficult to cope if I have a new baby who wakes two or three times a night for so many months and a toddler to look after in the day. But I am worried that if I follow a strict routine my baby may be denied food when he or she is really hungry.

A The whole reason why there are nine routines for the first year in this book is to ensure that the needs of individual babies are met, and that young babies are never denied food when they are hungry. You will see I give advice on how to adjust each routine to ensure that your baby's feeding needs are met, but also make sure that when your baby is ready to go a longer spell between feeds, that it happens at the right time – between 10pm and 7am. My main concern about demand feeding with very young babies is that a great many babies do not demand to be fed in the very early days. This can lead to many serious problems, the main one being that a baby who is not feeding enough during the day from the breast, will not stimulate the breast to produce enough milk. If this happens it can result in a situation where a pattern begins to emerge in which the mother is feeding the baby every 1–2 hours, night and day, to try to satisfy his needs, but by this time, exhaustion has set in. I believe that exhaustion is one of the main reasons why the milk supply decreases and women decide to give up breast-feeding very early on.

After the birth I advise a mother that her baby will need a minimum of eight feeds a day, and possibly more, and to offer her baby the breast every three hours. The time is taken from the beginning of one feed to the beginning of the next feed, and I also stress that if the baby is crying before the next feed is due, then hunger is probably the main reason and the baby should be fed. However, I do stress that, if a baby is continually crying and unhappy, you should also look for reasons why the baby cannot last the two hours between feeds.

The main cause for this is that the baby has not latched on properly to the breast and, while he may appear to be constantly sucking for up to an hour, much of the time he is not actually drinking well. This is why I advise mothers who are breast-feeding and finding that their baby is not going happily for two hours between feeds to seek advice from an experienced breast-feeding counsellor.

If you follow my advice on feeding your baby after the birth you should find that your baby quickly regains his birth weight and once this happens you can progress onto the first routine for one to two weeks. As the routine stresses, you do not need to move on to the next routine until your baby shows all the signs listed that he is ready to go longer between feeds. This is the advice given in all nine routines, so please do be reassured that your baby will never go hungry following them.

Q I was very lucky that my first-born did not catch his first cold until he was nearly a year old. My second baby is just over seven months and has already had two colds. How strict should I be with the routines when she is unwell?

A Some babies will need to sleep for longer when they are ill. Having said this, it would not be a good idea to let your baby sleep for too long during the day; firstly, you need to keep an eye on her fluid intake and, secondly, you might find that, if she sleeps all day, she will be awake all night. You should, therefore, relax the sleeping routine, but still have some influence on it. If she is unsettled during nap-times and in the evening, you may find it helps to settle her in her pram downstairs, with the mattress slightly elevated. If her sleep is being disturbed you can attend to her more easily if you do not have to keep running up and down stairs.

A feeding routine is very likely to change when a baby is ill, and she may go off solids, so don't press these if your baby is not interested. It is, however, vital to ensure that fluid levels are kept up, so do make sure your baby is drinking enough to avoid dehydration, which can become a serious problem. You may also need to reintroduce a night feed during this period, even if your baby has previously been sleeping through, and offer extra milk during the day if she is refusing solids. Once she is well again, you can quickly eliminate any milk feeds by reducing it by an ounce or so every night. If she has been feeding between 12am and 6am, you should count this milk as her breakfast milk and go straight on to solids at breakfast time, offering a small amount of milk after. This will help increase her appetite for solids. It can sometimes take a couple of weeks for a baby who has been ill to regain their appetite; as long as you gradually reduce any extra milk she has been having she will eventually get back to eating as normal.

The most important thing when your baby is ill is to concentrate on getting her well again, just try and stick to the sleeping and feeding times as best as you can and don't worry too much if the routine is altered slightly.

Finally, if you are concerned about anything to do with your baby's health, please consult your health visitor or GP.

Q **My baby is nearly four weeks old. I am trying to follow the CLB routines but for the last week my baby rarely settles for naps at the times the routines suggest and cries and feeds on and off all evening. She eventually settles at 11pm, but only after I have topped her up with formula. I think she may be suffering from colic, as she brings her legs up and screams as if in terrible pain when she cries. This goes on all evening, no matter how many times I put her to the breast. While we have managed to follow all the sleeping and feeding times of the CLB routine, I haven't managed well with the expressing times.**

A I suspect that your baby is unsettled due to hunger and not colic. It's likely that, as you haven't been able to express at the right times, when your baby went through a growth spurt at three weeks, she did not get the extra milk she required. The reason why it is so important to express during the early days of following the CLB routines is to ensure that you always produce more milk than the baby actually requires. This means that when a baby goes through a growth spurt the mother can express slightly less at the first feed of the day, ensuring that there is extra milk to satisfy the baby's increased needs.

I suggest you increase the number of breast-feeds you give your baby for several days to help increase your milk supply. I would advise that you top-up your baby with a breast-feed before the first two naps of the day to ensure that she gets the extra milk she needs and sleeps well. Instead of giving her a top-up of formula at 11pm, I would advise that, until your milk supply has increased, you offer it after the bath, so that she sleeps well between 7pm and 10pm. If she sleeps well at this time, and you manage to eat a good dinner and rest, you should find that you will make enough milk to offer her a full feed at the late feed. I would also urge you to attempt the plan on page 285 to help increase your milk supply so that you can eliminate the need to top-up with formula. If you find that you cannot fit in all of the extra expressings, if you could at least express 2–3oz milk first thing in the morning before you feed the baby, this expressed milk could be used instead of formula to top-up the baby after the bath. I always advise to express before a feed, as the baby is always more efficient at extracting the hind milk from the breast than the electric pump is. When you are expressing before the feed, you will probably find that your baby will need to feed slightly earlier and for longer than the times suggested in the routine. This is absolutely fine, as the longer feeds combined with the top-up feeding and expressing will help increase your milk supply.

Q To enable me to get out and about more easily with my very active toddler, I only ever used the sling for my second baby's daytime sleep. At six weeks I find that she is refusing to settle to sleep in her Moses basket or cot in the evening. She feeds well and looks sleepy but, the minute I put her down, she wakes up screaming, only to fall asleep in our arms as soon as either my husband or I pick her up. We are now spending the whole evening picking her up and putting her down, with her getting more and more distressed. We do want to establish a good routine but do not want to do this by leaving her to cry.

A It sounds as if your baby has learned the wrong sleep associations, having got used to being carried for much of her sleep-time. I understand you don't want your baby to be left to cry herself to sleep for any length of time, and this is not something I would recommend anyway. What I would suggest is that for several days you use a method I call 'assisted sleep routine'. The aim is to get your baby used to sleeping at regular times during naps and in the evening. Once your baby is used to sleeping at the same times for several days you should find that you can settle your baby in her Moses basket or cot with the minimum of fuss.

For this method to work it is important that it should be done consistently and by only one parent. For the next three days, don't even attempt to put your baby in her cot at nap times or early evening. Instead, one or the other of you should lie in a quiet room with her and cuddle her throughout the whole of the sleep-time. Try to ensure that she is held in the crook of your arm, not lying across your chest. It may help if she gets upset to use your right hand to hold both her hands across her chest, this way she will not wave her arms around and get so upset. It is important that the same person is with her during the allocated sleep-time and that you do not hand her back and forth or walk around from room to room. Once she is sleeping soundly for three nights, you should then settle her in the Moses basket or cot, but have it right next to you, so you can hold her hands across her chest and 'shh shh' her. For the fourth, hold both her hands across her chest until she is asleep, and on the fifth night hold only one of her hands across her chest until she is asleep. By the sixth night you should find that you can put her down sleepy but awake in her Moses basket or cot, checking her every two to three minutes and shh-ing her until she falls asleep. Once you find she is settling within 10 minutes you should leave her to self-settle using the crying down method described on page 212.

During the day it will help her get used to her Moses basket or cot by putting her in it for short spells at some of her awake time, with a small soft book or toy to look at.

Q **I did not follow your routines with my first child, but am trying to follow the four-week-old routine with my second baby. The problem is that he is not managing to stay awake for the two hours during the day, managing at the most an hour after each feed. He settles well in the evening and is waking only once in the night at around 2.30am.**

A If your baby is feeding well and gaining regular weight each week, is sleeping well between feeds in the night, and is alert for some of his awake periods during the day, he is just one of those babies who needs more sleep.

At some stage your baby will start to show signs of wanting to stay awake for longer. When this begins to happen, try to ensure that the times when he is awake and alert are happening during the day and not the night. If you aim to gradually extend the time he is awake by five minutes, every two to three days, between the 7am and 9am awake period, this will happen naturally. Once he is happily staying awake for the full two hours, you can try to do the same at the 10am to 12 noon awake period, and once this is successful aim to extend his wakeful period by five minutes, every two to three days, between the 2pm to 4pm period. Using this technique, you are reducing the amount of sleep your baby is having very slowly and this will ensure that you are not trying to encourage your baby to stay awake longer than he is able, but it will also mean that when he begins to need less sleep it happens between 7am and 7pm and not during the night.

Q I have been trying to follow your routines for six weeks with my second baby. I feel I am constantly struggling to keep her awake or keep her going for a feed. This is something I never had to do with my first baby, who followed the routines to the letter.

A Whether you have a routine or not, looking after a new baby and a toddler can be very challenging. My routines make sure the hard work is limited to as short a period as possible. Every baby is different, so try not to compare what your new baby is doing now to what your toddler was doing at the same age.

Start each day at 7am and attempt to follow the day's routine as best you can, but if it has gone 'pear-shaped' by lunchtime because your baby is wide awake at nap time and sleepy during the social times, I recommend that you don't panic. Keep repeating the same pattern of feeds and sleeps every day as best you can and your baby will pick it up very soon. If she is crying for food before the time the routine for her age recommends, she should be fed, and if she falls asleep long before her nap time is due, then do a split nap so that she does not exceed the daily amount of sleep recommended. During the first few weeks do not worry if you have to do lots of split feeds and split naps to fit in with your toddler's routine, the important thing is that you structure feeding and sleeping so that the baby settles well at 7pm. The older she gets the easier it will be to keep the daytime sleep and feeding on track. Remember, my methods are intended to make life easier. Try not to dwell on the times when the routine does not go exactly to plan, just start each day as a new day.

When your baby does start to follow the routines more consistently, as she very soon will, I can guarantee you will never regret the effort you put in to following them in the first few weeks. By establishing a routine, it will, in the long term, enable you to look after the needs of both your children more easily. Think how difficult it would be if your baby were still waking up in the night at nine months old … It is very hard work the first few months with a second baby, but keep persevering – it will be worth it.

Feeding problems

Q I would like to follow a routine with my second child, but how will I know when my baby is ready to drop his night feeds? If I follow your advice and stop feeding my baby at night at 12 weeks, I am worried that I will have to leave him to cry for lengthy periods.

A How quickly a baby sleeps through the night is very much determined by his weight and the amount of milk he is capable of drinking at each feed during the day. Those babies who are only capable of drinking small amounts at each feed will obviously need a feed in the night for longer than a baby who is capable of drinking a larger amount at each feed during the day.

The aim of the CLB routines is not to push the baby through the night as quickly as possible, or to deny the baby a feed in the night if he genuinely needs it. It is to ensure that the baby receives most of his nutritional needs during the day so that when he is physically and mentally ready to go through the night he will automatically do so. The feedback I have had from thousands of parents, along with my many years of experience caring for babies, confirms that this approach works.

The majority of babies I have cared for personally, would go to sleep during the night (i.e. from the last feed at 11pm to 6–7am) somewhere between eight and 12 weeks. The huge amount of feedback that I receive from readers indicates that this is the average age at which babies forming routines sleep for a longer spell. Every baby is, of course, different. Some babies, particularly breast-fed babies, may need to be fed once in the middle of the night until they are five or six months old. By following the routines and advice in this book you should find that your baby will gradually start to sleep for longer spells in the night and, eventually, when he is ready, sleep right through the night. This will all happen naturally and as long as your baby does not develop the wrong sleep associations you should never experience any crying in the night.

Q My two-week-old baby wakes up yelling for a feed, only to fall asleep after five minutes on the breast. He then demands to be fed two hours later, leaving me absolutely exhausted trying to cope with constant feeding and the demands of my very energetic two-year-old son. I feel that I am not meeting the needs of either of my children right now and, although I will feel guilty doing so, I am seriously thinking of switching the baby to formula so that I can see how much he is getting at each feed.

A Some babies are sleepy feeders in the first few weeks, and I do not think that changing to formula would resolve what is really a very short term problem. It is very important that sleepy babies are kept cool while feeding. Your baby should not be overdressed and the room should not be too warm. Have a play mat next to you on the floor and, the minute he gets sleepy, put him on the play mat. If necessary, remove his Babygro, as this will encourage him to stretch and kick. Within a few minutes he will probably protest about being put down, so pick him up and give him a few more minutes on the same breast. This procedure often has to be repeated two or three times. Once he has had 20 minutes on the first breast, burp him well and change his nappy. He can then be put back on the first breast if he has not finished it, or be transferred to the second.

Always make sure your baby is fully awake before you attempt to feed him. Unwrap him while he's in the cot, take his legs out of his Babygro and allow the cool air to get to his skin. Give him time to wake up by himself (see pages 59–60).

On the days you take your toddler to playgroup, you could express some milk prior to leaving the house, and ask one of the other mothers to feed the baby so you can give your toddler some undivided attention. If you are not already doing so, it is also a good idea to express some milk at 9.30pm and get your partner to do the 10–11pm feed. This way, you will at least manage to get an uninterrupted few hours' sleep for one part of the night, which will help give you more energy for dealing with your toddler and baby during the day.

The first few weeks of trying to meet the needs of a second baby and a toddler can be really exhausting, but take heart that this stage will not last forever – once your baby reaches four to six weeks he will begin to be more alert during feeds.

Q **I successfully followed the CLB routines with my first child, and am now trying to do the same with my second baby, aged four weeks. At the moment she is feeding at 10am and 2pm, but I know that eventually the feeds and sleeps will become a little later, which means she will be feeding at 2.30pm. The problem is that I have to pick up my eldest from nursery at 3pm, which means leaving the house at 2.45pm. My daughter is such a slow feeder, taking up to an hour, and if I follow the routines and feed her at 2.30pm, then there is no way that she would have taken a full feed by 2.45pm, at the time I need to be leaving the house.**

A I suggest that you gradually move the 10am feed on as the routines suggest, but continue to feed your baby at 2pm. If you feel that she has not taken a good enough feed at 2pm, and you have to leave for the school run, you can easily offer her the remainder of the feed on your return. If she refuses to feed on your return from the school run, you may find that she will be hungry slightly earlier than 5pm, and that feed will need to be brought forward a little.

Another option would be to express at 1.45/2pm and offer her a bottle of expressed milk at 2.30pm. Although not always the case, *some* babies do feed quicker from the bottle than the breast. Remember too, as she gets older, your baby will start to feed more quickly: some breast-fed babies will take a full feed in 10 minutes, so once you notice that she is taking a feed in less time, you can start to make the 2pm feed slightly later.

Q I have followed *The New Contented Little Baby Book* and for the most part my son is a 'Gina' baby. He sleeps from 7pm until 7am and for two hours after lunch. He is full of energy and fun to be with. The only problem is his feeding. I waited until he was six months old to introduce solids. For the first month of weaning he refused to open his mouth despite everything I tried. By seven or eight months he was still only on baby rice and puréed apple and pear. Every stage has been slower since then. He loved breakfast and after his milk he would eat one or two Weetabix and then either some of my toast or cereal. By mid-morning he would have a couple of rice cakes, oatcakes or breadsticks, and the same in the afternoon. His lunch and tea were nearly always the same – blended casseroles and soups. I kept some lumps, which he usually spat out. After most meals I gave him puréed apple and pear for dessert, which he liked. I sometimes added natural plain yoghurt.

At 19 months, I am still struggling to get him to eat

lumps and eat a more varied diet. He's started to refuse any type of savoury food, turning his head away when I try to feed him his usual soup or casserole. As an alternative, I end up giving him toast, which he feeds to himself. He also eats a few cheese triangles. I'm seven months pregnant with my second baby and am really concerned about how I will cope with a new baby and a toddler who is becoming an increasingly fussy feeder.

A Toddlers of this age can become fussy with their food, some days eating lots and other days eating very little. I would advise that you keep a detailed feeding diary so that you can monitor what he is eating and drinking. It will also help you structure his meals and snacks so that the right type of food is being served at the right time of the day, and so he doesn't fill up on juice and biscuits in between meals. I feel that your son's appetite for his lunch and tea could be affected by eating an excessive amount of carbohydrates at breakfast and snack times. I suggest that you temporarily change breakfast to puréed fruit and half a tub of yoghurt, and reduce the milk at breakfast to 114ml (4oz). For lunch, give him a protein meal, and for dinner, try some soup and sandwiches or some other carbohydrate foods. Include lots of finger foods at both meals. Instead of biscuit-type snacks, offer a little chopped fruit between meals. As a last resort, if he doesn't eat well in the evening, give him cereal so that he isn't going to bed on an empty tummy. It's important not to make a fuss or cajole your son at mealtimes. Allow no longer than 20–30 minutes for your son to eat his meal. If he refuses to eat or begins to fuss, the meal should be removed immediately. He should not be offered any other foods until the next snack or mealtime. At his age, it is important to allow him the control to decide how much he wants to eat.

Once your son is eating better at lunch and tea you can rein-troduce cereal and toast at breakfast, but I would give no more than one Weetabix or serving of cereal so that he continues to eat well at lunch and tea.

Sleeping problems

Q I followed the CLB routines with my first child, who slept through the night from 7pm to 7am at 18 weeks. At nearly three years of age, she has only ever woken up a handful of times in the night. But since the birth of our second baby six weeks ago she has started waking up several times a night. This doesn't coincide with the time the baby wakes, so we know that she is not being disturbed by her sibling. We are making sure that she gets lots of love and attention during the day, but we can't work out how to solve her night-time wakings.

She had dropped her daytime sleep and settles well at 7.30pm, is very sweet with the new baby and has shown no obvious signs of jealousy. Friends have advised us that we should try to make very little of her night-time wakings, otherwise we risk encouraging her.

But it is so out of keeping, and she has been such a consis-tently good sleeper, that we would really like to resolve it. I am sure she is more tired in the day as a result of a disturbed night – she also risks waking her brother when she calls for us. We are finding it tiring looking after our newborn, and it

is doubly so trying to settle a wakeful three-year-old in the early hours.

A This problem is fairly common when a new baby arrives. In my experience, quickly reassuring a toddler who has been used to sleeping well rarely leads to long-term waking problems. When your daughter wakes, either you or your husband should go straight to her and reassure her, using the same simple phrase every time. I would recommend something along the lines of 'shh shh, it's night-time, Mummy's here, cuddle up to teddy'. It is important not to get into a conversation with your daughter, not to switch the light on and not to stay in the room for more than a few minutes. You may have to repeat this a few times a night for several nights, but once you see she is settling back to sleep quickly you can then try not going into the room when she wakes; instead, open the door and use the same words of reassurance as you did when you went into the room. This method will work best if the same person does the checking all night. I have found that, if parents take it in turns to check their child, the toddler can begin to play one or the other up.

You might find that starting this method on a Friday night makes it easier, since it will enable the parent who has been up several times in the night to catch up on lost sleep during the day. I advise using this method along with a star chart, and lots of praise, as your daughter's sleeping improves. Once she is down to waking only once in the night, and you have not had to go in to her, give her a small star on the chart. When she sleeps through without calling out, give her an extra big star on the chart.

From that point work on a goal of a certain number of big stars for sleeping through. When she achieves a certain amount, reward her with a special treat. Perhaps you could promise her a special outing to her favourite place with either Mummy or Daddy, leaving the baby at home with the parent who stays behind.

If you are consistent and persistent with this method, your daughter's sleeping will gradually improve and the waking will get less and less – soon your daughter will be sleeping through the night again.

Q **My daughter was a CLB from eight weeks old, although she always needed much more sleep than the average baby – as an example, at five months of age she was still sleeping for five hours in the day and 12½ hours at night! Now my son is six and a half months old and he is still waking in the night, I'm not sure what to do. He naps from 9–9.45am, 12 noon–2pm and 4.30–5pm, and is settled for the night at 6.30pm. I'm sure hunger isn't the issue as he is a big baby and has taken to solids well without a reduction in his full milk feeds (which he still has at 7am, 2pm and 6.15pm).**

A It's very important to remember that, while your daughter needed a lot more sleep than the average baby, this is exceptional! Your son is showing that he is much more average in his sleep needs. A 'sleepy baby', while needing more daytime sleep, would also be sleeping soundly during the night. The fact that your son is waking in the night tells us that he is ready for less sleep in the day. Start by slowly reducing and cutting out his late afternoon sleep. Keep afternoons quiet and allow him lots of rest time while you do this to avoid him becoming overstimulated. Once you have cut out the afternoon nap, you should start to reduce the morning nap to 30 minutes and move it to 9.30am, which will allow you to make the lunchtime nap later. Once this happens it's important to keep moving his bedtime closer to 7pm.

Ensure that you settle him as quickly as possible should he wake in the night, even if this means offering him a milk feed. It is much easier to reduce and cut out a small feed in the night than it is to solve the sleep problems of a baby who is awake for long periods and trying to make up for this lost sleep in the daytime. After his daytime sleep has been reduced, you can gradually reduce and eliminate any milk he is having in the night.

Q My baby is seven months old and, despite following your routines and introducing solids at six months, he is still feeding at 10pm, continuing to wake up twice in the night and refusing to settle back to sleep unless I breast-feed him. He weighs nearly 7.7kg (17lb) and is exclusively breast-fed. He settles well at all his other sleep times, so I know it is not a sleep association problem. I have been advised that a baby of his age should not need to be fed in the night, and that I should consider sleep training him to end the middle-of-the-night feeds. We did try leaving him to cry a couple of times and he just worked himself up into such a hysterical state that it took a couple of hours to calm him down.

He breast-feeds during the day at 7am, 10.30am, 2.30pm, 6.15pm, 10pm and then at around 2am and 5am in the night. We offer him solids at 8am, 11.30am and again at 5pm. He rarely takes more than a tablespoonful at a time, and gets very upset if we try to push him to take more. He refuses any food that contains protein, which is also very worrying.

A In my books I advise that most babies of your son's age can sleep through the night, provided all their nutritional needs are met during the day. Taking into consideration your baby's weight, and the amount of solids he is taking, I suspect that most of his night wakings are due to genuine hunger, and that you cannot realistically expect him to go 12 hours until solids are more established. Because he is feeding three times in the night, this is probably affecting his appetite for solids during the day, hence the reason he is so fussy about eating them. When this happens, an unwanted pattern emerges of the baby needing to feed in the night, because he is not getting enough solids during the day.

Sleep training for this type of problem should never be contemplated, as your baby is genuinely hungry. I would suggest that you gradually reduce the amount of milk that your son is drinking in the night, which will in turn encourage him to eat more solids during the day. The first thing I would advise is to drop the 10pm feed. As he is waking at 2am and 5am, it is pointless to continue with this feed because it is not helping him sleep a long spell in the night. He will then most likely wake between midnight and 2am. It is important that when he wakes at this time you offer him a really good feed, and do not restrict the length of time that he is on the breast. A really good feed should hopefully take him to between 5am and 6am.

As your baby is being fussy about solids, I would advise that you work on establishing solids at lunch and tea first. I would advise not giving solids at breakfast until your baby is taking between 5–6 tablespoonfuls of solids at lunch and tea.

If you are not giving breakfast, you may have to bring the time of lunch forward slightly if your baby is showing signs of being hungry before the recommended time. With a baby who is being fussy about lunchtime solids, this is preferable to giving solids at breakfast. As your baby is still feeding twice in the night, I would suggest that you offer the solids first at lunchtime, followed by a breast-feed. As he is still taking two milk feeds in the night, you do not need to worry at this stage that his daily milk intake is dropping too low. The aim of this plan is to increase your baby's daytime solids, without leaving him to cry with hunger in the night. You will find that, once your baby increases the solids he is eating during the day, he will automatically need to feed from the breast less in the night.

Once your baby has been happily taking 5–6 tablespoons of solids at lunchtime and teatime for several days, you can then introduce small amounts of protein into your baby's food. When your baby is happily taking 5–6 tablespoons of protein-based meals (see page 191) at lunchtime, you can then introduce breakfast. I would suggest that you start off with a small amount of yoghurt and fruit, then progress to breakfast cereal and fruit. The important thing to remember when introducing breakfast is that you should not increase it so much that it takes away your baby's appetite for lunch. Also, it will really help if your baby has had all of his milk and solids by 8am. Remember that the aim of solids is to establish your baby on a feeding pattern of three meals a day, with bigger gaps between meals. If you give milk at 7/7.30am, then delay breakfast until 8/8.30am, it could affect your baby's appetite for lunch.

After breakfast has been introduced, I would count any breast-feeds in the night as his breakfast milk, and reduce the amount of milk that he has at 7am, to encourage him to take solids. This can be done by offering first the solids then a breast-feed.

Once your baby has increased the amount of solids that he is taking during the day, he should automatically start to sleep a longer spell in the night, leading to him waking up somewhere between 3/4am, instead of 2am and 5am. I would continue to give him a big enough feed at this time, until he sleeps regularly until 7am for at least a week. Once he is doing this, you can gradually decrease the length of time he is on the breast by a couple of minutes every few nights. Once you reach a stage of him taking a breast-feed of only a few minutes in the night, and sleeping until 7am, you can then look at dropping this feed, confident in the knowledge that the waking is not due to genuine hunger.

Dropping this feed will be easier if you get your husband to go to the baby when he wakes, and settle him with a small drink of cool boiled water and a cuddle. It may take several nights of your husband having to pick him up and resettle him several times. Follow the same procedure until your son shows signs of settling back to sleep more quickly in the night. Once this happens, your husband should progress to settling your son back to sleep without taking him out of the cot. Although it may take a week or two, by being persistent and consistent you should get your son sleeping through, without resorting to leaving him to cry for lengthy periods.

As you decrease the time on the breast in the night, it is then important to remember to allow your son more to drink during the day. What you are now aiming for is a full breast-feed at 7am, followed by solids, then lunchtime solids at around 11am/12 noon, followed by a breast-feed. He will then need a further breast-feed at around 2.30pm, followed by solids and a small breast-feed at 5pm, then a full breast-feed at bedtime. Once your baby is well established on three solid meals a day, and four to five good breast-feeds, you can feel sure that any night waking is not due to hunger.

I also suggest that you discuss with your health visitor the types of foods that you give your baby. Getting the right balance of protein, carbohydrates, vegetables and fruit also plays an important role in establishing healthy sleep habits.

Finally, it is important to keep an eye on how much sleep your baby has during the day. Although all babies are different, and some will need more than others, I would recommend that you aim for a nap of no more than 30/40 minutes in the morning and two hours after lunch if you want your son to sleep well at night.

If he sleeps less than two hours at lunchtime, then he may need a short catnap between 4pm and 5pm to avoid overtiredness.

Q My nine-week-old son has recently slept until 6.15am for two nights in a row and then 5.30am for another three, so I thought we were gradually getting to the holy 7am, but the other night (and again last night) he woke at 4am. The first time, I tried to use the core night method [see pages 280–2] of settling him with patting or a dummy; patting had no effect so I gave him a dummy, which kept him quiet, but I could tell he wasn't asleep so I eventually fed him at 5am, and he went back to sleep until 7am. He was then irritable all day, which I put down to the disrupted night. Last night I tried to settle him at 4am with water, but he refused to settle and then I had to offer him 100ml (3½oz) of expressed milk to get him back to sleep. After this he woke at 6.50am and wasn't interested in a top-up at 7.30am, but wouldn't settle for the 9am nap until I topped him up with 60ml (2oz) of expressed milk.

The core night method doesn't seem to be working – unless I am doing it wrong? I am a bit worried he will drop the wrong feed if I keep feeding him in the night.

As your baby is nine weeks old, and possibly going through a growth spurt, I recommend that you go back to feeding him when he wakes in the night for the next week or so, even if it means he takes less at the 7am feed in the morning. There is always a stage in the routines where a baby will feed at 4/5am and not be so hungry at 7am. If he refuses a top-up at 7.30am, then you will have to top him up prior to his morning nap, so that he sleeps well. If he takes a top-up at 7.30am, you may find that you will have to feed him at around 10/10.30am, with a top-up at lunchtime to keep the routine on track.

The most important thing to remember when establishing good sleeping habits is that your aim should be to encourage your baby naturally to sleep soundly for long spells, even if it means a quick feed in the night. It can take slightly longer for breast-fed babies to sleep through the night. If you try to push your baby through the night before he is ready, you will end up with a baby who gets into the habit of being awake on and off in the night and, as you have already found out, is tired and irritable during the day. A negative pattern will begin to evolve where the baby stays awake longer in the night, and needs to sleep more during the day. Because he is sleeping too much during the day, a vicious cycle of him continuing to wake in the night will evolve. This is a far worse problem to resolve than getting rid of a night feed. At this stage I suggest that you give him as big a feed as he needs in the night to get him back to sleep quickly until 7am. It is pointless restricting the amount you give him, if then he wakes up at 6am!

Once he has been sleeping through regularly until 7am for at least a week, you could try the core night method again. But always bear in mind that it should not be pursued unless the baby is settling back to sleep quickly with the aid of the dummy, water or a cuddle. If he hasn't settled within 20 minutes, it is best to feed him so that he is not awake for too long. As long as he is settling back quickly, with one of the suggested ways of settling and perhaps a small feed, you could continue using the core night method, provided he is sleeping until 7am. If he does settle back to sleep without a feed, but then wakes again an hour later, he should be fed immediately. The aim of the core night method is not to eliminate the night feed totally, but to encourage him to gradually sleep for longer and longer between feeds. If you attempt to settle him a second time in the night with the dummy or water, that in itself could establish the wrong sleep association.

Q My second baby is now almost two weeks old and I am keen to get started on the routines. Her sister was a CLB from birth and now, at two years old, still thrives on the routine, so I know how beneficial it can be. The days are falling into place, but I find myself really struggling from 6pm onwards. I know how important a good bedtime routine is, but I'm finding that I'm ending up with both my girls screaming and impossible to settle. What can I do to make it easier for all of us?

A Firstly, ensure that your new baby is napping well between 4pm and 5pm to avoid overtiredness, which will prevent her from settling at bedtime. It's crucial to allow plenty of time for the bath and bedtime routine in the early days – even more so if you are doing this on your own. Is there someone who could help you out with this for a couple of weeks? Another pair of hands really can help. If you have a friend or neighbour with a teenage daughter looking to earn extra pocket money they could be a great help entertaining your toddler while you bath the baby.

I would also advise you to begin the bathtime routine no later than 5.30pm and to bath your baby and toddler separately as explained in the one- to two-week routine on page 102. Try to involve your toddler in helping you cream the baby as this can amuse her while also helping them bond – but don't force her if she is not interested. Feed your baby while your toddler sits next to you having a cuddle, then you can read your toddler a story while you finish the feed. If neither child is settling well at bedtime, you need to decide which one to settle. If the baby is reasonably happy sitting in her bouncy chair or lying in her pram, then settle your toddler. At least that way you will be keeping one of them in a routine, which is preferable to ending up trying to get the routine right for both.

Q My daughter will be just over two years old when the new baby arrives in three months. We live in a flat with two bedrooms, so at some stage in the future we intend the children to share a room. We plan to have the baby in our room for the first six months, but wondered at what age we should aim to move our baby into her sister's room. My two-year-old has a cot bed, and we wondered when you would advise us to safely take the sides off this?

A If both your baby and toddler are sleeping well, there is no reason why you could not put them in the same room once the baby reaches six months. However, I would be inclined to keep the sides of your toddler's cot on until the baby is at least a year. I know many toddlers who sleep happily in their cots until they are well past three, so as long as your daughter is not climbing out of her cot, it should not be a problem.

I have known parents who put their children together at a much younger age, without any problems. But I have also known incidents of toddlers who are sleeping in beds getting up early in the morning and trying to climb into the baby's cot – one taking a blanket with him to tuck the baby in! Even with both children sleeping in their cots, I would do a careful safety check of the room. Ensure that no furniture or chairs are near your toddler's cot that she could climb up on to and get out of the cot. Be careful about how many toys and what type of toys you allow her to have in her cot. Throwing toys into the baby's cot can become a fun pastime for many toddlers. Likewise, make sure that both children are put in sleeping bags at night, and that your toddler does not have access to loose covers, cushions, etc.

I also recommend that you buy either a night light on a timer, or a bunny alarm clock, and use this along with a star chart to encourage your daughter to lie quietly in bed until the light goes on or the alarm goes off. A monitor with a webcam would also be a good idea, so that you can check on any suspicious noises!

Q My second daughter, who is seven and half months, has
begun to wake up earlier and earlier. This last week it
has been at around 5.30am every morning. I have tried leaving her to cry, but she works herself up into a state and it
wakes my toddler up. She eats really well and sleeps well for
an hour between 9am and 10am, and from 12 noon for two
hours. She used to go to bed at 7pm but, since the early
morning waking, I am having to put her down at around
6.30pm as she is so tired. With a toddler of 18 months, I am
struggling to cope with such an early start.

A Babies differ in the amount of sleep they need, and I think
that your daughter is one of those babies who probably
needs slightly less sleep. Leaving a baby to cry at this time of the
morning rarely works in my opinion, and usually just enforces the
early-morning waking even more. It is better to get to the cause
of the early-morning waking and, in your daughter's case, I think
it is due to her morning nap being too long.

In order to push the morning nap on and reduce it to 20 to
30 minutes, your daughter needs to sleep until nearer 7am.

It is important that for a few days you feed her as soon as she
wakes up at 5.30am to help settle her back to sleep. Once she is
settling back to sleep, you can move the morning nap on by 5–
10 minutes every couple of days until she is going down to sleep
at 9.30am for 20/30 minutes. You should then also push the
lunchtime nap to 12.30pm, and allow no more than two hours,
making a total daytime sleep of no more than two and a half
hours. If for some reason your baby sleeps less than two hours at
lunchtime, you may need to give her a short nap between 4pm
and 5pm, to avoid her becoming overtired. It is also important

that you count any sleep after 7am as part of her daytime sleep allowance. If she sleeps even 10 or 15 minutes past 7am, reduce the morning nap to 15 minutes. Once you have pushed on your daytime naps, your daughter should manage to get to nearer a 7pm bedtime.

By reducing the morning nap and pushing the naps on, your baby should start to sleep later in the morning, and the 5.30am waking will naturally disappear, but until this happens I would continue to settle her back to sleep with a feed – this is preferable to her getting into the habit of being awake from 5.30am every morning. Any milk that she is given at 5.30am should be counted as her breakfast milk, and at 7am she should be offered solids first, then a small drink of milk.

Weaning problems

Q I followed your routines with my first baby and, when she was six months, started weaning her according to your advice. Now my second baby is 18 weeks old and he has started waking in the night demanding a full feed (having slept through from his late feed at eight weeks old). He's also waking up halfway through his lunchtime nap for the first time ever! I'm not sure what to do. I had really wanted to wait until he reached six months until weaning him but he seems so unsettled all the time. He weighs 15lbs 6oz and is fully breast-fed, taking both breasts at each feed (with a bottle of expressed milk at 10.30pm).

A It is possible that your son is going through a growth spurt and introducing some extra feeds will help resolve his unsettled sleep. I would suggest that you do split feeds at 10am and 11.30am, also 5pm and 6.15pm, and 10pm and 11pm, which will help increase the daily amount of milk your baby is getting. If you find, after following these feed times for one week, that he still remains unsettled, I would suggest that you discuss with your health visitor or GP whether your baby may need to be weaned slightly earlier than six months. While the Department of Health does recommend waiting until six months before introducing solid food, I am aware that in some cases with larger babies, who are waking excessively in the night or who are unsettled during the day despite being offered extra milk feeds, parents are often advised to wean slightly earlier.

I do also advise that some babies, who have been sleeping through the night for several weeks, may need to go back to feeding in the middle of the night again until solids are introduced. However, sometimes a baby who wakes up in the middle of the night and will not settle back to sleep without a feed refuses to feed at 7am. If this happens I usually advise to try dropping the 10pm feed, in the hope that the baby will then sleep until nearer 1am or 2am, feeding only once in the night, and then sleep until nearer 7am and then feed well.

Fussy eating

Q My two-year-old daughter used to eat most of what she was offered but in the last few weeks, shortly after her younger sister was born, she has started to refuse many types

of food and she rarely finishes her meal. I am starting to get very stressed by her behaviour and I'm worried about the effect on her health.

A If you are concerned that your toddler is not eating enough, the first step is to keep a full and complete food diary for a fortnight. Detail all the timings and amounts of meals, snacks and drinks (including water) that she consumes. Many parents find, when they average it out, that their toddler eats a good range and a fair amount of all the required food groups. However, having completed your diary, if you still feel that there is a problem, it is important to speak to your health visitor or your GP and take their advice on how to proceed.

Below I have listed the most common causes of food refusal and fussiness together with some tips on how to encourage your toddler to eat well long-term. You can find further information in two of my other books: *The Contented Child's Food Bible* and *Feeding Made Easy*.

- **Excessive milk intake.** Toddlers need a minimum of 350ml (12oz) and a maximum of 600ml (20oz) of milk per day (inclusive of yoghurt, cheese and milk used in cooking and on cereal). An intake of more than 600ml is a major cause of food refusal. If your toddler is still having a large drink of milk 2–3 times a day (possibly from a bottle), it's a good idea to reduce the amount she is having to 350ml (12oz) morning and evening from a beaker or a cup. This should ensure that her milk intake is not adversely affecting her appetite for solid food.

- **Timings of other drinks.** Drinks (juice or even water) given less than an hour before meals, or even immediately before food is served, can sometimes take the edge off a toddler's appetite. Try to ensure that any drinks are offered no later than two hours before meal times. Obviously, if the weather is hot and your toddler is saying she is thirsty, then you cannot deny her water but it is a good idea to encourage her to sit down and have a good drink at scheduled snack times between meals – this also discourages constant 'grazing' of drinks and snacks which can really cause problems in toddlers with small appetites.

- **Timing of meals and snacks.** Schedule meals and snacks at regular times and stick to these times. If, after 20 minutes, your toddler is showing no interest in eating, remove the food without making any comment on her lack of eating. However, she should not be allowed anything to eat or drink until the next scheduled snack time. Ideally there should be a two-hour gap between meals and snacks. In my experience it works best if breakfast is finished by 8am, so that your toddler is ready for lunch between 12 noon and 1pm, and tea no later than 5pm. A mid-morning snack and a drink should be offered between 9.30am and 10am, with a mid-afternoon snack and drink around 3pm.

- **Size of meals.** If you notice that your toddler is particularly fussy at lunchtime, it is worth paying particular attention to the size of her breakfast. All too often I see parents worried about their child's small appetite saying 'Breakfast is her best meal of the day!'. When I look at their food diary it is clear to me that their toddler is eating a vast amount of breakfast – sometimes double what a child of this age and size would be expected to consume – which is often the reason why she is not hungry enough for lunch. If you feel this may be the case with your toddler, try reducing the amount of food you are giving at breakfast. This will mean she is hungry at lunchtime and may be more inclined to try new foods.

● **Type of snacks.** If your toddler has a small appetite or is going through a fussy phase, eating even the smallest of snacks less than two hours before a meal can be enough to affect her appetite. The type of snack given is significant. If your toddler is refusing her meals, stick to very small pieces of easy-to-digest fruit (such as a small piece of apple or two pieces of soft fruit) and steer clear of heavier snack foods such as banana, biscuits or rice cakes.

● **Avoid bribes.** Whatever the situation, don't use food as a reward or punishment. The child who is told 'If you don't eat your lunch, you can't have pudding' immediately thinks that her main meal can't be as good as what might follow! Instead, offer fresh fruit, natural yoghurt, or cheese and crackers, and avoid sugar-laden fromage frais and other commercial yoghurts marketed towards children – some of which can have as much as 14.5g (½oz) of sugar in a 100g (4oz) pot!

● **Never force-feed.** It is important to let your toddler take control of how much she wants to eat, and for her to learn that she eats when she's hungry and stops when she's full. If you are constantly coaxing her or getting her to take 'just one more spoonful' then she is likely to exercise her will and may stop eating certain foods altogether. The result can be extremely distressing for all concerned and is likely to result in extreme food aversion. Mealtimes should be happy, relaxed occasions where your toddler feels free to try new foods, or refuse if she's not hungry. If you have structured the timings, size and type of drinks and snacks as I've described above, she will be hungry enough and will eat as much as she needs.

Bedtime battles

Q Since my second child was born I have found it impossible to establish a calm bath and bedtime routine for both children. The whole thing seems to take forever and always ends up resembling a battleground. None of us enjoy it and I end up feeling fraught and exhausted. Help!

A Here are my suggestions on how to plan, prepare and carry out a stress-free bedtime for two children, or a toddler who has become difficult to settle:

● Try to ensure that your toddler has her main protein meal of the day at lunchtime. This means that tea can be something quick, easy and 'unchallenging', such as pasta and sauce, or thick soup and mini sandwiches.

● Sometime in the afternoon (maybe just after your baby and/or toddler have gone down for their lunchtime nap) lay out everything that you will need for the bath and bedtime routine. Flannels, towels, creams, nappies, nightwear, etc. should all be put in the places where you will need them later.

● At 4.30pm encourage your toddler to start tidying away at least most of her toys. It can be a good idea to have her seated at the table before 5pm (maybe occupied doing a quiet activity like looking at a picture book, or doing some sticking or drawing) while you get the tea things on the table.

● Tea should be ready at 5pm sharp, so you can sit down and feed the baby while your toddler is eating her tea.

- Both children should be taken upstairs no later than 5.45pm to allow plenty of time for the bath and for winding down. I know some parents like to put on some gentle classical music at this time as they find it helps everyone relax!

- Try to have both children bathed and dressed by 6.15pm to allow enough time for the baby to take the second half of his feed. Wait until you are all settled and ready to watch a quiet DVD and have a cuddle before allowing your toddler to drink her milk, while you feed your baby.

- Even if the baby does not look tired, settle him in his bed. Dim the lights and prop a small cot book or mirror next to him. I have found that, if this habit is established early enough, most babies will learn to settle quickly and easily on their own.

- In the early days, most babies will need to be asleep by 6.30–6.45pm, which should allow you enough time to settle the toddler with her night-time story before she becomes overtired.

Socialising – out and about, sibling rivalry

Q My toddler is two and a half years old and is showing signs of being ready to potty-train. My second baby is due in a month's time, so I would prefer to postpone training him until after the baby arrives. However, friends and family seem to think I am leaving it too late and that I should do it now. What do you think?

A I always say that one of the most important things about potty-training is that not only should your toddler be showing signs that he is ready but you should be too. Potty-training is also best avoided when either a new baby is due within a couple of months or a new baby has arrived within the last nine weeks. By all means start the preparation stage of potty-training, by encouraging your son to sit on the potty at certain times of the day (for example, after his lunch and before his bath), but don't be too disheartened if he doesn't 'perform', and also accept that there may be a certain amount of regression from him after his sibling is born. If this is the case and he gets upset about being asked to sit on the potty, then I would abandon stage one altogether, and put the potty away for a month or so, before trying again. Overall, follow his lead and there will be a much greater chance of potty-training, when you do start in earnest, being successful. See my book *Potty Training in One Week* for more details.

Q **My 21-month-old has always been a very gentle little boy, and I did not anticipate the sudden change of behaviour since the arrival of his sister, who is just over three months old. He loves playing with her, and is generally very kind and loving to her, but occasionally he snatches her toys from her, making her cry, and once or twice he has hit her and pushed her. At the moment I feel that I can't leave him alone with her, even to answer the door, since I am really afraid that he will one day seriously hurt the baby. I have tried putting him on the naughty step each time he is aggressive towards her, but so far this has not improved his behaviour.**

A This is a fairly common problem and it is important that a toddler of this age is never left alone with a baby, not even for one moment. If you need to answer the door or fetch something from another room, you should always take your toddler with you. This type of behaviour is always more likely to happen when a toddler is hungry, tired and bored. When you see the signs looming, keep an extra-close watch on your son and be ready to divert his attention when he's about to pounce. If he does actually hit his sister, make it very clear that hitting is not allowed. Get down to his level so you have eye-to-eye contact, hold his hands so he can't run away and say firmly, 'Mummy doesn't hit the baby, Daddy doesn't hit the baby and you mustn't hit the baby either.'

Instead of rough play, you can encourage your toddler to massage or tickle the baby's feet. I often find that allowing a toddler to do something like creaming the baby's feet (even if it gets a bit messy) is better than constantly saying 'Don't touch the baby'. Then you can say something like, 'Baby loves it when you touch her feet. Why don't you give them a little rub?'

Try to encourage your son to be kinder to the baby by reminding him of all the nice things he has done, instead of all the naughty things. Encouragement and praise always work better than criticism and nagging, and using lots of role play when he is playing with his toys is also a good way of enforcing the message to be kind. For example, try saying something like 'Teddy loves it when you stroke him so gently' or 'Mr Bunny looks so happy when you hold him so gently'.

Remember, at this age there are lots of new things happening in a toddler's life and your son needs lots of extra hugs and kisses, so he feels as important as the baby.

Q I have a very energetic two-year-old who is used to going out most mornings to either toddler group or play dates. I am concerned about how I am going to establish a feeding and sleeping routine for my second baby, while ensuring that my toddler's day is not too disrupted. Will I have to restrict my toddler's outings for the first few months in order to establish a routine for the new baby?

A For the first couple of weeks, it is really beneficial if you can take things as easy as possible, to help you get off to a good start with breast-feeding your new baby. Hopefully, you will have some sort of help in the early days after the birth, either from your husband, family or a good friend. Try to arrange, in advance, for someone who your son knows well, and likes, to take him to at least some of his regular playgroups. Expecting him to play happily around the house all day and every day, when he has been used to getting out and about, is unrealistic. But you are right that, if you wish to get off to a good start with breast-feeding, taking your son to toddler groups every morning a few days after you have given birth is counterproductive and runs the risk of being detrimental to establishing breast-feeding.

It is a challenge, but it is possible, to establish a balance that suits you, your new baby and your son during those first weeks. It will help if you can give it some advance thought, and make some arrangements for those early days when you have no one at home, and the demands of a newborn baby and toddler to meet.

If your son enjoys going to a playgroup, ask a friend to take him for the first couple of weeks after your baby is born. If it is to a playgroup where you can leave your little boy, check with the other mums to see if they'd be prepared to collect you son and bring him home.

Try to plan some of your toddler's favourite play dates prior to your baby arriving. If your son has enjoyed his normal activity in the morning, you can do something low-key with him in the afternoon – a trip to the park, having a couple of friends around to your house, or visiting them, will keep some sort of normality to the day, without exhausting you or being too disruptive to the new baby.

After the first couple of weeks, you can start to build up a new morning routine that meets the needs of both your toddler and the baby. Depending on how long it takes to get to the play date, you can transfer the baby to his car seat or pram at around 9.30/9.45am so that you arrive at the play date at around 10am in time for the baby's feed. I think you will find that the other mums will be understanding and help you keep an eye on your toddler while you give the baby his feed. Some mothers also find it easier to offer a bottle of expressed milk at this time; if you choose to do this, you will need to express at around 9.15am to get enough milk for the feed. Once the baby has had his 10/10.30am feed, he should be happy to sit in his chair and watch all the children playing.

I suggest that, prior to leaving the playgroup, you change your baby's nappy, so that you can pop him straight into his bed as soon as you get home. He may stir from his sleep when you transfer him from the car seat to his bed. If this happens, offer him a quick top-up feed to help settle him back to sleep quickly.

Q How can I adjust my baby's routine so that I can take her swimming once a week with her elder brother? She normally feeds at around 10.30am at the moment. I don't want to feed her just prior to her swimming, but am concerned that she will not enjoy the pool if she is starting to get hungry. The class starts at 10.30am and lasts 30 minutes, and I would need to leave the house around 10.15am to allow enough time to get to the pool and the children into their swimming costumes.

A I advise you to offer your baby a small feed at 9.45am so that she does not start looking for a feed during the lesson. Then, when you get home, offer her a further feed at around 11.30am. As you will be travelling back at around 11.15am, it is possible she may fall asleep or get very sleepy on the journey. Therefore, I would suggest that you leave everything ready so that you can pop her straight into her bed as soon as you arrive home, once she has had the top-up feed.

Q My second child, Jane, is a few months old and my toddler, Luke, is finding it very hard to deal with the fact that his sister is being breast-fed. Every time I try to feed her he yells and yells and tries to push Jane away from me. Then he tries to breast-feed and becomes very cross, throwing himself on the floor and howling, when I say no. He even comes up to me and tries to pull my top up himself to breast-feed. It seems as if he is regressing back to baby-hood. He had no problems weaning and moved on to bottles without any apparent difficulties. I am finding it hard to understand why he is behaving like this and it is difficult to deal with.

A   This is not actually that unusual a scenario, and it can be quite common for toddlers to want to revert to what they did as babies when a new baby is introduced to the household. The impact of a new baby is immense and despite the most thoughtful preparation, it is almost impossible to gauge the reaction of a toddler to the arrival of a sibling. Breast-feeding is clearly one of the most exclusive activities between mother and baby and it can be one of the most fraught areas for the toddler to deal with.

One of the most obvious theories is that your toddler feels jealous of the new baby and sees the closeness the baby has with you and feels excluded. There is a realisation that being very small means having more 'Mummy time' and watching breast-feeding is a very visual reminder that the baby is getting something the toddler is not.

Behavioural psychologist Liz Collins explains: 'Another consideration is the memories the toddler has of his own experiences of breast-feeding. It is difficult, for obvious reasons, to explore very early infant memories and so it is difficult to tell exactly what the memories may be of the experiences. This will also depend on how long the breast-feeding went on for, as it is less likely that there will be clear experiential memories if the baby was breast-fed for only a few weeks, compared to the baby who was breast-fed for most of the first year, for example. However, rather than wondering about the toddler's memories per se, it is likely that there is an association for the toddler between breast-feeding and feeling nurtured, safe and secure as well as the warm, satisfying feeling of being fed. It is these feelings that the toddler may be unconsciously relating to when indicating the need to engage in breast-feeding once more.'

So what to do about it? Having taken some time to mull over the reason for the sudden interest in breast-feeding, the management of the issue will generally be the same, no matter why a toddler has developed this interest.

Attention-seeking is very likely to be a cause, so it is important to give Luke lots of attention for more age-appropriate behaviour. Often actions speak louder than words to toddlers: have a special activity that you can do with Luke that is very specific to him. This can be something very simple like reading a book, doing a puzzle, singing nursery rhymes together; the type of activity does not matter really, but the essence of it should be total, undivided, focused attention that involves being close to him and being tactile. You can plan this in advance and say to Luke that you will be doing the chosen activity at a certain time so that he knows it will happen and be able to anticipate it. You can obviously have a range of activities and get him to choose which one to do, and talk about them as special activities for big boys (i.e. something that makes them specific and important to him).

Liz Collins suggests: 'It might also be that Luke is very interested in the whole process of breast-feeding and, if so, you could encourage him to breast-feed his own teddy. This can look rather amusing to begin with and feel a bit strange to be suggesting it, but it does give the toddler a focus of his own and encourages him to explore what it is he is interested in. It also satisfies his need to be participating in important events, and role play is a highly effective strategy in helping young children make sense of difficult or confusing events.'

If Luke is being very persistent in his attempt to try to breast-feed by pulling at your top, you need to explain gently that he cannot do this. You need to pull your top down firmly and say

'No' in a firm and clear voice. This needs to be done consistently whenever he attempts to do it so that a clear message is given to him that it is not appropriate behaviour. Try to ignore him when he is having a temper tantrum about it but, as soon as he stops, immediately turn your attention back to him and chat to him, cuddle him and engage him in something interesting. Do not be discouraged by his behaviour; it is very likely to pass.

Q My baby is due in a couple of weeks and I am really worried about how my two-year-old is going to react to our new arrival. He is very clingy to me and I'm concerned that he's going to be really upset at having to share my attention. Is there anything I can do to help my toddler adjust to becoming a big brother?

A I often hear of advice given to second-time mums to encourage a positive first meeting between a toddler and his new sibling – for example, buying your toddler a present 'from' the baby, and ensuring you are not holding the baby when he first sees you after the birth, so that you can give him a cuddle, and allow a gradual introduction to the new arrival. I agree all this is good advice, but please do not be disheartened if your toddler has a negative reaction in the moments (or days or weeks) after the baby is born. It is by no means indicative of how their relationship will be long-term. Give your toddler plenty of attention whenever the baby is sleeping or happy on the play mat. Gently try to encourage your toddler to get involved with washing, creaming and helping with the baby – although, if he's not keen, do not push him. Make a big deal about what a 'kind' and 'special' big brother he is and repeatedly remind him how much the new baby loves him. When the baby starts to respond and smile, encourage your toddler to tickle the baby's feet and rattle toys nearby – your son is sure to love the interaction this creates! Lastly, accept that there may well be times when your son is upset, angry and jealous regarding the baby and your relationship with the newest member of the house. This is entirely natural and it is really important that you acknowledge the difficult feelings that your son has. Saying something like 'I know it's really hard for you, sometimes our baby makes you feel angry and upset' is a more helpful response than getting upset with him and trying to dismiss his feelings.

Q My second son, Daniel, is six months old and his two-year-old brother, George, has taken to hitting, scratching and biting him from time to time. He will also try to sit on him when I put him on his play mat. It does not happen all the time and George does seem to love Daniel, lighting up when he sees him, and he loves spending time with him. He can be very good to him, bringing him toys and giving him kisses. However, when he is being 'heavy-handed' he can be quite aggressive and so I can't ever leave him alone with him even for a few minutes. I am not sure of his motivation for this as it seems to happen at random times.

A This is one of those very emotive areas and a situation that is often pondered upon when pregnant with number two: 'What will number one think? Will he be nice to the baby or will he be jealous and reject him?' These are thoughts that often run through parents' minds. On a general note, the arrival of a sibling is a landmark event in a young child's life. Indeed, it is for the whole family as it shifts the dynamic once again and brings about all sorts of changes for everyone involved.

Behavioural psychologist Liz Collins explains: 'The arrival of a new baby can evoke powerful feelings in small children. A sibling can provide the first taste of having to share, competitiveness, jealousy, loss and rivalry but, hand in hand with these, it will also provide the opportunity for invaluable learning experiences such as negotiation, resolving conflict, respecting differences, empathising and learning how to share and to tolerate not sharing. I think it is fair to say that most parents have an ideal vision of their offspring playing happily together, but the reality of this is not always so. Most people with siblings have stories to tell of how a sibling has inflicted some wound or other on them. However, as amusing as it may seem in the years afterwards, actually witnessing it and trying to deal with it is less amusing and causes many anxious moments for parents.'

It is hard to see the loved first child, who has been the centre of attention for so long and who possibly has had to be protected from other older and bigger children (e.g. at playgroup), as the perpetrator. There is an instinctive reaction to protect the small, vulnerable baby from any hurt, but there is also concern about not making a villain out of the older one and potentially exacerbating the negative feelings about the new sibling. However, it is obviously not the sort of behaviour that can be ignored.

Liz Collins continues: 'Just a point of interest, siblings under the age of five average four conflicts per hour, that is one every 15 minutes. Clearly, the nature of the conflicts change with age and in the early stages it is very one-sided, with the older one being in control. These early signs of anger, jealousy and rivalry towards a baby are not indicative of the future relationship in any way. As a young child is unable to verbalise feelings, he will use behaviour to do so instead.'

To begin with, it is very positive to hear that there can be lovely times and that George can be kind to his little brother. He is obviously very interested in him and recognises that he might enjoy being given toys and kisses and so on. However, it sounds as if his feelings can be mixed at times. Toddlers can react negatively to babies for all sorts of reasons, many having been highlighted above. However, it may be that George is curious to see how his brother reacts to being poked, hit, pinched and so on. This demonstrates a toddler's genuine curiosity as he investigates cause and effect. He might think, 'What will this little person do if I pinch him?' The baby may well scream, but it is also likely that there will be a strong response from Mummy (or another adult) and it is this response that may well reinforce the behaviour. The toddler sees it as a good way to get immediate attention and divert attention away from the baby. This is a very useful thing to do if you are young and suddenly find your position in the family being displaced.

This behaviour does need to be dealt with firmly. In the first instance, it is important to note when it is most likely to happen. Is it when your attention is diverted – are you busy doing something in the house or talking to someone? What else is going on at the time? Is there anyone else around? What time of day is it occurring? Is George hungry or tired at the time? Has he been stopped from doing what he wants to do – e.g. playing? These are all questions to think about to see if there is any pattern to the behaviour that will help you to work out how to manage it. It is important to establish firm boundaries for George and make it very clear to him what is appropriate behaviour. Praising and labelling the positive behaviour is as important as telling him not to do the negative behaviour. If he is being very physical, help him to think of different ways to interact with his brother – for example, instead of hitting, stroking him gently. If the behaviour is very aggressive, he needs to be taken away from Daniel until he calms down, but should then be given the opportunity to show you that he can be gentle.

Liz Collins explains: 'Research has shown that to foster positive sibling relationships it is important to keep the sibling feeling involved rather than in competition with the baby. Ask George to help look after Daniel and take care of him, giving him specific jobs to do, such as fetching the nappy, his toy, choosing his clothes. Put him in a position of being important such as asking him to look after Daniel while Mummy makes the dinner or answers the phone and so on. George is in a very new role, that of older sibling, and the importance of that should be emphasised to him. Also, it is important to give him special Mummy time so that there is a feeling of Mummy's attention being equally distributed.'

Although it is obviously important to remain calm, it can be difficult to deal with the feelings of anger that aggression does often evoke. It is important to show you can bear the negative feelings being expressed by George towards his brother. Keeping in your mind how George might be feeling about Daniel will help you do this and, with your help, George will gradually begin to learn that his positive behaviour will be more rewarding than his negative behaviour.

15

Common Problems
in the First Year

My advice in this book is based on the hundreds of babies I have
personally cared for. However, each baby is an individual and it is
natural that problems may occur.

Drawing on the feedback on my website and consultancy serv-
ice, in this chapter I have collected together the most common
problems encountered by parents during the first year and I hope
it will cover the majority of your concerns. Remember to consult
your GP or health visitor with any worries – even if they seem
small and you fear looking like a neurotic mother. It's better that
you are not beset with worries and can enjoy your baby and this
precious first year together.

You can use the list of headings on page viii to find the problems that concern you. I have divided the information up into
general, feeding and sleeping problems but many of them overlap.
Sleeping and feeding are interdependent so you may find it more
helpful to read the entire chapter.

General problems

Burping

It is important to follow your baby's lead regarding when to stop to wind him during feeding. If you constantly interrupt his feed to try and get his wind up, he is likely to get upset and frustrated, and the crying that results will cause more wind than the feed itself. Time and time again I watch babies being thumped endlessly on the back, the mother refusing to continue with the feed as she is convinced the baby has wind. The reality is that very few babies need to be burped more than once during a feed and once at the end.

A breast-feeding baby will pull himself off the breast when he is ready to burp. If he has not done so by the end of the first breast, you can try burping him before putting him on the second breast. Bottle-fed babies will normally drink half to three-quarters of their feed and pull themselves off to be burped. Regardless of whether you are breast-feeding or bottle-feeding, if you adopt the correct holding position, your baby should bring his wind up quickly and easily both during and at the end of the feed. If your baby does not bring up the wind within a few minutes, it is best to leave it and try later. More often than not he will bring it up after he has been laid flat for his nappy change.

Occasionally, a baby passing excessive wind from his rear end can suffer considerable discomfort and become very distressed. A breast-feeding mother should keep a close eye on her diet to see if a particular food or drink is causing the wind. Citrus drinks or fruits taken in excess can sometimes cause severe wind in some babies. The other culprits are chocolate and excessive dairy intake.

Special care should be taken to make sure that the baby is reaching the hind milk (see page 57). Too much fore milk can cause explosive bowel movements and excessive passing of wind.

With a bottle-fed baby, who is already feeding from the special anti-colic bottles, the cause of the excessive wind is usually over-feeding. If your baby is regularly drinking 90–180ml (3–6oz) a day more than the amount advised on the packet, and constantly putting on in excess of 226g (8oz) of weight each week, cut back on a couple of his feeds for a few days to see if there is any improvement. A 'sucky' baby could be offered a dummy after the smaller feeds to satisfy his sucking needs.

Sometimes a teat with a hole either too small or too large for your baby's needs could cause excessive wind. Experiment with the different sizes of teats; sometimes using a smaller hole at a couple of the feeds can help a baby who is drinking some of his feeds too quickly. It may be the case that too small a teat is forcing your baby to suck harder than necessary to get the milk out.

Colic

Colic is a common problem for babies under three months. It can make life miserable for the baby and the parents and, to date, there is no cure for it. There are over-the-counter medications, but most parents with a baby suffering from severe colic say that they are of little help. Although a baby can suffer from colic at any time of the day, the most common time seems to be between 6pm and midnight. Parents resort to endless feeding, rocking, patting, driving the baby round the block, most of which seem to bring little or no relief. Colic usually disappears by four months of age, but by that time the baby has often learned all the wrong sleep associations, so the parents are no further forwards.

Parents who contact me for help with their 'colicky' baby describe how the baby screams, often for hours at a time, thrashes madly and keeps bringing his legs up in pain. The majority of babies all seem to have one thing in common: they are usually being fed on demand. Feeding this way all too often leads to the baby having another feed before the first one has been digested, one of the reasons that I believe may cause colic. (See also the advice on feeding bottles on page 28.)

Not one of the babies I have cared for from birth ever suffered from colic and I am convinced that it is because I structured their feeding and sleeping from day one. When I used to go in to help an older baby who was suffering from colic it would disappear within 24 hours of them being put on to the routine.

Firstly, I would check that the colic was being caused by demand feeding and not the mother's diet. Then, depending on the age, the symptoms of the baby, and how often he was feeding throughout the evening and the middle of the night, I would introduce sugar water. With a baby between one and three months of age, who was feeding excessively in the night, and consistently putting on more than the recommended weight gain each week, I would make up a solution of boiled water – usually 120ml (4oz) boiled water mixed with half a teaspoon of sugar. I would offer small amounts of this solution in the night to try and settle the baby, before offering the first two milk feeds in the night. This usually had the effect of settling the baby back to sleep on less milk, thus reducing the overall amount of milk drank in the night. Once the baby was waking up only once in the night, I would stop giving the sugar water solution and give the baby a big enough milk feed to get through to 7am. When dealing with excessive night-time waking and colic, I found that plain cool boiled water did not have the same effect. When following this plan it is important to wake the baby at 7am, regardless of how little sleep he has had in the night, and then proceed with the routine throughout the day to 6.30pm. At this time I would always offer a breast-fed baby a top-up of expressed milk to ensure that he has had enough to drink. This avoids him needing to feed again in two hours, which is a common pattern for babies suffering from colic. With a bottle-fed baby I would always make sure that the 2.30pm feed is smaller so that he feeds well at 6.30pm.

A low milk supply in the early evening is often the cause of a baby feeding little and often, which is another reason babies can be unsettled in the evening.

More often than not, offering the top-up feed ensures that the baby settles well in the evening but occasionally I would get a baby who had developed the wrong sleep associations as a result of the colic. With these babies I would use the 'assisted sleep routine' method (see page 219). Within a week I usually found that they are going down happily and sleeping well until the 10.30pm feed. Because they have slept well and have gone a full four hours since their last feed, they feed well and will go on to last for an even longer spell in the night.

This method, along with the routines, should very quickly encourage a baby who has suffered from colic and developed the wrong sleep associations to sleep longer in the night. Parents are often concerned that it will encourage their babies to develop a sweet tooth, or even worse rot their teeth. Because of the short period of time the sugar water is used I have never seen any of these problems evolve. I am also pleased to say that my advice has now been backed up by recent research on colic by Dr Peter Lewindon of the Royal Children's Hospital, Brisbane, Australia. Research shows that sugar stimulates the body's natural painkillers and that some babies suffering from colic can be helped by the sugar water solution.

Crying

I have read in many leading baby books that most young babies cry on average a total of two hours in a day. This is also the information given by the Thomas Coram Research Unit at London University. They claim that at six weeks crying reaches a peak, with 25 per cent of babies crying and fussing for at least four hours a day. Dr St James-Roberts claims that 40 per cent of the crying occurs between 6pm and midnight. Dutch researchers Van de Rijt and Plooij, authors of *Why They Cry: Understanding Child Development in the First Year* (Thorsons), have spent over 20 years studying baby development and they claim that babies become troublesome and demanding when they are going through one of the seven major neurological changes that occur during the first year.

I have noticed that very young babies go through a more unsettled stage around three weeks and six weeks, which tends to coincide with growth spurts. However, I would be absolutely horrified if any of my babies cried for even one hour a day, let alone two to four hours! The one thing that parents comment upon time and time again is how happy their baby is on my routines. Of course, my babies did cry; some cried when they had their nappy changed, others cried when having their faces washed and a few fought sleep when put in their cots. With the ones that fought sleep, because I knew that they were well fed, burped and ready to sleep, I would let them fuss and yell for 10–12 minutes until they had settled themselves. This is the only real crying I experienced, and even then it was with the minority of my babies and lasted for no longer than a week or two. Understandably, all parents hate to hear their baby cry; many are worried that to put their baby down in a cot to sleep and leave him to cry like this could be psychologically damaging. I would like to reassure you that, providing your baby has been well fed, and that you have followed the routines regarding awake periods and wind-down time, your baby will not suffer psychological damage. In the long-term you will have a happy, contented baby who has learned to settle himself to sleep. Many parents who have followed the demand method with the first baby, and my routines with their second baby, would confirm wholeheartedly that my methods are by far the best and, in the long-term, the easiest.

Dr Marc Weissbluth, Director of the Sleep Disorders Center at the Children's Memorial Hospital, Chicago, says in his book *Healthy Sleep Habits, Happy Child* (Vermilion) that parents should remember they are allowing their baby to cry, not making him cry. He also says that it will be much harder for an older baby to learn how to settle himself.

Listed below are the main reasons why a healthy baby would cry. Use it as a checklist to eliminate the possible causes for your baby crying. At the top of the list is hunger.

Hunger

When your baby is very tiny and fretful and unsettled it is, of course, wise to assume when he cries that the problem is hunger and offer him a feed, even if it is before the time recommended in the routine for his age. I find that hunger is one of the main reasons why very young breast-fed babies are unsettled in the evening. If you find that your baby feeds well, stays awake for a short spell after feeds, then sleeps well until the next feed, but is unsettled in the evening, it is very possible the cause is hunger. Even if your baby is putting on a good amount of weight each week, you should not rule out hunger. Many mothers I know can produce a lot of milk early on in the day, but, come the evening when tiredness has crept in, the milk supply can decrease dramatically. This is certainly often the case with a second baby, and I would strongly recommend that for a few nights you try topping your baby up with a small amount of expressed milk after bathtime. If he settles well, then you will know that your milk supply is low at that time of the evening, and you will then have to decide on how best to deal with this problem. Please see page 283 for suggestions.

However, if you find that your baby is unsettled in the evening, or indeed any other times of the day, despite being well fed, it is important that you try to eliminate other reasons for him being fretful. All too often I hear people saying that it is normal for babies to cry a lot in the early days as 'that is what babies do'. During my many years of caring for young babies, I did have some who indeed were very fretful in the early days, no matter what I did to try and help calm them. But I have to stress that, out of the hundreds of babies I cared for, there could only have been a handful who did this. If I found that I had a very unsettled baby, I would go through every possibility before accepting that there was nothing I could do to help improve things. Babies do have many needs other than feeding, sleeping and being held.

Tiredness

Babies under six weeks tend to get tired after one hour of being awake. Although they may not be quite ready to sleep, they need to be kept quiet and calm. Not all babies show obvious signs of tiredness, so in the early days, after he has been awake for one hour, try not to allow your toddler or visitors to overstimulate the baby during this wind-down period.

Overtiredness

Babies under three months should not be allowed to stay awake for more than two hours at a time, as they can become very over-tired and difficult to settle. Overtiredness is often a result of overstimulation, which is mentioned above. An overtired baby reaches a stage where he is unable to drift off to sleep naturally and, the more tired he becomes, the more he fights sleep. A baby under three months, who is allowed to get into this state and stays awake for more than two hours, can become almost impossible to settle.

In a situation like this, sometimes a short period of 'crying down' has to be used as a last resort to solve the problem. This is the only situation where I would advise that young babies are left to cry for a short period, and even then it can only be done if you are confident that the baby has been well fed and winded.

Boredom

Even a newborn baby needs to be awake some of the time. Encourage your baby to be awake for a short spell after his day feeds. Babies under one month love to look at anything black and white, especially pictures of faces, and the ones that fascinate them most will be the faces of their Mummy and Daddy. Try to divide the toys into ones that are used for wakeful periods and ones that are used for winding-down time: bright, noisy ones for social time and calm, soothing ones for sleepy times.

Wind

All babies take a certain amount of wind while feeding; bottle-fed babies more so than breast-fed ones. Given the opportunity, most babies bring up their wind easily. If you suspect that your baby's crying is caused by wind, check that you are allowing enough time between feeds. I have found over-feeding and demand feeding to be the main causes of colic in young babies. A breast-fed baby needs at least three hours to digest a full feed, and a formula-fed baby should be allowed three and a half to four hours. This time is always from the beginning of one feed to the beginning of the next feed.

I also suggest that you keep a close eye on your baby's weight gain. If his weight gain is in excess of 226–283g (8–10oz) a week, and he appears to be suffering from wind pains, it could be that he is over-feeding, particularly if he weighs over 3.6kg (8lb) and is feeding two or three times in the night. For details of how to deal with this problem, refer to page 68.

Dummies

I have always believed that, if used with discretion, a dummy can be a great asset, especially for a sucky baby. However, I have always stressed the importance of never allowing the baby to have the dummy in his cot or allowing him to suck himself to sleep on the dummy. My advice was that it is fine to use it to calm a baby and, if necessary, settle him at sleep times, but it must be removed before he falls asleep. In my experience, allowing a baby to fall asleep with a dummy in his mouth is one of the worst sleep association problems to try and solve. He can end up waking several times a night, and each time he will expect the dummy to get back to sleep. That is why I always advised that the dummy is removed just before he drops off to sleep.

Since 2007, The Foundation for the Study of Infant Deaths (FSID) has recommended the following advice on how the use of a dummy at all sleep times may help reduce the risk of cot death:

'Using a dummy every time you settle your baby to sleep – day and night – can reduce the risk of cot death. If breast-feeding do not begin to give a dummy until your baby is one month old to ensure breast-feeding is well established. Don't worry if the dummy falls out while your baby is asleep, and don't force him to take a dummy if he doesn't want it. Never coat the dummy in anything sweet. Gradually wean him off a dummy after six months and before one year.'

In response to the advice from the FSID, the UNICEF UK Friendly Initiative issued the following statement:

'While welcoming any research which may help to reduce the risk of sudden infant death syndrome (SIDS), there are considerations which must be taken into account before using this latest data to make recommendations to parents.

'Firstly, we must look at other research into dummies and SIDS. This tends to show that babies who used a dummy during their last sleep were less likely to die, but that routine dummy use is not protective. This may indicate that infants are at greater risk of SIDS if they routinely use a dummy but have not been given their dummy on a particular night.

'Secondly, the potential risks of dummy use need to be considered. These include:

- Interference with good establishment of breast-feeding in the early weeks

- Increased risk of otitis media infection

- Increased dental malocclusion

- Risk of accidents such as obstruction of the airway

'Thirdly, we need to ensure that the advice being proposed is realistic. If dummy use is really protective against SIDS but only if used every night, parents must be informed of this. The possibility that missing a night will increase risk among routine dummy users creates confusion and concern. We must be secure that parents will never forget to give the dummy once they have started to use it.

'It is therefore clear that we must support parents to make informed decisions about using a dummy, based on their own personal circumstances. This should include a discussion of the benefits and risks of dummy use, and acknowledgement that we do not know everything about the issue.'

If you have any concerns about the use of a dummy to reduce the risk of cot death, I would urge you to contact the FSID directly so you can discuss the matter with them personally. When using the dummy at all sleep times during the first six months, it is possible that your baby will get into the habit of waking up several times a night looking for the dummy to be replaced. If this happens you will have to accept that when you start to eliminate the use of the dummy from six months, some form of sleep training will probably be needed to break the habit of your baby waking for the dummy. How best to eliminate the dummy after six months should be discussed with your health visitor.

There are two types of dummy available: one has a round cherry-type teat, the other has a flat-shaped teat, which is called an orthodontic teat. Some experts claim that the orthodontic teat shape is better for the baby's mouth, but the problem with this type is that most young babies cannot hold them in for very long. I tend to use the cherry-type teat, and so far none of my babies appear to have developed an open bite, which is often the result of a dummy being used excessively once the teeth have come through. Whichever type of dummy you choose, buy several, thus allowing them to be changed frequently. The utmost attention should be paid to cleanliness when using a dummy; it should be washed and sterilised after each use. Never clean it by licking it, as so many parents do; there are more germs and bacteria in the mouth than you would believe.

Hiccups

Hiccups are very normal among tiny babies, and very few get distressed by them. Hiccups often happen after a feed. If it has been a night-time feed and your baby is due to go down for a sleep, it is advisable to go ahead and put him down regardless. If you wait until the hiccups are finished, there is a bigger chance of him falling asleep in your arms, which is something to be avoided at all costs. If your baby is one of the rare ones who gets upset by their hiccups, then try giving him the recommended dose of gripe water, which can sometimes help.

Possetting

It is very common for some babies to bring up a small amount of milk while being burped or after a feed. It is called possetting, and for most babies it does not create a problem. However, if your baby is regularly gaining more than 226g (8oz) of weight each week, it could be that he is drinking too much. With a bottle-fed baby the problem is easily solved, as you are able to see how much the baby is drinking and therefore slightly reduce the amount at the feeds during which he appears to possett more. It is more difficult to tell how much a breast-fed baby is drinking. But by keeping a note of which feeds cause more possetting, and reducing the time on the breast at those feeds, the possetting may be reduced.

If your baby is possetting excessively and not gaining weight, it could be that he is suffering from a condition called 'reflux'. If your baby does have reflux, your doctor can prescribe a medication to be given either before or with a feed, which helps to keep the milk down. With babies who are inclined to bring up milk, it is important to keep them as upright as possible after a feed, and special care should be taken when burping.

Any baby bringing up an entire feed twice in a row should be seen by a doctor immediately.

Reflux

Sometimes a baby displaying all the symptoms of colic actually has a condition called gastro-oesophageal reflux. Because the muscle at the lower end of the oesophagus is too weak to keep the milk in the baby's stomach, it comes back up, along with acid from the stomach, causing a very painful burning sensation in the oesophagus. Excessive possetting is one of the symptoms of reflux. However, not all babies with reflux actually sick up the milk, and suffer from what the medical profession call 'silent reflux'. These babies can often be misdiagnosed as having colic. They are often very difficult to feed, constantly arching their backs and scream-ing during a feed. They also tend to get very irritable when laid flat and no amount of cuddling or rocking will calm them when they are like this. If your baby displays these symptoms, insist that your GP refers you to a paediatrician without delay. I have seen too many cases of babies being diagnosed as having colic, when in fact they were suffering from reflux, despite not being sick. If you think that your baby is suffering from reflux, it is essential that you do not allow anyone to dismiss the pains as colic. Reflux is very stressful for the baby and parents, and it is essential that you get ongoing advice and support from your GP and health visitor. If you feel that you are not getting the help you need, do not be frightened to ask for a second opinion. If reflux is not the prob-lem, you will have at least eliminated it as a possible cause. If it is the problem, with the help of the right medication, your baby will have been saved months of misery from the pain it can cause. It is important that a baby with reflux is not over-fed and is kept as upright as possible during and after feeding. Some babies may need medication for several months until the muscles tighten up. Fortunately, the majority of babies outgrow the condition by the time they are a year old.

Common feeding problems

Difficult feeder

The majority of newborn babies take to the breast or bottle quickly and easily. However, I sometimes find that some babies who have undergone a particularly difficult birth can be more difficult to feed.

If you find that your baby becomes tense and fretful when he is due to be fed, try to keep things as quiet as possible during feeds. With a boisterous toddler around this can sometimes be difficult, and you may find that you have to use a DVD more often than you would like in the early days, to occupy her while feeding the baby. Try not to get too stressed if this happens; remember, things will get better with your baby's feeding, and the DVD watching can then be reduced. The following guidelines, regardless of whether you are breast- or bottle-feeding, should help make feeding a tense baby easier.

- It is essential that the handling of tense babies is kept to the minimum. Avoid overstimulation and handing the baby from person to person, especially before a feed.

- The feed should be given in a quiet room with a calm atmosphere. Check page 17 for details of how to keep your toddler occupied while feeding the baby.

- Prepare everything needed for the feed well in advance. Try to make sure that you have rested and have eaten.

- If using a DVD to occupy your toddler during a feed, try to keep the volume as low as possible, unplug or turn off the telephone and keep visitors to a minimum.

- When the baby wakes for his feed, do not change his nappy as this may trigger crying. It is very important to prevent the baby becoming tense before a feed.

- Try swaddling him firmly in a soft cotton sheet to prevent him thrashing his arms and legs around. Make sure that you are comfortable before you start feeding.

● Do not attempt to latch the baby on to the breast or put the bottle straight in his mouth if he is crying. Hold him firmly in the feeding position and calm him down with continuous gentle patting on the back.

● Try holding a dummy in his mouth. Once he has calmed down and has sucked steadily for a few minutes, very quickly ease the dummy out and offer him the breast or the bottle.

If your baby has been feeding well and suddenly starts to refuse the breast or bottle, it could be because he is feeling unwell. Infections can easily go undetected and are a very common cause of a baby not wanting to feed. If your baby shows any of the following signs, it would be advisable to consult your doctor:

● Sudden loss of appetite, and becoming upset when offered a feed

● Disruption to the normal sleep pattern

● Suddenly becoming clingy and whingey

● Becoming lethargic and unsociable

Excessive night feeding

I have found that all babies, even demand-fed babies, are capable of sleeping one longer spell between feeds by the time they reach 4–6 weeks of age. Beatrice Hollyer and Lucy Smith, authors of an excellent book called *Sleep: The Secret of Problem-free Nights* (Cassell), describe this longer stretch of sleep as the 'core night'. They advise parents to take their cue from the core night, which they believe is the foundation of encouraging a baby to sleep right through the night.

I believe that, by the end of the second week, a baby who weighed 3.2kg (7lb) or more at birth should really only need one feed in the night (between midnight and 6am). This is provided, of course, that he is feeding well at all of his daytime feeds and gets a full feed between 10pm and 11pm. In my experience, regardless of whether he is breast- or bottle-fed, a baby who continues to feed two or three times in the night will eventually begin to cut back on his daytime feeds. A vicious circle soon emerges, where the baby cuts back so much on his daytime feeds that he ends up genuinely needing to feed in the night so that his daily nutritional needs can be met.

With bottle-fed babies, it is easier to avoid a pattern of excessive night-time feeding evolving by monitoring the amounts they are getting during the day.

Excessive night-time feeding is considered normal for breast-fed babies and is actually encouraged by many breast-feeding experts. Much emphasis is placed on the fact that the hormone prolactin, which is necessary for making breast milk, is produced more at night. The theory is that mothers who feed their babies more in the night than in the day, are much more likely to sustain a good milk supply. This advice obviously works for some mothers, but breast-feeding statistics prove that it clearly doesn't for many others, as so many give up in the first month. I believe that the exhaustion caused by so many night-time feeds is one of the main reasons why so many mothers give up breast-feeding.

In my experience, from working with hundreds of breast-feeding mothers, I have found that a good stretch of sleep in the night results in the breasts producing more milk. A full and satisfying feed in the middle of the night will ensure that the baby settles back to sleep quickly until the morning.

The following guidelines give the main causes of excessive night-time feeding and how it can be avoided:

- A premature baby or a very tiny baby would need to feed more often than three-hourly, and medical advice should be sought on how best to deal with these special circumstances.

- If he feeds well at every feed (a baby over 3.6kg (8lb) should always be offered the second breast) and is sleeping well at all the other sleep times, he may not be getting enough from the 10–11pm feed.

- If a low milk supply at the last feed is the problem, it is worth offering a top-up of expressed milk using the milk you expressed earlier in the day, or replacing the feed with a full feed of expressed milk. If you decide to offer expressed milk, you will need to allow enough time to express for the feed, which can be added to milk from the morning expressing.

- Many women are concerned that introducing a bottle too early may reduce the baby's desire to take the breast. All of my babies are offered one bottle a day as a matter of course and I have never had one baby who had nipple confusion or refused the breast. It also has the added advantage that the father can give the last feed and enable the mother to get to bed slightly earlier.

- If after one week of giving a full feed at this time there is no improvement, and your baby still is waking several times a night or more, it is more likely that your baby has a problem with his sleeping than with his feeding. I suggest that you continue to offer the bottle for a further week and refer to page 302 for more advice on night waking.

- Babies under 3.6kg (8lb) in weight who are changed to the second breast before reaching the fatty, rich hind milk in the first breast will be more likely to wake more than once in the night.

- If a baby weighs over 3.6kg (8lb) at birth and is only feeding from one breast at a feed, then he may not be getting enough milk, and should be offered the second breast at some or all of his feeds. If he has fed for 20–25 minutes on the first breast, then try to get him to take 5–10 minutes from the second. If he refuses, try waiting 15–20 minutes before offering it again.

The majority of the babies on my routines who are only feeding once in the night gradually push themselves right through the night, dropping the middle-of-the-night feed as soon as they are physically capable. However, occasionally I get a baby who reaches six weeks and continues to wake at 2am looking for a feed. In my experience, allowing these babies to continue to feed at this time usually results in them reducing the amount they take at 7am, often cutting this feed out altogether. When this happens, I would use the core night method to ensure that, when the baby is ready to reduce the number of feeds he is having over a 24-hour period, it is always the middle-of-the-night feed that he drops first.

The core night

The 'core night' method has been used for many years by maternity nurses and parents who believe in routine. It works on the principle that, once a baby sleeps for one longer spell in the night, he should never again be fed during the hours slept in the course of the core night. If he wakes during those hours, he should be left for a few minutes to settle himself back to sleep. If he refuses to settle, then other methods apart from feeding should be used to settle him. Hollyer and Smith recommend patting, offering a dummy or giving a sip of water. Attention should be kept to the minimum, while reassuring the baby that you are there. They claim that following this approach will, within days, have your baby sleeping at least the same number of hours as his first core night. It also teaches the baby the most important two sleep skills: how to go to sleep, and how to go back to sleep after surfacing from a non-REM (rapid eye movement) sleep.

Dr Brian Symon, author of *Silent Nights* (OUP Australia and New Zealand) and a senior lecturer in general practice at the University of Adelaide, recommends a similar approach for babies over six weeks. Babies who are putting on a good amount of weight each week, but who are still waking at 3am, should be offered the dummy or some cool boiled water. If the baby refuses to settle, then give the shortest feed possible that will allow him to settle.

Neither of these methods of dealing with night feeding is new in babycare. Babycare expert Christine Bruell, who has advised over 35,000 mothers during her 40-year career, also advises offering cool boiled water to a thriving baby over four weeks of age if he keeps regularly waking at 2am.

Before embarking on these methods, the following points should be read carefully to make sure that your baby really is capable of going for a longer spell in the night:

- These methods should never be used with a very small baby or a baby who is not gaining weight. A baby who is not gaining weight should always be seen by a doctor.

- The above methods should only be used if your baby is regularly gaining weight each week, and if you are sure that his last feed is substantial enough to help him sleep for the longer stretch in the night.

● The main sign that a baby is ready to cut down on a night feed is a regular weight gain and the reluctance to feed, or feed less at 7am in the morning.

● The aim of using any of the above methods is gradually to increase the length of time your baby can go from his last feed and not to eliminate the night feed in one go.

● The core night method can be used if, over three or four nights, a baby has shown signs that he is capable of sleeping for a longer stretch.

● It can be used to try to reduce the number of times a demand-fed baby is fed in the night and to encourage a longer stretch between feeds, or after his last daytime feed.

Sleepy feeder

Sometimes a very sleepy baby may be inclined to keep dozing during the feed, but if he does not want to take the required amount he will end up wanting to feed again in an hour or two. This is a good time to change his nappy and burp him and encourage him to finish his feed. Making a little effort in the early days to keep your baby awake enough to drink the correct amount at each feed, and at the times given on the routine, will in the long-term be well worthwhile. Some babies will take half the feed, have a stretch and kick for 10–15 minutes and then be happy to take the rest. The important thing that I have found with sleepy babies is not to force them to stay awake by talking too much or jiggling them about. By putting your baby under the play gym or cot mobile and leaving him for 10 minutes, you will probably find that he will get enough of a second wind for him to take more of a feed.

During the first months, allow 45 minutes to one hour for a feed. Obviously, if he does not feed well at a particular feed, and wakes early from his sleep, he must be fed. Do not try to stretch him to the next feed, otherwise he will be so tired that the next feed will also become another sleepy feed. Top him up and treat the feed like a night feed, and try to settle him back to sleep so that you can get his feeding back on track for the evening.

Low milk supply

As they grow, all babies will increase the amount they drink. However, the feeds must be structured to co-ordinate with the baby's growth, thereby encouraging him to take more milk at individual feeds. If this doesn't happen, he will be very likely to continue to feed little and often.

All too often, I get calls from the parents of older babies who are still following the demand rules of milk feeding. While the majority of these babies are over 12 weeks and are physically capable of drinking more at individual feeds, they continue to feed as they did as newborns – often between 8–10 times a day.

Many breast-fed babies are still having only one breast at each feed, while bottle-fed babies may only be taking 90–120ml (3–4oz) of formula. In order to go for longer spells between feeds, these babies should be taking from both breasts at each feed, or have a formula-feed of 210–240ml (7–8oz). It is my firm belief that it is during those early days of milk feeding that the foundation is laid for healthy eating habits in the future. To avoid long-term feeding problems that can affect your baby's sleep, it is advisable to structure and solve any milk-feeding problems early on.

Not producing enough milk, especially later in the day, is a very common problem for breast-feeding mothers and one of the major reasons breast-feeding goes wrong. I believe that hunger is one of the main reasons why so many babies are fretful and difficult to settle in the evening. If the problem of a low milk supply is not resolved in the early days, then a pattern soon emerges of the baby needing to feed on and off all evening to try to satisfy his needs. Mothers are advised that this constant feeding is normal and the best way to increase the milk supply but, in my experience, it usually has the opposite effect. Because the amount of milk the breasts produce is dictated by the amount of milk the baby drinks, these frequent feeds signal the breasts to produce milk little and often. These small feeds will rarely satisfy the baby, leaving him hungry and irritable.

I believe that the stress involved in frequently feeding a very hungry, irritable and often overtired baby can cause many mothers to become so exhausted that their milk supply is reduced even further. Exhaustion and a low milk supply go hand in hand, and are the main reasons why so many mothers give up breast-feeding. I am convinced that by expressing a small amount of milk during the early weeks of breast-feeding, when the breasts are producing more milk than the baby needs, the mother can help to avoid the problem of a low milk supply.

If your baby is under one month old and not settling in the evening, it is possibly due to a low milk supply. Expressing at the times suggested in the routine below should help solve this problem. The short amount of time you will spend expressing will ensure that, during any future growth spurts, you will be producing enough milk to meet any increase in your baby's appetite immediately. If your baby is over a month old and not settling in the evening or after daytime feeds, the following six-day plan will quickly help to increase your milk supply. The temporary introduction of top-up feeds will ensure that your baby is not subjected to hours of irritability and anxiety caused by hunger, which is what usually happens when mothers resort to demand feeding to increase their milk supply.

Plan for increased milk supply

Days one to three
6.45am

- Express 30ml (1oz) from each breast.

- Baby should be awake, and feeding no later than 7am, regardless of how often he fed in the night.

- He should be offered 20–25 minutes on the fullest breast, then 10–15 minutes on the second breast.

- Do not feed baby after 7.45am. He can stay awake for up to two hours.

8am

- It is very important that you have a breakfast of cereal, toast and a drink no later than 8am.

9am

- If your baby has not been settling well for his nap, offer him 5–10 minutes on the breast from which he last fed.

● Try to have a short rest when the baby is sleeping.

10am

● Baby must be fully awake now, regardless of how long he slept.

● He should be given 20–25 minutes from the breast he last fed on, while you drink a glass of water and have a small snack.

● Express 60ml (2oz) from the second breast, then offer him 10–20 minutes on the same breast.

11.45am

● He should be given the 60ml (2oz) that you expressed to ensure that he does not wake up hungry during his midday nap.

● It is very important that you have a good lunch and a rest before the next feed.

2pm

● Baby should be awake and feeding no later than 2pm, regardless of how long he has slept.

● Give him 20–25 minutes from the breast he last fed on, while you drink a glass of water. Express 60ml (2oz) from the second breast, then offer 10–20 minutes on the same breast.

4pm

● Baby will need a short nap according to the routine appropriate for his age.

5pm

● Baby should be fully awake and feeding no later than 5pm.

- Give 15–20 minutes from both breasts.

6.15pm

- Baby should be offered a top-up feed of expressed milk from the bottle. A baby under 3.6kg (8lb) in weight will probably settle with 60–90ml (2–3oz); bigger babies may need 120–150ml (4–5oz).

- Once your baby is settled, it is important that you have a good meal and a rest.

8pm

- Express from both breasts.

10pm

- It is important that you express from both breasts at this time, as the amount you get will be a good indicator of how much milk you are producing.

- Arrange for your husband or another family member to give the late feed to the baby so you can have an early night.

10.30pm

- Baby should be awake and feeding no later than 10.30pm. He can be given a full feed of either formula or expressed milk from a bottle.

In the night

A baby who has had a full feed from the bottle at 10.30pm should manage to sleep through until 2–2.30am. He should then be offered 20–25 minutes from the first breast, then 10–15 minutes from the second. In order to avoid a second waking in the night at 5am, it is very important that he feeds from both breasts.

If your baby fed well at 10.30pm and wakes earlier than 2am, it may not be due to hunger. The following checklist gives other reasons why he might wake earlier:

- Kicking off the covers may be the cause of your baby waking earlier than 2am. A baby under six weeks who wakes up thrashing around may still need to be fully swaddled. A baby over six weeks may benefit from being half-swaddled (under the arms) in a thin cotton sheet. With all babies, it is important to ensure that the top sheet is tucked in well, down the sides and at the bottom of the cot.

- The baby should be fully awake at the 10pm feed. With a baby who is waking up before 2am, it may be worthwhile keeping him awake longer, and offering him some more milk just before you settle him at around 11.30pm.

Day four

By day four, your breasts should be feeling fuller in the morning and the following alterations should be made to the above plan:

- If your baby is sleeping well between 9am and 9.45am, reduce the time on the breast at 9am to five minutes.

- The top-up at 11.45am can be reduced by 30ml (1oz) if he is sleeping well at lunchtime, or shows signs of not feeding so well at the 2pm feed.

- The expressing at the 2pm feed should be dropped, which should mean that your breasts are fuller by the 5pm feed.

● If you feel your breasts are fuller at 5pm, make sure he totally empties the first breast before putting him on to the second breast. If he has not emptied the second breast before bathtime, he should be offered it again after the bath, and before he is given a top-up.

● The 8pm expressing should be dropped and the 10pm expressing brought forward to 9.30pm. It is important that both breasts are completely emptied at the 9.30pm expressing.

Day five

● Dropping the 2pm and 8pm expressing on the fourth day should result in your breasts being very engorged on the morning of the fifth day; it is very important that the extra milk is totally emptied at the first feed in the morning.

● At the 7am feed, the baby should be offered 20–25 minutes on the fullest breast, then 10–15 minutes on the second breast, after you have expressed. The amount you express will depend on the weight of your baby, as it is important that you take just the right amount so that enough is left for your baby to get a full feed. If you managed to express a minimum of 120ml (4oz) at the 10pm feed, you should manage to express the following amounts:

○ Baby weighing 3.6–4.5kg (8–10lb) – express 120ml (4oz)
○ Baby weighing 4.5–5.4kg (10–12lb) – express 90ml (3oz)
○ Baby weighing over 5.4kg (12lb) – express 60ml (2oz)

Day six

By the sixth day, your milk supply should have increased enough for you to drop all top-up feeds, and follow the breast-feeding routine laid out in my first book that is appropriate for your baby's age. It is very important that you also follow the guidelines for expressing as set out in the routines. This will ensure that you will be able to satisfy your baby's increased appetite during his next growth spurt. I would also suggest that you continue with one bottle of either expressed or formula milk at the 10pm feed until your baby is weaned on to solids at six months (see page 177). This will allow the feed to be given by your husband or partner, enabling you to get to bed earlier which, in turn, will make it easier for you to cope with the middle-of-the-night feed.

Refusal of milk

The amount of milk a six-month-old baby drinks will gradually begin to reduce as his intake of solid food increases. However, up to the age of nine months, a baby still needs a minimum of 500–600ml (18–20oz) a day of breast or formula milk. This daily amount gradually reduces to a minimum of 350ml (12oz) at one year of age. If your baby is losing interest or refusing some of his milk feeds, and taking less than the recommended amounts, careful attention should be given to the timing of solids and the type of food given.

The following guidelines will help you determine the cause of your baby refusing his milk feeds:

● Up to the age of six months, a baby should still be taking a full milk feed morning and evening. A full milk feed consists of 210–240ml (7–8oz) or a feed from both breasts. Babies under six months who are weaned early on the advice of a health visitor or doctor should not be given solids in the middle of their milk feed. They will be more likely to refuse the remainder of their formula or the second breast. Give the full milk feed first, then the solids.

● A baby under six months of age still needs a full milk feed at 11am, even if he is being weaned early on medical advice. Introducing breakfast too soon or offering too much solid food first thing in the morning can cause a baby to cut down too quickly or to refuse the 11am feed.

● The 11am milk feed should be reduced gradually between the ages of six and seven months.

● Giving lunchtime solids at 2pm and evening solids at 5pm is the reason many babies under seven months cut down too quickly or refuse their 6pm milk feed. Until he is used to solids, it is better to give a baby his lunchtime solids at 11am and his evening solids after he has had a full milk feed at 6pm.

● Giving hard-to-digest foods, such as banana or avocado, at the wrong time of the day can cause a baby to cut back on the next milk feed. Until a baby reaches seven months, it is better to serve these types of food after the 6pm feed, rather than during the day.

● Babies over six months of age who begin to refuse milk are often being allowed too many snacks in between meals or too much juice. Try replacing juice with water and cutting out snacks in between meals.

● Between nine and 12 months, some babies begin refusing the bedtime milk feed, which is a sign that they are ready to drop their third milk feed. If this happens, it is important to reduce the amount given at the 2.30pm feed, before eventually dropping it altogether.

Refusal of solids

With babies six months or older, the refusal of solids often occurs because they drink too much milk, especially if they are still feeding in the middle of the night. Every day I speak to parents of babies and toddlers who will barely touch solids, let alone eat three meals a day. In the majority of these cases, the babies are still being milk-fed on demand, some feeding as often as two or three times in the night. While milk is still the only important food for babies up to six months, failing to structure the time of milk feeds and the amounts given can seriously affect the introduction of solids. If your baby is refusing solids, the following guidelines will help you determine the cause:

● The recommended age to introduce solids is at six months. If your baby is under six months, gaining weight well and sleeping through the night from his 10pm feed, he simply may not be ready to be weaned yet.

● A baby is ready to be weaned when he shows signs that his appetite is no longer satisfied with 5–6 full milk feeds a day. A full milk feed is either a formula-feed of 240ml (8oz) or a feed from both breasts.

● If your baby reaches six months and is having more than five full milk feeds a day, his refusal of solids is certainly caused by drinking too much milk. It is important to cut right back on his 11am milk feed to encourage him to eat more solids at that time. By the end of six months, a baby's milk intake should be around 600ml (20oz) a day, divided between three to four drinks a day and small amounts used in food. If your baby is still refusing solids at this age, despite cutting down on his milk intake, it is important that you discuss the problem as soon as possible with your doctor or health visitor.

Fussy feeder

If milk feeding is structured properly during the early days of weaning, the majority of babies will happily eat most of the solid foods they are offered. By the time they reach nine months, babies are expected to be getting most of their nourishment from eating three solid meals a day. Parents are advised to offer their babies a wide variety of foods to ensure they receive all the nutrients they need. However, it is often around this time that many babies start to reject food they have previously enjoyed.

If your baby is between nine and 12 months of age and suddenly starts to reject his food, or becomes fussy and fretful at mealtimes, the following guidelines should help to determine the cause:

- Parents often have unrealistic expectations of the amounts of food their baby should have, and serving too-large portions can mislead them into thinking that their baby has a feeding problem. The following list showing the amounts of food a baby aged between nine and 12 months of age needs in a day will help you decide if your baby is eating enough solids:

  - 3–4 servings of carbohydrate, made up of cereal, wholemeal bread, pasta or potatoes. A serving is one slice of bread, 30g (1oz) of cereal, two tablespoonfuls of pasta or a small baked potato.
  - 3–4 portions of fruit and vegetables, including raw vegetables. A portion is one small apple, pear or banana, a carrot, a

    couple of cauliflower or broccoli florets, or two tablespoons of chopped green beans.

○   One portion of animal protein or two of vegetable protein. A portion is 60g (2oz) of poultry, meat or fish or 120g (4oz) of lentils and pulses.

● Self-feeding plays an important role in a baby's mental and physical development as it encourages hand–eye co-ordination and increases his sense of independence. Between six and nine months of age, most babies will start to pick up their food and try to feed themselves. The whole business of feeding can become very messy and mealtimes take much longer. Restricting a baby's natural desire to explore his food and feed himself will only lead to frustration and, very often, a refusal to be spoon-fed. Introducing lots of finger foods and allowing him to eat part of his meal by himself, regardless of the mess he makes, will make him much more inclined to take the remainder from you off a spoon.

● By the time a baby reaches nine months of age, he will become more interested in the colour, shape and texture of his food. A baby who is still having all the different foods mashed up together will quickly begin to get bored with even his favourite foods and this is one of the main reasons why babies lose interest in vegetables.

● Offering your baby a selection of vegetables of various textures and colours at each meal in small amounts will be more appealing to him than a large amount of just one or two vegetables.

● Sweet puddings and ice-cream desserts served on a regular basis are major causes of babies and toddlers refusing their main course. Even babies as young as nine months can quickly learn that, if they refuse the savoury foods and fuss enough, they will more than likely be given the pudding. It is better to restrict puddings and desserts to special occasions, and serve your baby fresh fruit, yoghurt or cheese as a second course.

● If your baby rejects a particular food, it is important that he should be offered it again a couple of weeks later. Babies' likes and dislikes regarding food fluctuate a good deal in the first year and parents who fail to keep reintroducing food that is rejected usually find that their baby ends up eating a very restricted diet.

● Giving large amounts of juice or water prior to a meal can result in a baby not eating very well. Try to offer him drinks midway between meals, not an hour before. Also, at mealtimes encourage him to eat at least half of the solids before offering him a drink of water or well-diluted juice.

● The timing of meals also plays a big part in how well a baby eats. A baby who is having his breakfast solids later than 8am is unlikely to be very hungry for his lunch much before 1pm. Likewise, a baby who is having teatime solids later than 5pm may be getting too tired to eat well.

● Giving too many snacks in between meals, especially hard-to-digest foods like bananas or cheese, can often take the edge off a baby's appetite. Try restricting snacks for a couple of days to see if his appetite improves at mealtimes.

If you are concerned that your baby is not taking enough solids, it is advisable to seek advice from your health visitor or GP. Keeping a diary for a week, listing the times and amounts of all food and drinks consumed, will help to determine the cause of your baby's feeding problems.

Common sleeping problems

Difficulties in settling

If your baby is difficult to settle at nap times, it is essential that you pay particular attention to the time you begin settling him and how long you spend trying to do this. With the majority of babies, the main reason they are hard to settle is overtiredness or overstimulation. However, it is important that hunger is eliminated as a possible cause of your baby not settling. I would suggest that for several days you offer your baby a top-up feed before each nap. If your baby settles to sleep well, then hunger is obviously the reason why he has not been settling to sleep. I would suggest that you continue to top-up, but also look to increase the amount he takes at feeds so that top-ups can eventually be phased out. When offering a top-up it is important it is done just prior to the nap, but it is equally important that your baby does not fall asleep while drinking the top-up feed. If breast-feeding, offer the breast you last fed on at the top-up feed. If your baby continues to fight sleep despite being topped-up, I would strongly advise you to help your baby learn how to settle himself to sleep. Although it will be very difficult to listen to him cry, he will very quickly learn how to go to sleep by himself. Refer to page 212 for details on crying down, a method that allows you to reassure your baby without assisting him to sleep. From my experience in helping hundreds of parents with babies who have had serious sleeping problems, once a baby learns how to settle himself, he becomes happier and more relaxed. Once proper daytime sleep is established, night-time sleep will also improve.

The following guidelines should help your baby learn how to settle himself:

● A baby who is allowed to fall asleep on the breast or bottle and is then put in the cot will be more likely to have disruptive nap times. When he comes into a light sleep 30–45 minutes after falling asleep, he will be less likely to settle himself back to sleep without your help. If your baby falls asleep while feeding, put him on the changing mat and rearrange his nappy. This should rouse him enough to go down in the cot semi-awake.

● Overtiredness is a major cause of babies not settling and not sleeping well during the day. A baby under three months who is allowed to stay awake longer than two hours at a time may get so overtired that he goes on to fight sleep for a further two hours. After three months, the majority of babies, as they get older, will manage to stay awake slightly longer, sometimes up to $2\frac{1}{2}$ hours at a time. A close eye should be kept on all babies after they have been awake for $1\frac{3}{4}$ hours so that you do not miss the cue for sleep.

● Over-handling prior to sleep time is another major problem with young babies. Everyone wants just one little cuddle. Unfortunately, several little cuddles add up and can leave the baby fretful, over-tired and difficult to settle. Your baby is not a toy. Do not feel guilty about restricting the handling in the early weeks, especially prior to sleep time. Allow a wind-down time of at least 20 minutes before nap time.

● Overstimulation prior to sleep time is another major cause of babies not settling well. Babies under six months should be allowed a quiet time of 20 minutes before being put down to sleep. With babies over six months, avoid games and activities that cause them to get overexcited. With all babies, regardless of age, avoid excessive talking at put-down time. Talk quietly and calmly using the same simple phrases: 'Night night, teddy. Night night, dolly'.

The wrong sleep association can also cause long-term sleep problems. It is essential that a baby goes down in his cot awake and learns to settle himself. For a baby who has already learned the wrong sleep associations, this problem can rarely be solved without some crying. Fortunately, the majority of babies, if they are allowed, will learn to settle themselves within a few days. Refer to chapter 14 for advice on crying down and sleep training.

Early-morning waking

All babies and young children come into a light sleep between 5am and 6am. Some will settle back to sleep for a further hour or so but many do not. I believe there are two things that determine whether a baby will become an earlier riser. One is the darkness of the room where the baby is sleeping. It would be an understatement to say I am obsessed with how dark this should be, but I am totally convinced that it is the reason the majority of my babies quickly resettled themselves to sleep when they come into a light sleep at 5–6am. Once the door is shut and the curtains drawn, it should be so dark that not even the faintest trace of toys or books can be seen. As the baby will be sleeping in your room for the first six months, it would be worth investing in black-out linings for the curtains and, if need be, black-out blinds to ensure that the room is really dark. Even a glimpse of toys or books will be enough to fully waken a baby from a drowsy state, wanting to start the day.

How parents deal with early wakings during the first three months will also determine whether their baby will become a child who is an early riser. During the first few weeks, a baby who is waking and feeding between 2am and 2.30am may wake around 6am and genuinely need to feed. However, it is essential to treat this feed like a night-time feed. It should be done as quickly and quietly as possible with the use of only a small socket night light and without talking or eye contact. The baby should then be settled back to sleep until 7–7.30am. If possible, avoid changing the nappy as this usually wakes up the baby too much.

Once the baby is sleeping and feeding nearer to 4am, waking at 6am is not usually related to hunger. This is the one and only time I would advise parents to help their baby return to sleep. At this stage the most important thing is to get him back to sleep quickly, even if it means cuddling him and offering him a dummy until 7am. Listed below are guidelines that will help your baby not to become an early riser:

- Avoid using a night light or leaving the door open. Research shows that chemicals in the brain work differently in the dark, preparing it for sleep. Even the smallest chink of light can be enough to awaken the baby fully when he enters his light sleep.

- Kicking off the bedcovers can also cause babies under six months to wake early. In my experience, all babies under this age sleep better if tucked in securely. The sheet needs to be placed length-ways across the width of the cot to ensure that a minimum of 20cm (8in) is tucked in at the far side and a minimum of 10cm (4in) is tucked in at the near side. I would also advise rolling up a small hand towel and pushing it down between the spars and the mattress at the near side.

- Babies who work their way up the cot and get out of the covers will benefit from being put in a lightweight (0.5tog) 100 per cent cotton sleeping bag and tucked in with a sheet as described above. Depending on the weather, blankets may not be necessary. It is important to adjust the layers of clothes and bedding according to the temperature of the room.

- Once a baby starts to move around the cot and is capable of rolling, I would advise that you remove the sheets and blankets and use only the sleeping bag. This will allow your baby to move around unrestricted, without the worry that he might get cold in the middle of the night. It is important to choose a sleeping bag that is suitable for the time of year.

- Do not drop the 10pm feed until your baby has reached six months and is established on solids (see page 177). If he goes through a growth spurt before he starts solids, he can be offered extra milk at this time. This reduces the chances of him waking early due to hunger, which can occur if the 10pm feed is dropped too soon.

- A baby who is over six months and has dropped the 10pm feed should be encouraged to stay awake until 7pm. If he is falling into a deep sleep before this time, he will be much more likely to wake before 7am.

If your baby is over four weeks old, waking twice in the night or refusing to settle back to sleep at 6am, and then ready for his nap at 8/8.30am (or falling asleep on the school run, see page 87), and then sleeping until nearer 10am, it is worth trying to reduce the amount of sleep that he has in the morning. It is possible that the extra amount of sleep he is having in the morning is the cause of the night waking and early morning waking. The easiest way to do this is to introduce a split nap. You can do this by allowing your baby to have a short nap at around 8/8.30am and then another nap at 9.30/9.45am. How long you allow him to sleep at each nap will depend on his age. If he is between four and eight weeks old you should allow him to sleep for no more than 45 minutes, divided between the two naps. For babies aged between eight and 12 weeks you should allow a total of no more than 40 minutes, and babies over 12 weeks should be limited to a split nap of no more than 30 minutes. It is always best to ensure that he is awake by 10am in order to keep the rest of the day on track.

Once the amount of time your baby sleeps in the morning is reduced, the problem of the night-time sleep/early-morning waking should improve. When this happens you should find that your baby will then start to stay awake until nearer 9am, and you can go back to giving one nap in the morning.

I have noticed some babies aged four months and older being allowed a longer nap in the morning because they wake early, and cannot be settled back to sleep despite being offered a feed. Unfortunately, when this happens it quickly creates a cycle where a baby will need less sleep at night because they have had more daytime sleep than needed for their age. At this age I recommend these babies should be given a nap of no more than 30 minutes if they are to sleep nearer 7am.

If your baby will not return to sleep on waking at 5/6am, splitting the morning nap is a good way of ensuring that your baby has less sleep overall but is not overtired for his lunchtime nap. Allowing a total of 30 minutes between the two naps should quickly help resolve the problem of early-morning waking. Start off by giving 15 minutes at 8.30am and a further 15 minutes between 9.40am and 10am. If your baby is over five months you may have to reduce the total of the two naps to no more than 30 minutes. Ensure your baby is wide awake at 10am so as not to affect the time he'll be ready for his lunchtime nap.

The very first morning your baby sleeps closer to 7am it is important to push the nap to the times suggested in the routine for your baby's age. This will ensure that you make good progress and that early-morning waking will soon be a thing of the past.

Excessive night waking

Until the mother's milk comes in, a newborn baby may wake and need to be fed several times a night. By the end of the first week, a baby who weighs over 3.2kg (7lb) should manage to sleep for a stretch of four hours from the 10–11pm feed, provided his feeding needs are being fully met during the day. Smaller babies may still need to feed three-hourly round the clock. In my experience, all babies who are healthy and well fed will, between four and six weeks of age, manage to sleep one longer spell of 5–6 hours. By following my routines, this longer spell should happen in the night. The main aim of my routines is to help parents structure their baby's feeding and sleeping needs during the day to avoid excessive night-time waking.

How long a baby will continue to wake for a feed in the night depends very much on the individual baby. Some babies aged between six and eight weeks sleep through after the 10pm feed, others not until 10–12 weeks. Some may even take longer. All babies will sleep through the night as soon as they are physically and mentally able, provided the daytime feeding and sleeping is being properly structured. Listed below are the main causes of excessive night-time waking in healthy babies under one year old:

● Sleeping too much during the day. Even very small babies need to be awake some of the time. The baby should be encouraged to stay awake for 1–1½ hours after daytime feeds. Between six and eight weeks, most babies are capable of staying awake for up to two hours.

● Not feeding enough during the day. If excessive night feeding is to be avoided, the baby needs to have six feeds between 7am and 11pm. To fit in this number of feeds, the day must start at 7am.

● Not feeding enough at each feed. In the early days a baby needs a minimum of 25 minutes on one breast. A baby who weighs over 3.6kg (8lb) should be offered the second breast.

● Breast-fed babies will be more likely to wake several times a night if they do not get enough to eat at the 10pm feed and may need a top-up after this feed.

● Babies under six weeks have a very strong Moro reflex and can wake themselves several times a night by the sudden startle and jerk. These babies will benefit from being swaddled in a light-weight stretch cotton sheet.

● Older babies often wake several times at night because they have kicked their covers off and are cold or they may have got their legs caught between the spars of the cot. A sleeping bag will help them avoid becoming cold and will prevent them from getting their legs caught in the spars. Refer to page 156 for advice on sleeping bags and tucking in.

● The baby has learned the wrong sleep associations. Between two and three months his sleep cycle changes and he will come into a light sleep several times at night. If the baby is used to being fed, rocked or given a dummy to get to sleep, he will need the same assistance to resettle himself in the night.

- Parents who leave their room door open or leave on a night light are more likely to be woken several times a night.

- If the baby's milk feeds are reduced too quickly when solids are introduced, he will begin to wake in the night genuinely needing a milk feed.

Illness: the effect on sleep

The majority of my first babies manage to get through the first year without suffering the usual colds and coughs that seem to plague my second and third babies. By the time most first babies I have cared for experience a cold, their sleep is so well established that night-time waking is very rare. With second and third babies this is not the case as they usually catch their first cold at a much younger age from a brother or sister and disrupted nights are inevitable. A baby under three months of age will usually need help to get through the night when he has a cold or is ill. A young baby with a cold can get very distressed, especially when he is feeding, as he will not have learned to breathe through his mouth.

When a sick baby needs attention in the evening and during the night, it should be given calmly and quietly. I believe that a sick baby needs more rest than a healthy baby. Lots of visitors and activity in the nursery during the evening and in the night should be avoided. When I have had to care for a sick baby over six months who was sleeping in his own room and waking several times at night I found it less disruptive if I slept in the same room as the baby. It enabled me to attend to him quickly and I was less likely to disrupt the sleep of older siblings by to-ing and fro-ing along the corridor.

Occasionally, I found that an older baby who had dropped night-time feeds would, once he had recovered, continue to wake up in the night looking for the same attention he received when he was unwell. For the first few nights I would check him and offer him some cool boiled water, but once I was convinced he was totally recovered I would allow him to cry down so that he settled himself. In my experience, parents who are not prepared to do this usually end up with a baby who develops a long-term sleep problem.

If your baby develops a cold or cough, regardless of how mild it appears, he should be seen by a doctor. All too often I hear from distressed parents of babies with serious chest infections, which could possibly have been avoided if they had been seen by a doctor earlier. Too many mothers delay taking their baby to the doctor, worried that they will be classed as neurotic, but it is important that you discuss with your doctor any concerns you have about your baby's health, no matter how small. If your baby is ill, it is essential that you follow to the letter your doctor's advice, especially on feeding.

The lunchtime nap

The lunchtime nap is a fundamental part of my Contented Baby routines. Research shows that children up to the age of two years benefit physically and psychologically from a proper, structured nap in the middle of the day. As your baby grows and is more active, this nap will become his time to rest and recover from the morning's activities and will enable him to enjoy his afternoons with you and others. Establishing a regular lunchtime nap for the baby also allows you time for a short rest or quiet time with your toddler.

However, I am well aware that in the early days a lunchtime nap may sometimes go wrong. I understand totally the feelings of frustration when a baby wakes up fully, usually 30–45 minutes into the lunchtime nap and, despite still being tired, refuses to settle back to sleep. Assuming that the wrong sleep associations have not been established, there are several things you can do to try and improve the lunchtime nap.

The first thing is to allow your baby a short time to settle himself back to sleep. Normally I would find that over a period of a week or so, if a baby was allowed five to 10 minutes of crying down, they would then learn to settle themselves back to sleep. Obviously, if you find that after 10 minutes your baby is not crying down, but in fact crying up, then he should of course be attended to. With a baby who is crying up, I would offer half of the 2pm feed, treating it like a night feed, so that the baby does not become overstimulated by lots of talking or eye contact. I would then assume that the reason why the baby may not be able to settle himself back to sleep, is that his coming into a light sleep coincides with him starting to get hungry.

Hunger – young babies
To eliminate the possibility of hunger causing a disturbed lunchtime nap, I would bring forward the morning feed of very young babies to 10/10.30am, then offer them a top-up just before they go down for their lunchtime nap. This way you can be confident about allowing them a short crying down period, without worrying that they could be genuinely hungry.

If they continue to cry up and not settle back to sleep, it is worth looking at the amount of sleep your baby is having at the morning nap.

Morning nap – younger babies

If your baby is over one month and under six months, and having more than one hour sleep in the morning, it could be that too much morning sleep is affecting his lunchtime nap. Depending on how much sleep your baby is actually having at the morning nap, I would try reducing it to between 45 minutes and one hour, maximum. If you find that you cannot push your baby on to 9am for his morning nap, I would suggest that you do a split morning nap for a short time, in order to reduce his overall morning sleep time. Allow him 15/20 minutes at the first part of the split nap, then a further 15/20 minutes at the second part of the split nap. By offering your baby a top-up before his lunchtime nap and reducing his morning nap to between 30 and 40 minutes, and allowing him a short spell of crying down when he does wake up after the 45 minutes, he should fairly quickly start to sleep a longer spell again.

Hunger – older babies

With a baby who is weaned, you can try offering him a top-up of milk just prior to his lunchtime nap. If you find that he is taking quite a large top-up it could be that you need to look at the amount of solids that you are giving, and ensure that you are getting the right balance of protein, carbohydrates and vegetables.

By seven months, your baby should be eating three meals a day and solids should be well established. Check *The Contented Little Baby Book of Weaning* for the recommended amounts. If you have weaned at six months, you will need to move through the guide quickly to build up the right amounts of food.

If your baby is over nine months and is not having a good drink of water or well-diluted juice with his lunch, thirst can be a reason why a baby wakes from his nap, especially during hot weather. Therefore, it is worth offering him a further drink of water or well-diluted juice just prior to his lunchtime nap. Once the possibility of hunger is ruled out, if your baby continues to cry up instead of down, then you should look at the amount of sleep your baby is having in the morning.

Morning nap – older babies

With babies over six months, try to ensure that the nap is not before 9.15/9.30am. If you find your baby is sleeping longer than 45 minutes at this nap, it could well be the reason for him not sleeping for long at lunchtime. If your baby is between six and nine months, reduce the morning nap by gradually cutting it back by 10 minutes every three or four days until he is having only 20–25 minutes. If your baby is between nine and 12 months, try reducing it to 10–15 minutes. You might find that for a short time you will have to move lunch forward if he is getting tired and put him down earlier for his nap. Hopefully, the top-up before the lunchtime nap and the reduction in the morning sleep, should see an improvement within one or two weeks in the length of time he sleeps at the lunchtime nap.

What to do when it goes wrong

If you find that despite trying all the suggestions above your baby will not resettle back to sleep, then you will have to adjust his afternoon sleep so that he does not become overtired at bedtime. A younger baby won't be able to make it through the afternoon if he's only had 40–60 minutes' sleep at lunchtime and I find the best way to deal with this is to allow him a 30-minute nap after the 2.30pm feed and then a further 30 minutes at around 4.30pm. This should stop him getting overtired and irritable and you can get back on track again at 5pm and ensure he goes down well at 7pm. If he doesn't sleep at 2.30pm but falls asleep between 3–4pm on the school run he might be ready to sleep at 6pm. With a young baby you just have to accept this. I suggest you bring the 5pm feed forward to 4.30pm and have him in bed for 6pm. An older baby will usually get through the afternoon, with just one short nap of 45 minutes to an hour somewhere between 3pm and 4pm, although you may have to bring bedtime forward slightly.

If you 'tweak' the routines to allow him more sleep to make up for what he missed at lunchtime, you can follow my recommendations at the beginning of each routine for the maximum amount of daily sleep. Always make sure the baby is up and awake by 5pm if you want him to go down well at 7pm.

Checklist

- Rule out hunger as the possible reason.

- With older babies check that he is not thirsty by offering him a drink of water just before he goes down for his lunchtime nap.

- Correct any sleep associations such as falling asleep on the breast or the bottle and ensure he goes down, well fed, in his bed. Note that it might take some time to get him into good habits, so you will need to be patient.

- Eliminate all other reasons for waking, such as excessive noise or not being tucked in properly. (Remember that the Moro reflex – see page 303 – can be very strong in babies under six months, so tucking them in securely is very important if they are not to wake themselves up.)

● Always allow your baby to wake naturally and, provided he is not screaming for food, allow him a short awake spell in his bed before you pick him up, so that he does not associate being picked up with the minute he wakes.

When you have checked everything on the list above, and given any changes enough time to work, if the lunchtime nap still continues to be a problem and you feel your baby has gotten into the habit of waking when he comes into his light sleep, it may be worth trying the assisted sleep method, mentioned on page 219, which can help get babies into the habit of sleeping at regular times.

I would also suggest checking out *The Complete Sleep Guide for Contented Babies and Toddlers*, available from your library, which has extensive advice and lots of case studies on sleeping problems.

Teething and night waking

In my experience, babies who enjoy a routine from a very early age and have established healthy sleeping habits are rarely bothered by teething. Out of the 300 babies I have helped care for, only a handful have been bothered by teething in the night. In these cases it is usually when the molars come through and then only for a few nights. I have found that babies who wake in the night due to teething are more likely to have suffered from colic (see page 263) and have developed poor sleeping habits.

If your baby is teething and waking in the night, but quickly settles back to sleep when given a cuddle, drink or a dummy, teething is probably not the real cause of his waking. A baby who is genuinely bothered by teething pain would be difficult to settle back to sleep. He would also show signs of discomfort during the day, not just at night. I would advise you to check the section on excessive night waking (see page 302) and early-morning waking (see page 298) to eliminate other reasons why your baby may be waking.

If you are convinced that your baby's night-time wakings are caused by severe teething pain, I suggest you seek advice from your doctor regarding the best pain relief for babies. While genuine teething pain may cause a few disruptive nights, it should never last for several weeks. If your baby seems out of sorts, develops a fever and suffers from loss of appetite or diarrhoea, he should be seen by a doctor. Do not assume that these symptoms are just a sign of teething. Very often I have found that what parents thought was teething turned out to be an ear or throat infection.

Appendix I:
Baby and Toddler
Menu Planner

7–9 months

Breakfast

- Baby: Breast-feed or 210–240ml (7–8oz) of formula milk.

- Toddler: 150ml (5oz) of full-fat milk from a beaker.

Plus:

- Wheat cereal with milk and mashed fruit *or*

- Oat cereal with milk and finely chopped fruit *or*

- Mixed mashed fruit and yoghurt, lightly buttered toast fingers *or*

- Baby muesli with milk.

Mid-morning

Toddler: Drink of water or well-diluted juice from an open-top cup plus a small piece of fruit.

Lunch

Choose from the following for baby and toddler:

- Cheesy chicken gratin (*The Gina Ford Baby and Toddler Cook Book*, page 47) and broccoli florets *or*

- Chicken and butternut squash pie (*The Gina Ford Baby and Toddler Cook Book*, page 118) and green beans *or*

- Chicken and sweet potato casserole (*The Gina Ford Baby and Toddler Cook Book*, page 48) and peas *or*

- Chicken casserole (*The Contented Little Baby Book of Weaning*, page 85) and peas *or*

- Chicken risotto (*The Contented Little Baby Book of Weaning*, page 79) and sweetcorn *or*

- Cod with cheese sauce and broccoli (*The Gina Ford Baby and Toddler Cook Book*, page 40) and carrots *or*

- Fish Lyonnaise (*The Contented Little Baby Book of Weaning*, page 87) and sweetcorn *or*

- Fruity lamb tagine (*The Gina Ford Baby and Toddler Cook Book*, page 122) with couscous and peas *or*

- Individual fish pies (*The Contented Little Baby Book of Weaning*, page 93) and green beans *or*

- Lamb hotpot (*The Contented Little Baby Book of Weaning*, page 94) and broccoli florets *or*

- Quick chicken and vegetable gratin (*The Contented Little Baby Book of Weaning*, page 83) and mixed vegetables *or*

- Quick pilaf (*The Gina Ford Baby and Toddler Cook Book*, page 52) and mixed vegetables *or*

- Tuna pasta (*The Contented Little Baby Book of Weaning*, page 81) and mixed vegetables *or*

- Vegetable shepherd's pie (*The Contented Little Baby Book of Weaning*, page 97) and lightly buttered toast fingers.

Plus:

- Pieces of soft fruit.

- Water to drink (in a beaker for baby, and a cup for your toddler).

Mid-afternoon

- Baby: Breast-feed or 150–210ml (5–7oz) of formula milk.

- Toddler: Drink of water or well-diluted juice from a cup plus small piece of fruit or rice cake/plain biscuit.

Tea

Choose from the following for baby and toddler:

- Baked potato with baby baked beans *or*

- Bubble and squeak potato cakes (*The Gina Ford Baby and Toddler Cook Book*, page 98) *or*

- Bumper macaroni cheese (*The Contented Little Baby Book of Weaning*, page 92) *or*

- Cheesy peasy rice (*The Gina Ford Baby and Toddler Cook Book*, page 90) *or*

- Corn chowder (*The Contented Little Baby Book of Weaning*, page 91) with mini sandwiches *or*

- Creamy pasta with spring vegetables (*The Contented Little Baby Book of Weaning*, page 80) *or*

- Leek and potato soup (*The Contented Little Baby Book of Weaning*, page 95) with rusks, lightly buttered *or*

- Minestrone soup (*The Contented Little Baby Book of Weaning*, page 82) with rice cakes or corn cakes, lightly buttered *or*

- Neapolitan macaroni (*The Gina Ford Baby and Toddler Cook Book*, page 104) *or*

- Scotch broth (*The Gina Ford Baby and Toddler Cook Book*, page 30) with bread or rice cakes, lightly buttered *or*

- Spotty couscous (*The Contented Little Baby Book of Weaning*, page 90) *or*

- Thick courgette and leek soup (*The Contented Little Baby Book of Weaning*, page 84) with bread, lightly buttered *or*

- Thick lentil and carrot soup (*The Contented Little Baby Book of Weaning*, page 96) with lightly buttered toast *or*

- Vegetable broth (*The Contented Little Baby Book of Weaning*, page 86) with mini sandwiches.

Plus:

- Natural yoghurt (sweetened with a small amount of grated fruit if required) *or*

- Another choice of healthy pudding.

- Water to drink in a beaker for baby, and water or milk in a cup for your toddler.

Bedtime

- Baby: Breast-feed or 180–240ml (6–8oz) of formula milk.

- Toddler: 150–180ml (5–6oz) of full-fat milk from a beaker.

9–12 months

Breakfast

- Baby: Breast-feed or 150–180ml (5–6oz) of formula milk from a beaker.

- Toddler: 150ml (5oz) of full-fat milk from a beaker.

Plus:

- Wheat cereal with milk and finely chopped fruit *or*

- Oat cereal with milk and finely chopped fruit *or*

- Fruit yoghurt and lightly buttered toast fingers *or*

- Scrambled egg on toast *or*

- Muesli with milk.

Mid-morning

- Toddler: Drink of water or well-diluted juice from an open-top cup plus a small piece of fruit.

Lunch

Choose from the following for baby and toddler:

- Baby bolognese (*The Contented Little Baby Book of Weaning*, page 125) and broccoli florets *or*

- Beef and lentil pot supper (*The Contented Little Baby Book of Weaning*, page 122) and mixed vegetables *or*

- Chicken and butter bean burgers (*The Contented Little Baby Book of Weaning*, page 120) and sweetcorn *or*

- Chicken and leek lasagne (*The Gina Ford Baby and Toddler Cook Book*, page 50) and green beans *or*

- Chicken and vegetable oat crumble (*The Contented Little Baby Book of Weaning*, page 123) and peas *or*

- Chicken with tagliatelle (*The Gina Ford Baby and Toddler Cook Book*, page 58) and carrots *or*

- Fishy ribbons (*The Contented Little Baby Book of Weaning*, page 110), peas and oven chips *or*

- Italian fish stew (*The Gina Ford Baby and Toddler Cook Book*, page 42) and lightly buttered toast fingers *or*

- Kiddies' kedgeree (*The Contented Little Baby Book of Weaning*, page 124) and mixed vegetables *or*

- Minced beef cobbler (*Feeding Made Easy*, page 194) and peas *or*

- Quick salmon fishcakes (*The Gina Ford Baby and Toddler Cook Book*, page 82) and peas *or*

- Roast poussin (*The Gina Ford Baby and Toddler Cook Book*, page 46) and mixed vegetables *or*

- Shepherd's pie (*The Gina Ford Baby and Toddler Cook Book*, page 64) and sweetcorn *or*

- Tender lamb in a pot (*The Gina Ford Baby and Toddler Cook Book*, page 60) and broccoli florets.

Plus:

- Pieces of soft fruit.

- Water to drink (in a beaker for baby, and a cup for your toddler).

Mid-afternoon

- Baby: Breast-feed or 150–210ml (5–7oz) of formula milk from a beaker.

- Toddler: Drink of water or well-diluted juice from a cup plus small piece of fruit or rice-cake/plain biscuit.

Tea

Choose from the following for baby and toddler:

- American eggy bread (*Feeding Made Easy*, page 169) with grilled tomatoes and mushrooms *or*

- Baked barley risotto (*Feeding Made Easy*, page 212) *or*

- Baked potato with unsalted butter, and baby baked beans *or*

- Chickpeas in tomato sauce (*Feeding Made Easy*, page 164) with rice *or*

- Chinese noodles (*The Contented Little Baby Book of Weaning*, page 118) *or*

- Courgette cornmeal muffins (*Feeding Made Easy*, page 216) *or*

- Green monster pasta (*Feeding Made Easy*, page 173) *or*

- Hearty bean soup (*Feeding Made Easy*, page 180) with oatcakes (*Feeding Made Easy*, page 222), lightly buttered *or*

- Mini courgette rosti cakes (*Feeding Made Easy*, page 185) *or*

- Mixed vegetable frittata (*The Contented Little Baby Book of Weaning*, page 116) *or*

- Pick-up sticks (*The Contented Little Baby Book of Weaning*, page 126) *or*

- Pizza potatoes (*The Contented Little Baby Book of Weaning*, page 114) *or*

- Roast vegetables and couscous (*Feeding Made Easy*, page 174) *or*

- Scrambled egg surprise (*The Gina Ford Baby and Toddler Cookbook*, page 123) served on hot buttered toast.

Plus:

- Natural yoghurt (sweetened with a small amount of grated fruit if required) *or*

- Another choice of healthy pudding.

- Water to drink in a beaker for baby, and water or milk in a cup for your toddler.

Bedtime

- Baby: Breast-feed or 180–240ml (6–8oz) of formula milk from a beaker.

- Toddler: 150–180ml (5–6oz) of full-fat milk from a beaker.

Appendix II:

Foundation for the Study of Infant Deaths (FSID) Advice to Reduce the Risk of Cot Death

1. Babies do not need hot rooms; all night heating is rarely necessary. Keep the room at a temperature between 16–20°C (61–68°F), 18°C (65°F) is just right.
2. Adults find it difficult to judge the temperature in the room, so use a room thermometer in the rooms where your baby sleeps and plays. A simple room thermometer is available from FSID.
3. When you check your baby, if he is sweating or his tummy feels hot to the touch, take off some of the bedding.
4. Use lightweight blankets or a baby sleeping bag. If your baby feels too warm, reduce the number of layers or use a lower tog baby sleeping bag. In warm summer, your baby may not need any bedclothes at all. Do not use a duvet, quilt or pillow for babies under 12 months.
5. Even in winter, babies who are unwell and feverish need fewer clothes and bedclothes.
6. Babies need to lose excess heat from their heads. Make sure his head cannot be covered by the bedclothes by sleeping him 'feet to foot' (with his feet to the foot of the cot) so he doesn't wriggle down under the covers.

Useful Addresses

Breast pumps
Ardo Medical Ltd.
Unit 1,
Belvedere Trading Estate
Taunton
Somerset TA1 1BH
Tel: 01823 336362
Fax: 01823 336364
www.ardomums.co.uk

**Foundation for the Study
of Infant Deaths (FSID)**
11 Belgrave Road
London SW1V 1RB
Tel: 020 7802 3200
Helpline: 020 7233 2090
www.fsid.org.uk

La Leche League
Tel: 0845 456 1855
www.laleche.org.uk

NCT
Tel: 0300 33 00 770
www.nctpregnancyandbaby
care.com

Sure Start
Tel: 08700 002288
www.surestart.gov.uk
**Twins and Multiple Births
Association (TAMBA)**
2 The Willows
Gardner Road
Guildford
Surrey GU1 4PG
Tel: 01483 304442
Twinline: 0800 1380509
www.tamba.org.uk

UNICEF
UNICEF House
30a Great Sutton Street
London EC1V 0DV
Tel: 020 7490 2388
www.unicef.org.uk

Further Reading

The Complete Sleep Guide for Contented Babies and Toddlers by Gina Ford (Vermilion 2006)

The Contented Baby's First Year by Gina Ford (Vermilion 2007)

The Contented Child's Food Bible by Gina Ford (Vermilion 2005)

A Contented House with Twins by Gina Ford and Alice Beer (Vermilion 2006)

The Contented Little Baby Book of Weaning by Gina Ford (Vermilion 2006)

The Contented Toddler Years by Gina Ford (Vermilion 2006)

Feeding Made Easy by Gina Ford (Vermilion 2008)

The Gina Ford Baby and Toddler Cook Book by Gina Ford (Vermilion 2005)

The Great Ormond Street New Baby and Child Care Book (Vermilion 2004)

Healthy Sleep Habits, Happy Child by Dr Marc Weissbluth (Vermilion 2005)

The New Contented Little Baby Book by Gina Ford (Vermilion 2006)

Potty Training in One Week by Gina Ford (Vermilion 2003)

Remotely Controlled by Aric Sigman (Vermilion 2005)

Silent Nights by Brian Symon (OUP Australia and New Zealand 2005)

Sleep: The Secret of Problem-free Nights by Beatrice Hollyer and Lucy Smith (Cassell 2002)

Solve Your Child's Sleep Problems by Richard Ferber (Dorling Kindersley 1985)

What to Expect When You're Breast-feeding . . . And What If You Can't? by Clare Byam-Cook (Vermilion 2006)

Why They Cry: Understanding Child Development in the First Year by Hetty Van de Rijt and Frank Plooij (Thorsons 1996)

Your Child's Symptoms Explained by David Haslam (Vermilion 1997)

Contented Baby and Toddler Newsletter

Would you like to learn more about the Contented Baby and Toddler routines and Gina Ford's books? Why not visit Gina's official websites at www.contentedbaby.com and www.contentedtoddler.com and sign up to receive Gina's free monthly newsletter, which is full of useful information, tips and advice as well as answers to questions about parenting issues and even a recipe or two.

You may also want to take the opportunity to become part of Gina's online community by joining one or both of the websites. As a member you'll find there are a huge range of benefits with the opportunity to find support and solutions from like-minded parents on the forums, as well as a wealth of information and advice. You'll receive a monthly online magazine with a personal message from Gina, along with a selection of the latest exclusive features on topical issues from our guest contributors and members. You'll be able to access more than 2,000 frequently asked questions about feeding, sleeping and development answered by Gina and her team. You'll also find many case histories not featured in the Contented Little Baby series of books, and an extensive archive of fascinating articles on parenting and lifestyle issues from experts on nutrition, diet, child psychology and counselling as well as journalists and writers.

You'll be able to link up with other parents on the forums where you can discuss any parenting concerns, and you will be able to get in touch with other mothers in your area who are following the Contented Little Baby routines. You can even find out what Gina thinks about common dilemmas in her 'Gina Responds' column looking at parenting issues. What's more, you can benefit from online shopping recommendations and tips on family days out, as well as more general advice.

Index